THE SPIRIT BUILDER

THE LIFE AND TIMES OF DOROTHY BECKER

A BREAKTHROUGH VIEW OF AGING

By

Ursula Levy

July 28, 2004

Dear Helen,

Best wishes and I hope to meet you... in the near future, through our mutual friend, Yvonne Kant.

Ursula Levy

4124 West Oakton Street, Skokie, IL 60076
Phone 847.673.3703 FAX 847.329.0358

First Published in 2004 by the College Marketing Bureau, Inc.

Content Designed by Marie Jansen
Cover Designed by Mark H. Jansen

Manufactured in the United States of America.

ISBN# 0-9747830-0-5

I dedicate this book to my children

Gerard and Kareen

TABLE OF CONTENTS

ACKNOWLEDGEMENTS

I wish to thank Gerry Franks, Inge Hoffmann, Helen Ramirez Odell and Michaeline Rojek for the time they took to give me valuable suggestions and corrections to the first draft of the book. The interest Renate Reber and Ron Shaffer expressed in the book helped keep the project on track. My attorney, Leslie Bertagnolli took the time to explain the nuances of the copyright laws in terms understandable to the lay person. Dr. Ronald Morgan, a professor at Loyola University, added a pertinent dimension to the book by suggesting to link Dorothy Becker's views on aging with the current research on aging. I especially thank my computer teacher, Donna Cordon, for infusing her clear instructions with a contagious spark of enthusiasm. The elegance of Rae Paul, my editor, is reflected in her elegant editing style. It was my good fortune to discover Mark and Marie Jansen right in my neighborhood. Mark and Marie, the owners of "College Marketing Bureau, Inc." are experts in all aspects of preparing books and magazines for publication. I appreciate Marian Shaffer's friendship and value the spirit of trust with which she made her mother's photos and documents available to me. I thank my partner, Dominick Giovanetto, for his constant friendship.

INTRODUCTION

Friends thought I was exaggerating when I used words like "upbeat" and "festive" to describe the atmosphere at the Selfhelp Home for the Aged. After a hectic day at work, I always looked forward to visiting my aunt and uncle at the retirement home. I was struck by the contrast between the teachers at my school who passed each other in the hallways with eyes fixed in space and the Selfhelp residents who welcomed visitors with smiles, "hellos" and handshakes. The festive atmosphere of the Home - where the average age of the residents was 84 - pleased and perplexed me.

Friends thought it strange that I liked visiting my relatives at their retirement home after work, but it was like having a mellow glass of wine before dinner. Before my Aunt and Uncle, Dr. Joseph and Irmgard Mueller moved into the Home, I had made the rounds at a number of more upscale retirement homes in the area. At the other facilities, people were nicely dressed and looked well cared for, but they sat in silence, as if they didn't speak the same language. Not long after Aunt and Uncle moved into the Selfhelp Home for the Aged, it became apparent that they were *talking* with more people in one day than they had formerly *seen in months*. They could speak either English or German and they also liked the formal dress code for meals. It was part of their culture.

On the way to my aunt and uncle's apartment, Mrs. Dorothy Becker rushed past me with what I later came to know as her characteristic "Hi, Hi! Don't forget Mrs. Bloom's birthday party this afternoon! You'll like the cake; it's hazelnut", she whispered to me as if to let me in on a secret. I made her feel good by telling *her* a secret: that though Aunt and Uncle might occasionally be late for dinner, they actually got dressed for her parties two hours ahead of time. Mrs. Becker laughed; her blue eyes beamed. I remember, on that occasion, complimenting her on the stunning colors of her tweed suit. "Cranberry was my husband's favorite color", she confided in an intimate voice. Every wave of her thick white hair gleamed and her eyes sparkled behind thick glasses. She had been nearly blind in her right eye for years yet both eyes registered the range of emotions with equal intensity.

I had met Mrs. Becker for the first time about a year before I asked her to consider my aunt and uncle for admission to the Home. She listened intently, and seemed as interested in my background as in Aunt and Uncle's declining ability to care for themselves. I was beginning to worry that she might consider me a likely candidate for the Home as well.

She only asked me one question, "Have you ever gone back to Germany?" I told her that I had been back twice, and that I'll be going to Germany next year to talk to students about my Holocaust experiences. Her eyes flashed like black granite. She looked me straight in the eye and said, " I don't respect people who go back to Germany." Her anger was palpable and I was sure that my chances of getting Aunt and Uncle into Selfhelp had dropped to zero. She collected herself as she stroked her wedding band with her left thumb and said, "Don't take your Aunt and Uncle into your home. You deserve a life of your own." She invited the three of us to join her at the center table for Sabbath dinner the following Friday evening.

Several months later Aunt and Uncle moved into a studio apartment at the

Selfhelp Home. Whenever Mrs. Becker saw them, she would put an arm around each of them and tell them how happy she was that they were with her at the Home. They adjusted well to the Home, but their health was declining.

After Aunt and Uncle died, three years elapsed before I was able to return to the Home to visit Mrs. Becker. She was retired now and had more time to chat. Every piece of furniture in her apartment, and every cup and plate, told a story from the past. She was born in Germany around the turn of the century. Like my father, her husband had left high school to enlist in the First World War. Both men thought that they would not be persecuted by the Nazis because they had fought for the fatherland. Her parents had a clothing store in Berlin; my parents had a clothing store in Lippstadt, a small German town. The hours flew by as I listened to her talk about her childhood.

On several key issues, the two families differed drastically. Both of our families were assimilated German Jews, proud to fight for the fatherland, but many of *my* family members were apologetic about their Jewish background, whereas Dorothy Becker was proud to be Jewish. Having lost our home, business and all of our civil rights, my mother urged my father to leave Germany, but he refused. Dorothy Becker's family responded to the threat and left for America. These similarities and disparities between her family and mine fascinated me.

She surprised me when she told me that as a young girl, she had wanted to become a doctor and one of her best girl friends had hoped to become a judge. Most of the girls in her class of 1927 aspired to go to the university. In *my* graduating class of 1953, most of the girls hoped to get married after

3

high school. Girls of my generation became either secretaries, teachers, or nurses, but none of my classmates had hopes of becoming a doctor or a judge! Until I met Dorothy Becker, I had never quite believed Betty Friedan's contention that women had more career choices in the 1920s than in the 50s.

After WWII, women lost many of the rights they had gained since the earlier decades. After the men came home from the War, many women dreamed of homes in the suburbs and raising families. Dorothy Becker loved her family above all, but her search for fulfillment was not confined to home and children. She interested me because she seemed so modern and at the same time so Victorian. Our commonalties and our differences - her warmth and her uncompromising stance - her modern ways as well as her rigidity - and her unique style of caring for the elderly all intrigued me.

I remember asking her if she would allow me to write the story of her life. She thought for a moment and said, "yes." She explained she had always envisioned herself sitting in an overstuffed chair with the great grandchildren snuggling close while she told stories about their large family in Berlin. For her, "the beginning of Selfhelp was the most beautiful story of all." However, this fervent desire of the consummate storyteller had remained a dream because her daughter, the grandchildren and great - grandchildren lived in distant states.

On several occasions, her granddaughter Lori had asked her to write her memoir and several times Mrs. Becker had begun to write her life story but she had difficulty keeping the focus on herself. Lori said that she didn't want to read about everybody else, she wanted to read about her grandmother. "It was hard to write only about myself", commented Mrs Becker. "Why don't *you* try writing the story of my life?" she asked me pensively. I said I would be privileged to do so.

Front: Granddaughter Lori Shaffer, Dorothy Becker, Daughter Marian Shaffer

One of Dorothy Becker's strongest qualities, I believe, was her ability to inspire people to volunteer for Selfhelp. Without the hundreds of volunteers, mostly women, who worked for Selfhelp in every capacity imaginable, the Selfhelp Home would not exist today. So, both the officers and the foot soldiers of the organization are given the recognition they deserve in this, "The Life and Times of Dorothy Becker."

This biography emerged from taped interviews with Mrs. Becker and from conversations with her daughter, childhood friends, lifelong colleagues,

Selfhelp employees and volunteers. I loved and admired Dorothy Becker, and while writing her story, I had to make a conscious effort to remain objective. The issues I determined relevant to the "Spirit of Selfhelp," I insisted on including. The stories that she shared with me that are not relevant to the book, I have omitted. She exerted formidable control over the content, which made writing a credible story difficult at times.

Her priority was to present a flawless image of the organization in general and of the Selfhelp Board in particular. Mrs. Becker would have liked me to depict every person either sprouting wings or wearing a halo. I pointed to our biblical matriarchs and patriarchs who appear credible because of their fair share of weaknesses as well as virtues.

1

GENEOLOGY

Thea Westmann's great grandfather, Chaim Westmann, was very proud of the brick factory he owned on the outskirts of Berlin - and terribly disappointed when he had to sell it. A Protestant minister at the court of Wilhelm I had told the Kaiser that the Jews were getting too powerful. The Protestant minister (and politician), Adolf Stoecker (1835 to 1909), worked every angle to exploit his position of influence at the court of Kaiser William I. He preached anti-Semitism from the Court pulpit to win support for the Christian Social Workers, a political party he launched in 1878. He blamed the Jews for the evils of industrialization, urbanization and capitalism. In fact, his anti-Semitic outbursts probably influenced William I to seize land from the Jews. As a result, businessman Chaim Westmann lost his land and was forced to sell his factory in the late 1870's.

He felt cheated and angry but decided to open up a small clothing store in Berlin. His business began to flourish and most people thought that his initial "C" stood for Christian. They assumed his name was "Christian" because whenever a little girl would pick out a First Communion dress that her mother thought was too expensive, Chaim would reduce the price.

Chaim continued to send customers home with a smile long after his son Marcus took over the family business. Marcus Westmann and his wife, Rosalie, became Thea Becker's paternal grandparents. The store flourished with a reputation of reliable service and quality merchandise.

n Marcus and Rosalie died within one week of each other, Simon and

well prepared to take over the family business.

was the older son, the Westmann clothing store was list-

Berlin telephone book of 1894 and 1896 under Simon

in. The Berlin telephone book published in 1910 named both Simon

Sally Westmann as the owners of the Clothing Store, located at the

G   Frankf   er Street 115.

The Westmann store on 115 Frankfurther Street in 1910

The Westmann Store was right across from Herman Tietz, the first German

department store, the site from which decorators had traveled to Chicago to

learn the art of window display at the Marshall Field Department Store.

Sally Westmann, the future father of Thea Westmann, together with his brother Simon worked long hours to steer the business in a different direction. They decided to specialize in black mourning attire.

A second Westmann store - here specializing in black mourning attire

The Westmann Store featured the custom-made suits, dresses, coats, and hats customarily worn for an entire year after the death of a loved one. Sales people would go to peoples' homes with samples of the black dresses, coats, hats and veils needed for these lengthy periods of mourning. The five seamstresses working under the supervision of a professional dressmaker could hardly meet the demands of their growing number of customers.

Sally worked long hours at the store six days a week. He was in charge of the employees and Simon took charge of the finances. On one occasion, Simon became impatient with one of the employees who was late almost everyday. "I'm tired of his excuses," Simon complained. One time he was late because the horses pulling the streetcar refused to move; another time, a worker's strike blocked the street; another time, his right leg felt numb.

"Why don't you fire him?", Simon asked. Sally thought for a second and said, "When his excuses get boring, I'll fire him."

The Westmann store on Frankfurther Street with its employees out front

At 32, Sally was a prosperous business man, but he despaired of ever finding a wife because of the long scar that stretched across the right side of his face. When he was a teenager, the oral surgeon had made an incision through the outside of his cheek to remove an infected wisdom tooth. As a result, Sally Westmann was always shown with his *left profile* turned toward the camera.

Sally's life changed when he met the friendly, well-educated Natalie Mottek. She liked the affectionate Sally who exclaimed that she was the most beautiful woman he'd ever seen. Her parents liked him too because he came from a solid middle-class German Jewish family. Natalie's parents valued education above all. Her father had even agreed to let his daughter become a

10

teacher, but only if she promised never to *work* as one. (During the nineteenth century, respectable girls did not work outside the home.) Natalie obtained her teaching degree and she longed to teach, but dutifully stayed at home.

The friendship between Sally and Natalie turned to love. When one of her friends asked how she could love a man with a deformed face, she answered, "He is the kindest man I've ever met. I love him with or without the scar." On December 25, 1905, the entire family living in and around Posen arrived either by streetcar or in horse and buggy to celebrate the wedding of Natalie and Sally Westmann. They began their life together by moving into an apartment on the Grosse Frankfurter Street, not far from their store. Their exceptionally modern elevator building even had central heating! [Appendix A]

Eleven months later their son Kurt was born. The boy blossomed in the singular glow of his parents' love. He beguiled those around him - especially his mother - with his astute observations and handsome appearance. By the time he was four, he would share his parents' love with a new baby, without fear of losing his special place in their hearts. He could hardly wait to see the new baby born on October 24, 1910. Despite occasional anti-Semitic outbursts from opportunistic politicians, life under Kaiser Wilhelm II seemed as peaceful as the new baby girl nestled in her mother's arm. "Her name is Thea," his mother explained as she sat down to give him a better view of his sister. (*Thea Westmann later changed her name to Dorothy Becker.*) Her blond hair looked like his, he thought to himself; and at least she wasn't crying. He liked how she gripped his finger too whenever he touched her tiny hand.

One day he watched attentively as his mother changed the baby's diaper. The four-year old Kurt looked surprised as he inspected the baby's bare bottom, and told his mother not to worry, "It'll grow when she gets bigger." Kurt's exceptional good looks prompted the nanny to call him a prince. But he stomped his foot and said, "I'm not a prince; I'm Kurt Westmann from Berlin."

2

EARLY CHILDHOOD

"My brother and I always had a special relationship. He loved me, and he always protected me. Even when we were little, he was much nicer to me than I was to him. I could hit him and he would never hit me back."

At an early age, Thea discovered that not all boys refrain from hitting girls. One day while playing in the park, one of the boys called her a bad name. She slapped him across the face and to her surprise, he hit her back. She ran to her mother crying, "He hit me"! Her mother, who had watched the entire incident, asked, "What did you do?" Thea confessed, "I hit him first, but he called me a bad name. Besides, a boy isn't allowed to hit a girl," insisted Thea. "Not all boys are like Kurt," her mother explained.

On a family vacation in Bad Kissingen, a popular resort in Germany, Thea was struck with severe abdominal pain. World War I had just broken out, and their family doctor had enlisted in the army. In desperation, Mrs. Westmann called a friend of the family, a doctor who had been retired for 15 years. He agreed to examine Thea and determined she had acute appendicitis and needed surgery immediately.

The doctor refused to do the operation because he had been out of practice for a number of years. Unable to find another surgeon, her frantic parents finally convinced the elderly doctor to perform the surgery. Reluctantly, he agreed and removed the inflamed appendix.

Thea survived the surgery, which in those pre-penicillin days could have been life threatening. Temporarily, her mother stopped working at the Westmann store to spend most of the day at Thea's bedside. After a six weeks hospital stay, Thea went home but had to stay in bed for six months. A constant stream of friends, family and neighbors visited Thea daily. *"I loved it because I had so much company,"* she recalled. *"One day three people came at the same time!"*

Mitze, the 15-year old daughter of the head designer at the Westmann store, was Thea's nanny. Everyday, Mitze helped Kurt with his homework first and then took Thea and her friend Margo Kainer to the park. While Thea had to stay in bed, Margo brought her dolls to say "hello" to their Aunt Thea in the afternoon. The girls had to make sure that their dolls took the pink cough medicine that Thea's Uncle Jacob, the pharmacist, mixed specially for them. When they got older, Thea liked to play school with Margo because when they picked roles, she didn't mind that Thea wanted to be the principal of their girls' school.

On the weekend aunts, uncles and cousins usually took turns visiting one other, but now that Thea had to stay in bed, Uncle Simon and other relatives usually took the streetcar to the Westmanns' on Sunday afternoons. All this attention could cause the most stoic person to become a hypochondriac. To the contrary, throughout her life, Thea usually dealt with most aches and pains by ignoring them. Since birth, she had little vision in her right eye, but she never mentioned it. However, she did convince her mother to get the doctor to excuse her from gym, permanently. The doctor had no idea how much Thea hated to wear the school gym uniform!

Thea was surprised to learn that both of her parents loved both of their children. For years, she thought that her mother only loved Kurt and her father only loved her. In the evening, when her father came home, not even the delicious aromas from the kitchen could deter him from visiting his Thea first. She couldn't wait to see him. Her beguiling smile warmed his heart and erased any sign of whatever worried him.

Sometimes he brought her a perfectly tailored dress that one of the dress-makers had made for a favorite doll. "A Sunday dress is just what she needs," exclaimed Thea gazing affectionately at her father. Stroking the hint of a dim-ple in her cheek, he repeated the words she most loved to hear, "No one laughs like my Thea!" She hugged him tightly as he lifted her into his arms. "Soon you'll be completely well again, just in time for school," he whispered.

School Days

"In first grade I invited the entire class to my birthday party. I wasn't close to anyone in particular; I just liked all of them!"

Only Rebecca Plotke, a girl from an orthodox family could not accept the invitation because the Westmanns did not keep kosher. All of her other class-mates eagerly awaited the day of the party. Only one problem existed: Thea hadn't told her mother that 40 kids might show up on her birthday.

Mrs. Westmann first heard about the prospective party when several mothers called to find out what time they should bring their children to the Westmann home. Mrs. Westmann, who usually could take any emergency in stride, panicked at the thought of having 40 children at the house without being able to serve them any treats. During the First World War, one could not buy the sugar, butter, cocoa and milk needed for making cakes, cookies, and hot chocolate. She did not have the heart to disappoint her daughter and her enthusiastic classmates. Finally, 18 girls came to Thea's party and devoured the rye bread with thinly spread margarine as if they were savoring chocolate cake.

They sang, played a balloon game and squealed with excitement as the blindfolded players tried to pin the tail on the donkey. One of Thea's friends suggested they play school. The girl who played the teacher's role could imitate the angry voice of Mrs. Krech perfectly, especially when she lost her patience with Rebecca Plotke. Even before Mr. Plotke had enrolled Rebecca at the Margareten Lyceum, her father had asked the principal of the school to excuse his daughter from written work on Saturdays. In post-World War I Germany, children attended school six days per week. Rebecca's father explained that their religion did not permit them to write on the Sabbath. Dr. Engelman, the principal, who upheld the rights of all people to practice their religion, gave Rebecca a note to give to the teacher, excusing her from writing assignments on Saturdays.

The following Saturday the teacher - Mrs. Krech - told the children to take out their chalk and chalkboards. While her classmates rummaged inside their desks to produce the needed writing materials, only Rebecca did not follow the teacher's instruction. She sat perfectly still with her hands folded on top of her desk.

Glaring at the girl, the teacher repeated, "I said, take out your chalkboard."

In a barely audible voice the girl explained that her father did not permit her to write on Saturdays. "Why don't you go to a Jewish school?" yelled the teacher. The child's head drooped as she fixed her eyes on her tightly clenched hands. Neither the anger of her teacher nor the stares from her classmates could prompt her to disobey her father.

The teacher's angry outburst at Rebecca perplexed Thea who could not understand why Mrs. Krech wanted Rebecca to go to a Jewish school. On the way home from school, Thea and her friend, Ilse, could talk about nothing else. After dinner, Thea told her mother about the disturbing incident. Thea thought that most people were Jewish and just couldn't understand why Mrs. Krech had made a distinction between their school and a Jewish school.

She asked, "Aren't all people Jewish?" Her mother explained, "Most people in Berlin are Protestant or Catholic. The Protestant minister and the Catholic priest teach religion to the Christian children, while you and the four other Jewish girls in your class learn the Old Testament stories from Mr. Sommerfeld." But Thea wondered, "Why don't I go to a Jewish school?" "Why should you go to a Jewish school?" her mother responded. "I went to a public school and so did your grandmother." They talked until bedtime. Stroking the child's gleaming hair, she admonished, "Be proud of who you are." Thea fell asleep with those words imprinted on her heart.

Because she showed favoritism, Mrs. Krech was never one of Thea's favorite teachers. But Thea didn't dislike her until the teacher actually accused her of lying. During a writing lesson, she dictated a sentence which contained the German word, "Bäcker" which means "baker" in English.

Helene, the daughter of a minister, asked Thea, "How do you spell "Backer," with an "a" or an "e"? Before Thea had a chance to answer, Mrs. Krech demanded to know, "Who talked?" Helene, pointing her finger at Thea said, "She talked." The flustered Thea blurted out, "How can you say I talked when you asked me to spell Backer?" Fixing her stern gaze on Thea, Mrs. Krech pronounced her verdict calmly and irrevocably, "A minister's daughter doesn't lie."

Blood rushed to Thea's face as her heart beat furiously against her chest. The teacher had accused her of something she had not done, and she was powerless to defend herself. After school, on their way to the Westmann Store, Ilse tried to console Thea, who kept repeating between sobs, "She didn't even give me a chance to tell her what happened."

Thea always told everyone how she felt, but this time, "I was crying so hard I couldn't even talk." Ilse told Mrs Westmann that their teacher had falsely accused Thea of lying. Mitze's mother, suggested that Mrs. Krech might be a friend of Helene's family or a member of their church. "Regardless, a teacher should never show preference," countered Thea's mother. They talked until past Thea's bedtime. Her mother assured her, "You don't need to feel ashamed or guilty if you know you told the truth."

A few weeks later, she and Helene were in a class play together. The entire class came to school dressed in fancy clothes for the wedding they staged on the playground. Nobody wanted to play the mother-in-law. Because her mother always said nice things about her mother-in-law, Thea volunteered for the role. Besides, she'd have a chance to wear her blue velvet dress.

Helene, playing the minister, was dressed in black, and performed the wedding ceremony beneath the large elm tree. The groom had just kissed the giggling bride, when the bell rang.

As soon as Mr. Borg, Thea's math teacher entered class he noticed Thea. "How pretty you look. Are you going somewhere special today?" She reminded him, " I'm the mother-in-law, don't you remember?"

After that Mr. Borg always asked, "How is my little mother-in-law?" When she later married, he sent a telegram with best wishes to "My Favorite Little Mother-in-Law."

At this time, marriage was far from Thea's mind. She wanted to become a doctor, like Nesthackchen, the heroine of her favorite book. Like her role model, she wanted to become a children's doctor first, and then perhaps marry a doctor. Her friend Gerda Israel was determined to become a judge. This was not such an impossible dream because after World War I, the universities in Germany were beginning to open their doors to women.

Mr. Katzorke, Thea's French teacher, despised everything French, including the language. For him, World War I would not end until Germany had torn the Treaty of Versailles into shreds. His students didn't need to learn the correct pronunciation of words like Marseilles and Bordeaux because he believed that eventually Germany would conquer France and German would become the predominant language of France. Unfortunately, years later, some of his predictions came true. Thea disliked this teacher, and doing the homework he gave in French, poetry and geography was a drudgery she postponed as long as she could.

19

During one of his classes, he noticed that the pencils in his supply box were dwindling. He told the students to take everything out of their desks. He walked past the other students, but interrogated each of the five Jewish students as if he suspected them of stealing his pencils.

Looking suspiciously at the two pencils on top of Thea's desk, he ordered her to make sure that she had taken everything out of her desk. She felt embarrassed and said, "Everything is out of my desk." "Everything?" he asked in an accusing tone, as he checked the inside of her desk with a brusque sweep of his hand. Ilse, who sat near Thea, gathered her courage and asked, "Why do you question her like this?" Giving her a sidelong glance he muttered, "I have my reasons."

That evening at a parent teacher meeting, Mr. Katzorke spotted Ilse's father and warned him to keep a closer check on the "type of girls his daughter befriends." Ilse's father, a teacher at a boys' school, knew Thea well. On weekends, he had frequently taken her along on hiking tours and on steamship excursions. "If you are referring to Thea Westmann," he replied, "I'm delighted that she and Ilse are best friends."

Despite Mr. Katzorke's objections, Thea and Ilse remained inseparable. They thoroughly enjoyed the chance to poke some fun at Mr. Katzorke, who was also their geography teacher. During the previous semester, they had studied the lakes and rivers which border the large cities of North America. As soon as the semester ended, Else, one of their classmates, moved to the United States with her family. As soon as she arrived in Chicago, she sent her former classmates a card, assuring them that Mr. Katzorke, as always, was absolutely right. Chicago is indeed situated on the shores of Lake Michigan.

When Else's friend, with permission from the teacher, read the card to the class, everyone laughed uproariously, except Mr. Katzorke. He was furious. How dared they make fun of him? He doled out swift and immediate punishment by having the entire class write one hundred times, "Chicago is situated on the shores of Lake Michigan." But Mr. Katzorke was not the only one brimming with subversive ideas.

A Revolt at Their Doorsteps

"We were petrified as bullets shattered every window in our living room, but when Kurt yelled, 'Mother, I think I heard shooting!', we all burst out laughing."

Two hundred thousand communists, carrying flags and weapons, paraded through the streets of Berlin on January 5, 1919.[1] They marched down the Grosse Frankfurter Street, shattering the windows of shops, including those of the Westmann Store and the Tietz Department Store. The German Chancellor, Friedrich Ebert, ordered the German military to retaliate with flame throwers, artillery and machine guns. From the first day of the Spartacus Uprising, both the Westmann store and their apartment building were caught in the cross fire between the government troops and the communists who yelled, "Power to the proletariat."

Every window in their apartment and store was broken. They had no choice but to flee to Uncle Simon's house in a quiet section of Berlin. They dressed in a hurry. Thea's father suggested that they each take along the one article that was most important to them. He took his prayer book; his wife took her purse; Kurt lifted the bird cage from its stand, and Thea carried her favorite doll.

In the hallway, they met their friends, Margo and Herbert Kainer, who were waiting for their parents. Momentarily, the two girls forgot the raucous revolt outside and chatted as if they were going on a vacation. They hoped that the Uprising would last until spring break. Their street had become a war zone, the streetcar wasn't running, and the usual line of droshkes (horse and buggies) had all but disappeared.

Finally, Mr. Westmann flagged down a tired-looking driver with his horse and buggy. With the help of a little extra change, the driver allowed the two families to squeeze into the buggy which comfortably seated only four people. Gangs of militant communists shouted, "Bourgeois, bourgeois, bourgeois!", as eight people and a dog squeezed into the top-heavy carriage.

Halfway to Uncle Simon's house the weary horse didn't even have the energy to hold up its head. It pulled its heavy load at an ever slower pace until it stopped, refusing to take another step. The Kainer family had to get out, and luckily, found another carriage. After some rest and a generous helping of water and oats, their horse took the Westmanns to Uncle Simon's house in time for lunch.

When Thea and Kurt jumped out of the carriage, their three cousins were eagerly awaiting them, but they pretended surprise and asked, "Whose birthday is it?" The two families always celebrated holidays and birthdays together and on Sundays they visited each other by streetcar - but never on school days!

In Berlin, the fighting continued as the German military freed the

Vorwarts' newspaper building and the Telegraph Bureau from communist control. After two weeks, the Spartacus Uprising had claimed the lives of 100 communists and 13 free military corps men. The fighting ended on January 19, 1919 when two lieutenants brutally murdered the communist leaders, Rosa Luxemburg and Karl Liebknecht.[2]

When a child reached the age of 10, her teachers together with the parents decided which track she should follow. Some students stayed another four years at the elementary school, which was free of charge. Those girls who wanted to enter a profession transferred to the Lyceum (a secondary girls' school in Germany). Most of the girls in her class wanted to go on to the university. Thea's mother had been allowed to go to teachers' college only if she promised never to teach. She could have been a full-time wife and mother, but she preferred to work at their store. Like her mother, Thea aspired to have a profession and to someday realize her dream of becoming a pediatrician. She transferred to the Luisen Lyceum when she was 10.

The Luisen Lyceum

What Thea liked best about the gymnasium were the summers at the Landheim School. Dr. Engelman taught literature beneath shady elm trees on the lawn of the school. Thea, Ilse and Lieschen, a friend who hoped to become a music teacher, liked the informal atmosphere. They sat on the grass and didn't have to jump up every time the teacher entered the class. Before class, they jogged everyday along the paths through the park that separated their school from a school for mentally handicapped children.

On their afternoon strolls through the park, Thea befriended one of the handicapped children. One day, the little girl spotted Thea from a distance, dashed out of the sandbox, and ran straight into Thea's arms. The girl squealed with delight as Thea twirled her around. "Why do you play with her?" sneered one of the neighborhood boys. "She goes to the dummy school." When Thea told him that the little girl had a lot more sense than he had, he began to hurl more insults at them. The frightened little girl huddled closer within Thea's protective arms.

When their teacher asked the class to write about their most memorable experience that summer, the affectionate little girl from the school for handicapped children came alive in Thea's composition. She questioned how any one could be mean enough to call the child a "dummy," and tried to discover why the boy would taunt a handicapped child. She linked her affection for the handicapped child to the empathy she felt for her father who was disfigured by the scar on his face. The teacher read Thea's paper to the class and awarded her the first prize for her composition.

That experience strengthened her determination to become a doctor in order to help children like her little friend from the special school. Someday, she hoped to study at the well-known Children's Clinic in Munich. Her mother took her seriously, and so did Gerda Israel, one of her closest teenage friends.

Gerda, who was inclined to look at three sides of every problem, wanted to become a judge. She had a better than average chance of getting into to law school because her father had died fighting for Germany during the First World War. Widowed at a young age, Mrs. Israel struggled to provide for herself and her two children, Gerda and James. Both children wanted to go to the university, but she wondered how she was going to pay for their education. Her hard work and smart decisions paid off, and by the mid 1930's, she owned three millinery stores.

For at least another three years, Gerda and Thea spent carefree hours playing tennis together. They also went swimming everyday during their vacations in the Black Forest. During the 1920's, popular songs were played on the piano in every living room. The most prized article any relative could bring back from a trip to Berlin or Frankfurt was sheet music of a favorite song which usually originated in America. At the height of the Depression, some played the piano, others sang, but everybody danced!

Girls were always trying to get their brothers to practice a new dance step with them. Even Gerda, who usually preferred to read, attended dance classes on Saturday afternoons with Thea, Margo and their brothers. The fun began afterwards, when the 30 kids from the dance class would go to someone's house to eat and dance.

After second helpings of potato salad and sausages, they moved the furniture against the wall, placed a record on the phonograph and resumed their dancing. The boy with a balloon of a certain color had to ask the girl holding a matching balloon to dance.

A young doctor came to one of the Saturday dance parties at Thea's house. Thea had the feeling that he and Gerda liked each other, but she denied it. A few months later, Gerda sent Thea a card from Greece. She wrote: "Can you imagine, by chance, I met Victor while I was touring the Acropolis." Then she went to Egypt and wrote: "Can you imagine, by coincidence, I met Victor on the way to the pyramids." Years later, they got married.

Margo, an excellent dancer, had no difficulty finding partners. Since the popular Kurt was seldom available to practice with his sister, Thea danced with Herbert, who was studying medicine. She was 14 and he was 18. They danced a lot, and people thought they liked each other, but they never went out together. He was older and was studying to become a doctor. He tried to impress her with stories about the cadavers he dissected, but he seemed immature to her.

3

ROMANTIC AWAKENING

"I wanted so badly to go with Kurt to Westerland, an island in the North Sea. My parents wouldn't let me go with Kurt; they said, "Come with us to Wildbad." "I was so disappointed."

Initially, Kurt had asked Thea to go with him to Westerland, a vacation spot popular with the young people. Mostly older people went to the Wildbad Spa in the Black Forest. Thea doubted that her parents would let her go alone on a vacation with Kurt.

At a recent party, Thea's father, watching one of the boys say good-bye to Thea with a slightly prolonged hand shake, had darted toward the startled young man muttering, "That'll be all. It's time to go now; It's getting late."

Her father would never let his daughter stray too far from his watchful eye. Mrs. Israel and Gerda would go with them to Wildbad. Mrs. Israel, a good friend of the Westmanns, liked going on vacations with her friends. Her children, Gerda and James, were about the same age as Thea and Kurt. Mr. Westmann tried to persuade Thea that she and Gerda would have as much fun in Wildbad and Switzerland. Thea felt disappointed because most of the people at Wildbad were older.

In the 1920's many middle class families often took their daughters to fashionable spas to maximize their chances of meeting desirable marriage partners. This was not the intention of either the Westmanns or Mrs. Israel. Her daughter, Gerda, was intent on going to law school, and Thea wanted to study medicine. Someday, after graduation from the Children's Clinic in Munich, she hoped to meet the mature, intelligent man of her dreams.

At the Wildbad Spa, the two girls raced each other across the length of the swimming pool every morning. They played tennis in the afternoon, while the older people sitting near the court, liked to watch the two girls volley the ball across the net.

In the evenings, people danced to live music. Even during the week many young people from the neighboring villages came to the dances. Gerda, who preferred to wear slacks to hide her heavy legs, looked bored and hadn't danced once. Thea danced with everyone and the young men reserved dances with her for Saturday's ball.

In a letter to Kurt, Thea wrote, "Too many older people! The word 'boring' describes the place perfectly." Kurt read on with amusement. Despite her complaints, he remembered that plenty of young men from the nearby town of Pforzheim attended the dance parties on Wednesdays, Saturday evenings and Sunday afternoons. She casually mentioned the gold engraved announcements displayed on every table in the dining room inviting all music lovers and dancers to join the orchestra in the grand ballroom on Saturday evening. "Formal attire required." Feigning indifference, the cool teenager could barely conceal her excitement as she anticipated the gala event.

On the morning of the dance, every hair dryer at the hotel beauty shop hummed anxiously above the heads of impatient customers. The frenzied manager of the beauty shop admonished the girl assigned to wash Thea's hair to stop talking and get to work.

Trude and Thea had been classmates at the Margareten Lyceum, and here she was washing Thea's hair. Trude had left school early to help her widowed mother support the family. Usually Mrs. Westmann gave her daughter the tip for the woman who washed her hair. This time she asked her mother to give the tip to Trude herself.

Her less fortunate friend stimulated feelings of guilt as Thea considered the half dozen new dresses her father had bought her for the trip. He always said, "If my wife and daughter don't dress in style, how can I expect my customers to buy the latest fashions." Whenever his wife appeared in a new dress, he would ask relatives, friends or even strangers, "Have you ever seen anyone look more beautiful?" For the grand ball that evening, Thea chose her father's favorite red dress. The swirling skirt, fitted bodice and slightly revealing neckline, gently outlined her graceful figure.

After dinner that evening, gentlemen in tuxedos escorted ladies wearing long evening gowns to the grand ballroom. As soon as Thea's parents, Mrs. Israel and Gerda, stopped to admire a large bouquet of lilacs and roses on the antique table outside the ballroom, the singer on stage recognized Thea. She recalled:

"He waved to me from the stage. Once we were seated, he came to our table and sang a special serenade for me. I was only 16 years old; it was real kitsch, but I loved it."

Shimmering chandeliers swayed rhythmically to the lilting sounds of violins, as the parquet floor, buffed to a flawless sheen, awaited the eager dancers. Spurred by the whirl of a Viennese waltz, men rushed across the floor to ask the girls of their choice for the opening number. The first of several young men strode toward Thea, bowed slightly and asked her for a dance. She rose, smiling at the prospect of swirling around the dance floor in perfect time to the music. Those years of practice at the Saturday dance parties had prepared her well. He asked where she was from, and when she said, "Berlin," he replied, "You don't look like a girl from Berlin." Every man she danced with asked her the same question and made the same comment. She was getting tired of it. As they walked off the dance floor, the shy young man from the neighboring village asked if she planned to go to the tea dance the following Sunday. If so, would she please reserve a dance with him? She promised she would.

When she returned to their table, she discovered that her father and Gerda had gone upstairs to play a game of chess. Gerda, who had protested that she did not want to dance with every Harry, Hans or Ludwig, had not danced even once. The 17-year old Gerda said, "Why should I dance with a man just because he asks me. I just hate it." Thea, who was 16, danced with everybody. Gerda's mother didn't like the way her daughter was acting, but Thea's father said, "You're absolutely right. We didn't go on a vacation to sit in a smoky ballroom." Gerda's mother stayed. She liked the music and enjoyed watching the young people dance.

At a nearby table, a more confident, mature man had not ventured off his chair either. Nearly oblivious to the company of his brother, Richard, his father, and his Uncle Ike, he had spent most of the evening watching the gregarious Thea with increasing interest. Initially, he had not wanted to attend the ball, but Richard insisted that they should make an appearance anyway to please their father and their Uncle Ike. Their father and Uncle Ike, who lived in Chicago, considered the big band at Wildbad its main attraction.

Front: Wilhelm Becker - Back: Sally Westmann, Ike and Richard Becker

Richard had settled the matter by suggesting that his brother could always buy a tuxedo in the event he hadn't brought one with him. "Have you seen any nice girls?" the reluctant brother asked Richard, who had arrived at Wildbad a few days earlier.

At the ball, Richard pointed out two of the prettiest girls he had seen at the hotel the day before. The moment Richard directed his brother's attention to one of the girls he thought his brother might like, she took a cigarette out of her purse. "I don't like women who smoke," grumbled his brother. "Do you see the blond, blue-eyed girl in the red dress at the table to our left?"

His brother smiled, nodding with approval. He liked her feminine, yet stylish appearance. Her youthful spontaneity muted with inbred decorum appealed to him. She danced with everyone, yet maintained a discreet distance from the young men who led her across the floor. Above all, her engaging smile captivated him. Suddenly, he rose from his chair and with an aside to Richard declared, "I'll ask her for a dance."

Until he was standing by her side, Thea had not noticed the athletic looking man of medium height, who had fixed his eyes on her most of the evening. The intense gaze of his blue eyes startled her. Extending his hand to take hers, he asked, "May I have this dance?" His unwavering gesture elicited more than a routine response from her. She looked at him and said, "Yes, I would like to dance with you."

From the moment she had entered the ballroom she had been serenaded by the singer, she had been complimented by the stream of young men who had asked her to dance, but never before had she felt as exhilarated as she did while dancing with this compelling stranger. Her face flushed as she became aware of feeling totally protected within his arms.

She returned to earth when he asked her where she was from. When he told her that she didn't look like a girl from Berlin she had heard it once too often, and snapped, "Have you ever been to Berlin and do you know what the girls in Berlin look like?"

During one of the slower dances he introduced himself, "My name is Wilhelm Becker." When he told her that he was finishing a fellowship in orthopedic surgery at the University Hospital in Munich, she stopped in the middle of a waltz and exclaimed, "That's where I want to study, at the University Hospital in Munich. I want to become a pediatrician." He raised an eyebrow and she wasn't sure if he was teasing when he said, "Women doctors are masculine." Because she felt complimented by his admiring smile, his remark had hardly registered with her.

He asked her to dance a second time and told her, "I'd really like to see you again; I'll tell you more about the Clinic." Thea explained, "My father doesn't want me to go to Munich. He tells me that I can study in Berlin just as well. But when I'm 18, I can go." As he escorted her back to their table he told her how much he had enjoyed dancing with her. Their eyes met momentarily as they said "good-night."

Mrs. Israel leaned towards Thea's mother and whispered, "He will marry her." Startled by the definite tone in her friend's voice, Thea's mother protested, "She is only 16; besides, she wants to go to medical school." Mrs. Israel persisted, "I can tell by the way he looked at her. I'll bet you a Dresden doll, he'll ask her to marry him."

The following day, Richard lost no time informing Wilhelm that he had seen Thea in the writing room adjacent to the lobby. Wilhelm leaped down the stairs, two steps at a time. Just as she was writing Kurt that Wildbad was not so boring after all, Wilhelm suddenly appeared and she was thrilled to see him again.

The usually quiet Wilhelm had no trouble starting a conversation with the talkative Thea. She wondered if the University Hospital also treated children with mental disabilities. Wilhelm assured her that all children, regardless of their parents' ability to pay, were treated at the Children's Clinic in Munich. He told her about one of his favorite patients, an orphaned boy named "Schorschi." Willhelm had assisted with the surgery to correct the boy's feet. He loved the child and saved all the cookies and candies he could get for the four-year old Schorschi. Every morning, the boy sat and played outside Wilhelm's office, anticipating the moment he would emerge with the hoped - for treat.

They spoke with palpable excitement as they discovered mutual interests, despite their age difference. Wilhelm, who was 30, expected to finish his fellowship at the Hospital in 18 months. Engrossed in conversation, they had lost track of time. In the distance, Thea recognized her mother's footsteps hurrying toward them. She introduced Wilhelm to her mother. "It's nearly three o'clock," she reminded Thea. "You have to get dressed yet or you'll be late for the tea dance."

Before they went upstairs, Wilhelm asked, *"Do you have to go? Can we sit together, just the two of us?"* She was really more interested in him, but she had promised some of the young men that she would dance with them. He persisted: "Would you dance only with me?"

She wanted to say "yes" but she didn't think it was right to renege on her promises. Several of the young men had told her they would make the trip from Pforzheim just to dance with her.

She rushed upstairs, changed into a dancing dress and appeared at the tea dance 15 minutes later. Wilhelm, already waiting at one of the tables, rose when she entered the social room and held the chair for her until she was seated next to him. They danced two numbers, but both longed to be outside on that balmy Sunday afternoon. When he asked if she'd like to go for a walk, she wondered if he had read her mind.

Thea recalls, "We walked along the river and talked, and talked, and talked. It was so beautiful." Wilhelm told her he was from Rockenhausen, where his father owned a grain business. He explained that he was finishing his medical education later than usual because he had served two years in the army during World War I. He was 16 when the First World War broke out, and in a burst of patriotic zeal, he together with his entire class, had quit school to volunteer for military service.

Many of his former classmates did not come back. He considered himself one of the lucky ones, even though he had sustained an injury to his right arm. Initially, he thought his hope of becoming a surgeon had been shattered, but fortunately he *did* regain full use of his right hand.

After the War, he finished the gymnasium and entered the university to study medicine. After he finished his fellowship in orthopedic surgery, he hoped to obtain a teaching position at one of the university hospitals. He looked forward to earning a decent salary in the near future. His father and his Uncle Ike had invited him to join them in Wildbad, a welcome break from the long hours of work.

She told him, "At first I wanted to go to Westerland, but both of my parents disapproved of my going alone on a vacation with my brother Kurt." "Your parents definitely made the right decision," he commented. "I think so too," she confided. He wondered, "How else would we have met?" "I believe we would have met somewhere, somehow." Her steadfast glance and the caressing intimacy of her voice captivated him.

For as long as she could remember, she had always wanted to be 16. "Could he be the reason?" she wondered silently, casting a sidelong glance at the self assured man she had met only yesterday. This, the 16th summer of her life had already surpassed her fondest dreams. Once again they lost track of time.

The eerie stillness of the forest alerted them to the fact that most of the vacationers were probably in their hotel rooms getting dressed for dinner. As they hurried back, he asked, "Could we see each other again tomorrow? I'll pick an armful of flowers for you if we take the path that winds through the meadow," he promised. She beamed, "Only if you'll accept a flower from me."

The following morning, Thea and Gerda met at the swimming pool. Basking in the warm sunshine, Thea talked of nothing but Wilhelm. Gerda couldn't understand why Thea was smitten with him. The topic bored her. Thea realized that Gerda felt left out, but she could hardly wait to see Wilhelm again.

Later, while strolling through the flower-dotted meadow, Wilhelm told Thea about his deceased mother, a kind but formal woman who had expected her sons to wear jackets before they sat down at the dinner table. Not only did proper clothes make a good first impression, she said, but they reflected your upbringing and social class. Their parents' preoccupation with appearance seemed superficial to Thea. To have ideals and to help those in need seemed much more important. Wilhelm agreed. "My brother Richard maintains that he is the capitalist and I am the idealist of the family. I think he's right," he conceded.

Wilhelm Becker and Thea Westmann - Love at first sight!

Thea smiled. She knew that the word "idealist" applied to her as well. Near an alcove of trees they rested awhile as the sun's departing rays cast long shadows across the meadows. A final glimpse of the setting sun brought Wilhelm to his feet. He extended both hands to help her up. Thea trailed behind while Wilhelm darted sideways and forward to pick a bouquet of buttercups, poppies and corn flowers for her.

High in the sky an invisible star took note of that first tangible expression of his love for her. Inhaling the subtle scent of the meadow flowers, she removed one poppy, caressed its petals with her lips, and handed it to him. Church bells chimed their evening song as the last rays of the departing sun held the couple in a momentary embrace.

The Zavelstein Ruin

That evening, Richard, who had become aware of his brother's increasing interest in Thea, reminded Wilhelm of their plans to drive to the Zavelstein Ruin the following day. "Perhaps Thea and her family would like to go with us. There is enough room in the car to invite Mrs. Israel and Gerda also."

Mrs. Westmann, who had developed a painful swelling beneath her right arm had a doctor's appointment and declined the invitation. Mrs. Israel and Gerda appreciated the invitation, but they too had other plans that day. Thea, however, expressed a profound interest in seeing the ruins of a 12th century castle. Of course, she would have been equally eager to visit the city garbage dump if the tour gave her an opportunity to be near Wilhelm.

With the chauffeur behind the steering wheel, the car climbed steadily through a patchwork of meadows and forests until they reached the Zavelstein Ruin at the top of a mountain. Throughout the 13th and 14th centuries, the once majestic castle had dominated the surrounding valley until it was destroyed in 1692. Remnants of the dilapidated banquet hall with its stone fireplace evoked images of feasting and dancing to celebrate Christmas, weddings and military victories.

The voice of the tour guide droned on endlessly as Wilhelm removed his light meter to set the aperture on his camera. Taking Thea's hand, he led her to a higher, sunnier side of the crumbling castle. By the time the tour ended, he had taken two rolls of pictures - all of her - nevertheless chiding himself for not having brought more film.

No one objected when Wilhelm's father and Uncle Ike suggested stopping for refreshments at the Zavelstein restaurant. When the waitress arrived, Wilhelm's father asked Thea what she would like to have. Thea remembered what her father always told her, "Never accept money from any man. You always pay for yourself." She took two dimes out of her change purse and replied, "I'd like some lemonade but I want to pay for it myself."

The four men laughed uproariously. Uncle Ike took on the difficult task of convincing Thea to allow them to treat her to the lemonade. When he suggested she might even splurge and try a piece of cake with whipped cream, she laughed and put her dime back into her purse.

That night, the memory of Wilhelm's gentle touch kept her awake for hours. She had finally fallen asleep after midnight, but got up early to meet Gerda at the pool. Drying off on a sunny patch of meadow, the two girls talked about their plans for the future. Gerda, intent on pursuing a law career, found it difficult to listen to her friend's preoccupation with Wilhelm. Noticeably irritated, she exclaimed, "So what if he is the most intelligent man you've ever met! So what if he's a great surgeon!"

Disappointed that Gerda could not share her happiness, Thea stopped talking, but she could not stop thinking about Wilhelm. Although the two girls continued to swim and play tennis together, they were drifting apart, emotionally.

Irrevocably drawn to each other, Thea and Wilhelm wanted to be together whenever possible. She wasn't sure when she would see him again because she and Gerda had plans to visit the Sommerberg (Summer Mountain) the following day.

Every tourist visiting the Wildbad Resort rode the cable car to the top of the Sommerberg. Spectacular views, scenic trails, plus a slice of Black Forest cake, awaited each pilgrim at the top of the mountain. If necessary, Thea would gladly forego a piece of her favorite cake for the chance to catch a glimpse of Wilhelm.

Gliding on a gentle breeze, the cable car sailed effortlessly from the shining meadow to the carefree blue of the sky. As they climbed higher, their hotel withdrew deeper into the heart of the surrounding forest. From their elevated carriage in space, the sprightly Enz River appeared to wind a white ribbon in and around the Wildbad Spa. In the village of Wildbad, splashes of red geranium peered from window sills and balconies. White stucco houses, reinforced with dark wooden beams, proudly displayed the characteristic Black Forest architecture. As they stepped out of the cable car, the church bells proclaimed their indisputable dominion over the valley.

The strong pine scent wafting from the carpeted slopes, prompted Gerda and her mother to stop for a bratwurst at the restaurant, while Thea and her parents inquired about hiking trails. As soon as Thea walked toward the information desk, Wilhelm spotted her. He greeted Mr. and Mrs. Westmann, and with a playful wink, told Thea, "I had no idea you and your parents might visit the Sommerberg today, but I was hoping to meet you here." With a ripple of girlish laughter, Thea replied, "I was hoping to see you too."

Wilhelm relished the delightful mixture of honesty and shyness. "This is the blueberry season," he said, "I'd like to pick some for you." "We can pick them together," she laughed excitedly. Thea's parents, holding a map of the various trails, remained undecided until Wilhelm pointed them in the direction of a secluded corner of the forest, thick with patches of blueberries. The enthusiastic pair promised to pick a pail of berries for dessert that evening.

The Westmanns, the Beckers, Mrs. Israel and Gerda gladly let Thea and Wilhelm lead the way. Engrossed in conversation, the three families strolled leisurely along the trail while Wilhelm and Thea strayed through the underbrush to hidden corners of the forest floor in search of the illusive berries.

They dodged prickly pine branches to pluck the plump, sweet fruit from the vines. The enamored couple carefully selected the most succulent berries to give to each other. The rest they deposited in the large pail for their families.

Emerging from the dusky forest, Wilhelm had to take at least one picture of Thea before the sun disappeared. She sat down momentarily on the lawn in front of the Sommerberg Restaurant, when to her surprise, a baby deer strolled along side of her. The gentle young creature didn't resist her in the least, and she cradled it in her arms long enough to have their picture taken.

Looking for a Doctor

Mr. and Mrs. Westmann were seriously considering the need to return home early because of the painful swelling under Mrs. Westmann's right arm. Earlier that week, she had seen a doctor from the village of Wildbad.

When she noticed the rusty scalpel and surgical scissors inside his instrument cabinet, she rushed out of his office. She wondered if she would be able to find a competent doctor in one of the neighboring towns. She had the choice of either returning to Berlin early or living with the throbbing pain for the remaining weeks of their vacation.

Distressed by her mother's pain, yet eager to remain with Wilhelm for as long as possible, Thea ventured a suggestion. "Why don't you ask Wilhelm to look at the swelling under your arm? He's a doctor."

To Thea's surprise, her parents took her suggestion seriously. Wilhelm's intelligence and confident manner had made a favorable impression on them. They asked him to look at the red, swollen boil beneath Mrs. Westmann's arm.

The following morning, Wilhelm drove to Wildbad and bought a minor surgery kit and some sterile bandages. Thea held her mother's arm up while Wilhelm lanced the boil, drained the wound and applied the sterile bandages. Every morning, the surgical team arrived to change Mrs. Westmann's dressing. By the end of their vacation, the wound had nearly healed; and Wilhelm had secured their respect and confidence.

He took a chance on asking Thea to go for a walk with him - unchaperoned - on their last evening in the Black Forest. The Westmanns, who usually joined Mrs. Israel and Gerda for supper, had just finished dessert when Wilhelm walked into the dining room. After shaking hands with each person seated at the table, he asked Thea if she would like to take a walk with him along the river. She glanced at her father whose benign expression did not signal any strong objection to Wilhelm's request.

She jumped to her feet, said "good-bye" to her parents, Mrs. Israel and Gerda, and bounded out the door with him. Her dream of being alone with him one last time had come true. This would probably be their last evening together since her family was scheduled to leave for Lucerne, Switzerland the following day. She pushed the painful thought of leaving Wilhelm out of her mind. For the moment, his nearness and the idyllic beauty of the evening enraptured her.

God Intervenes

Ribbons of orange and crimson crisscrossed the heavens as the tranquil valley reclined in the golden glow of the departing sun. They walked in silence following the Enz River as it coursed through the vast woodlands surrounding the resort. In the stillness of the evening, the forest came alive with its own music. A chorus of crickets announced the start of the mating season. The occasional rustling of a squirrel contrasted sharply with the relentless rush of the river.

Reluctantly, Wilhelm broke the silence: " I didn't want to tell you earlier, but this is my last night at Wildbad." She felt downcast and replied, "Tomorrow, we're leaving too." " Tomorrow Uncle Ike and I are taking the train to Lucerne," he said. Thea couldn't believe her ears, and was barely able to contain her excitement: "We're going to Lucerne too." She wondered, was this a coincidence or had God intervened so they could spend another week together? Wilhelm explained that Uncle Ike wanted to spend the last week of his vacation in Switzerland before he returned to Chicago. He had made reservations at the National Hotel which was right across the street from the Hotel Schweitzerhof where Thea would be staying with her family. "We'll be together one more week," she concluded. The intimate tone of her voice just mesmerized Wilhelm.

Thea Westmann and Wilhelm Becker - Tying the knot!

They continued to walk, but as the path ascended on a steeper incline, he took her hand to guide her through the dimming forest. When he held her hand she felt the same sense of security that she had experienced the first time she had danced with him. His manly confidence thrilled her.

They stopped near a bench beneath an alcove of trees. Leaning against the back of the bench, she searched the sky for the faint outlines of the new moon. Wilhelm faced her directly and cupped his hands around her shoulders.

Searching her animated eyes, he held her with outstretched arms and declared, "With you I can walk forever, wherever the road might lead." His use of the informal, more intimate form of "you" for the first time since they had met six days ago caused her to gasp.

In German, the familiar form of "you" removes barriers and holds the promise not only of friendship, but of romance, perhaps even intimacy. With one word he had removed the boundary that had maintained a formal distance between them. Though she was enthralled by the anticipation of a more enduring relationship with him, she did not fully understand what he had meant by, "With you I can walk forever, wherever the road might lead."

His eyes captivated her as he declared, " I love you Thea. Will you marry me?" She responded wholeheartedly, "And I love you. Yes, I will marry you!" Gently, he drew her close to him and kissed her. In a fleeting embrace, their love was sealed forever. Brushing his lips against the golden strands of her hair, he whispered, "We'll get married as soon as possible." Entwined in each other's arms, they "floated" back to the hotel.

Mr. and Mrs. Westmann had already retired to their room when Thea bolted through the door, threw her arms around her mother shouting, "Mutti, Mutti, er hat du zu mir gesagt." (Momi, Momi, he said "you" to me.)

Although Thea's mother understood the implications of the familiar form of "you," she didn't fully grasp what the excitement was about. After she had regained her composure, Thea proceeded to tell her mother that Wilhelm had told her that he loved her and had asked her to marry him. He had kissed her and said they would get married as soon as possible.

Thea's Mother - Natalie Mottek Westmann

The perceptive Mrs. Westmann tried to make sense out of her daughter's state of excitement. She listened intently to Thea's account of the marriage proposal, but she didn't take it seriously. At 16, she is much too young to even consider marriage, thought Mrs. Westmann.

All the while her husband's expression had changed from mild amusement to serious concern the more he listened to his daughter's enraptured account. They liked Wilhelm but marriage at the age of 16 was out of the question. Besides, they had met not even a week ago. Her father asked, "Is he Jewish?"

"I didn't ask him." "You have to know if he is Jewish," insisted her father. "But I'm not interested," she replied. He spoke sternly, "But I am interested." He looked at the clock. It was too late to call Wilhelm at that hour, but he would talk with him the first thing in the morning.

The following morning, Mr. Westmann and Wilhelm met in a quiet corner of the hotel lobby. "I want you to know that we are Jewish." "That doesn't bother me," Wilhelm replied. He chose not to reveal that he too was Jewish. For many academics and professionals, it was safer to conceal their religion. "My daughter is talking about getting married. What is the meaning of this?"

Wilhelm gathered his composure and revealed that he had fallen in love with Thea the moment he had first seen her. Even though they had met only a week ago, they loved each other and hoped to get married as soon as possible.

"Be that as it may, she's only 16," protested Mr. Westmann. "I'll definitely not permit her to get married before she is 18." Wilhelm assured Mr. Westmann that he would be in a good position to provide for Thea as soon as he finished his fellowship at the end of the following year.

Returning to their hotel room, Mr. Westmann repeated to his wife what he and William had talked about. He had made clear to Wilhelm that he would not permit his daughter to marry before becoming 18. "Then we'll see what will happen." Thea's mother was relieved to hear that Wilhelm would not be finished with his residency for another year. She needed at least that much time to adjust to this sudden change of plans.

In Switzerland, they did everything together. The Westmanns, Mrs.

Israel and Gerda, and Uncle Ike and Wilhelm met for supper every evening. They rented a car and drove through Alpine valleys shielded by ice-capped mountains. Covered in white, Die Jungfrau or the Maiden dominated the region.

At the highest look out point of "Die Jungfrau" Wilhelm asked, "Are you sure you want to get married?" "Yes!" she answered unequivocally. He longed for the day they could wander alone, wherever they pleased, free from the watchful presence of well-meaning parents.

On the last day of their vacation, Wilhelm bought some Swiss chocolate for Schorschi, his little friend at the Children's Clinic. "Why don't we adopt him?" suggested Thea. Wilhelm laughed. "I don't think the nuns would let us adopt him, but I would like at least six children of our own." Thea mused, "I want a boy who looks exactly like Bubi." In the 1920s, Bubi was a popular child film star, who wore bangs and had shoulder length hair. Wilhelm objected, "No son of mine is going to look like a sissy."

She did not want this vacation nor their dreams of the future to end. The separation they both dreaded would soon become a reality. School, which seemed more like a return to kindergarten, had become unimportant to her. With her hand securely in his, she stepped from adolescence to adulthood. She could ruminate endlessly about their future life. But now, they had to part; her train was waiting. She recounted, "He was 14 years older than I, but he was and remained so young."

"Not thousands of miles, nor hundreds of days will ever separate us," he whispered.

"I missed him terribly. I wrote him everyday, and he wrote me everyday. For my 17th birthday, he couldn't take time off, but he sent me a big stuffed dog. I met him when I was 16 and I was engaged when I was 18. I had a big party. Apparently I made the right decision. I only felt safe when I was near him."

4

THE HAPPIEST YEARS DISRUPTED

She thought about Wilhelm by day and by night. She didn't think she could learn anything from her teachers who didn't seem to know half as much as the man she loved. School became a drudgery. She tried to do her homework, but she couldn't concentrate. They wrote each other everyday, but her formal, aloof letters puzzled him. When she was with him she was spontaneous, but in her letters she carefully avoided any expressions of affection. He wondered if she had changed her mind. Wilhelm discovered later that Mrs. Westmann had warned her daughter not to put her romantic feelings into writing, in case their courtship might dissolve.

That year, he couldn't come to Berlin for her 17th birthday, but he sent her a bouquet of 17 roses and a cuddly, stuffed dog. She was disappointed that he couldn't take time off from the clinic, but it didn't stop her from celebrating her birthday first with her friends and then again with her aunts and uncles on the weekend. After the last guest had left, Thea usually began to plan the next year's celebration. However, her mother, who had collapsed on the sofa, insisted she needed at least a year to recuperate.

Thea was delighted when Wilhelm suggested they announce their engagement on her 18th birthday. He took time off from the clinic and traveled to Berlin two months ahead of time to help with the preparations not only for their engagement but also for their wedding. Mrs. Westmann, Thea and Wilhelm compiled a list of the people they would invite. The large trousseau was designed to last a lifetime and comprised enough linens for a family of 12. They bought an oak dining room set that would withstand any rough treatment from children, grandchildren and even great grandchildren. They compared the food and the prices at several banquet halls before Thea's mother finally reserved a room at the Luther and Wegener Restaurant in the heart of Berlin.

Engagement - Wilhelm Becker and Thea Westmann. Berlin, Oct 24, 1928

The voice of Thea's father began to dominate the conversation when the young couple introduced the possibility of moving to Munich. Wilhelm, who preferred an academic career to the actual practice of medicine, had been offered a teaching position at the Children's Clinic in Munich. Mr. Westmann would not hear of letting his daughter move to Munich, and that was final! Wilhelm quickly realized the futility of arguing this point and began to look for a teaching assignment in Berlin. Thea was relieved when he accepted a position in orthopedic surgery at the Friedrichshainer Hospital, where he met Dr. Bernard Blumenthal.

Dr. Blumenthal owned one of the largest orthopedic clinics in Berlin. Scores of health care professionals served the 150 to 200 patients who came to the clinic everyday for consultation and treatment. Several orthopedic surgeons served on the staff plus eight physiotherapists and several highly - skilled technicians, who tailor-made the artificial limbs to match patients' specific requirements.

Dr. Blumenthal expected his staff - especially the physicians - to adhere to the highest standards of medical practice. He did not hesitate to voice his dissatisfaction, and had fired several young doctors before he finally hired Wilhelm Becker. He liked Wilhelm personally and respected his professional knowledge and skills; and before the year ended, he offered Wilhelm full partnership in his medical practice. Wilhelm never doubted his ability to provide for Thea, but he never dreamt of being this successful so early in his career. To celebrate their good fortune they went out to dinner and saw one of their favorite operettas, "The Merry Widow."

The Birthday Without Equal

On her 18th birthday - October 24, 1928 - Thea and Wilhelm became officially engaged. In the presence of 150 guests, they professed their love and commitment to each other. For Thea, birthdays provided the opportunity to celebrate the uniqueness of the person. When she became engaged, she felt that the very core of her being had been expanded to include her chosen lifetime partner.

They had set their wedding date with Uncle Ike in mind. Ike, who lived in Chicago, couldn't reserve a cabin on the Queen Mary until the last week in May. To accommodate him, Thea and Wilhelm set their wedding day for June 2, 1929.

Engagement Oct 24, 1928 - Thea Westmann and Wilhelm Becker

Wilhelm wanted Rabbi Max Weyl from Berlin to marry them. Rabbi Weyl had officiated at Wilhelm's bar mitzvah and had conducted the high holiday services in his home town of Rockenhausen. Wilhelm admired Rabbi Weyl, an avowed socialist, who was not afraid to speak out against the oppression of working people. Thea, who felt proud that her family members supported the slightly left-of-center Democratic Party, was impressed with what she heard about Rabbi Weyl. They made an appointment to speak with him.

He was a gaunt-looking man with a black beard, who did not believe in excesses of any kind; and the furniture of his living room consisted of one table and two chairs. He offered Thea the second chair, while Wilhelm stood as they spoke. Since he had also helped prepare Thea's brother Kurt for his bar mitzvah, he knew both families well.

Rabbi Weyl considered the young couple exceptionally fortunate in view of Germany's economic depression and high unemployment rate. More importantly, he sensed in both young people a spirit of compassion and concern for the poor. He checked the date: He had no other appointments for the second of June! He told them that he would be privileged to unite them in matrimony and entered the event in his calendar book. Both Thea and Wilhelm placed exceptional importance on having the socially - progressive Dr. Weyl perform their wedding ceremony. They had to tackle one last hurdle; they had to find an apartment.

At that time in Germany, only married couples could obtain the white card needed to apply for an apartment. To solve this problem, they were married privately by the justice of the peace on March 12, 1929. With the white card in hand, they were then able to rent an apartment, but continued to live apart until they were officially married. They found a large apartment with central heating on 31 Lessing Street in Berlin. [Appendix B] All of the appliances were electric; they remodeled the bathrooms and had new light fixtures installed.

The Wedding

On June 2, 1929, Thea and Wilhelm were married by Rabbi Weyl in the Fasanen Strasse Synagogue, the largest liberal congregation in Berlin. Relatives and friends from both families filled the magnificent synagogue. Before Thea and Wilhelm placed the wedding bands on each other's fingers, the Rabbi referred to the ring as, "an eternal symbol, without beginning or end. So may your love be."

His vision foreshadowed a love that would blossom throughout life and endure beyond the grave. The Rabbi reminded the fortunate couple to remember their responsibility to the poor and to others less fortunate than they. His admonition - indelibly imprinted on their hearts - became the guiding principle of their lives.

The large crowd followed the bridal party to an elegant lodge for the wedding reception. The two families gathered around festive tables and became acquainted as they celebrated. Many of them had composed poems; others had written lyrics to popular melodies. Aunt Fannie, Mr. Westmann's talented sister, had written a play, wickedly titled, "Auf der Jungfrau Ists Geschehen," Translated it means, "It Happened on the Maiden." It was a play on the word, "Maiden" the highest mountain in Lucerne, where Wilhelm had proposed to Thea a second time.

Her cousins teased, "What did happen on top of the Maiden?" "Nothing happened," insisted Thea. The characters in the play depicted 40 relatives trailing behind Thea and Wilhelm wherever they went. The young couple did everything except fall off the mountain, to dodge the family, but they never succeeded in getting rid of them. The concierge at their hotel befriended Aunt Fanny and never missed an opportunity to disclose embarrassing secrets about all the family members. He had provided Aunt Fanny with enough scandal for a two-hour musical.

After the applause subsided, Thea and Wilhelm rose to dance to their favorite song: "Wenn Der Weisse Flieder Wieder Bluht, ("When the White Lilacs Bloom Again"). The entire wedding party danced the next waltz, until all of the guests waltzed in a circle around the newlyweds.

Several relatives who had come from distant towns stayed with the Westmanns that night. Thea and Wilhelm spent their first night together in their beautiful apartment. He embraced her with utmost tenderness. Exhilarated and fatigued, they fell asleep in each other's arms.

At daybreak, he kissed her golden strands of hair, gingerly sliding out of bed to avoid waking her. An unexpected event forced him to leave the side of his young bride early that day. Dr. Blumenthal had suddenly died, leaving the responsibility for the clinic to Dr. Wilhelm Becker. Shortly after Wilhelm left the apartment, Thea called her mother and shared her happiness with her. Soon after they began talking, she revealed, "I'm completely fulfilled! And I wish I could have been married when I was eight."

Any worries her mother might have had disappeared. Thea had always been able to talk to her mother about personal matters. Even some of Thea's friends asked if they could speak with Thea's mother about some of their private concerns. When Thea repeated a second time, "I wish I could have been married when I was eight." Her mother asked what she meant by this unusual comment. Thea explained that when she was near Wilhelm she felt completely safe, but added, "on second thought eight would have been too young because I can't wait to become pregnant."

She told her mother that in his last will, Dr. Blumenthal had named Wilhelm the sole heir to the clinic. Because large sections of the clinic needed to be remodeled, Wilhelm spent the evenings with architects and contractors, discussing designs and construction materials. While he was busy from early morning until late at night, Thea found herself with excess time on her hands.

Even if the Beckers hadn't had a live-in cook, a maid and a laundress, it is unlikely that Thea would have found fulfillment in cleaning and cooking, except when preparing for a party. To fill the time, she enrolled in French and English classes, only to find them boring. One evening, while visiting their doctor friends, the Bernards, Thea told them that she did not find her classes the least bit stimulating. Dr. Bernard, a psychiatrist, asked why she didn't consider working in her husband's office.

That idea sparked Thea's interest immediately. The highest aspiration for most women of that era was to work in their husbands' offices or businesses. Thea's mother, an English teacher, never taught at a school, but as soon as Thea was born she went back to work in the family business. Since 1914, women had won greater access to the universities but not to the job market. Even during the more liberal climate of the Weimar Republic, men continued to object to women working outside the home.

Thea was delighted with the prospect of working in Wilhelm's large clinic. She began to take courses in physiotherapy at the Charite Hospital and hoped to become a licensed physiotherapist. However, she soon withdrew from this course of study because Wilhelm did not think that it was a proper occupation for the wife of a doctor. A wife acquired social status through her husband, and to be allowed to work side by side with him, was considered, the pinnacle of any wife's dream. They went to the clinic together early in the morning and left together in the evening. Some people might get claustrophobia from all this togetherness, but Thea thrived on it. She assumed responsibility for coordinating the range of services their large staff provided to 150 - 200 people each day. Thea considered the years she worked alongside her husband the happiest time of her life.

Thea felt like she was witnessing a miracle every time she watched a previously crippled child walk out of the clinic with a nearly normal gait. She shared the mother's joy when the child, in a burst of confidence, would let go of the maternal hand and run into Wilhelm's outstretched arms. Her heart soared with love and pride for the man who was not only her husband but one of the best orthopedic surgeons in Berlin.

She was happy that Wilhelm had not forgotten Rabbi Weyl's entreaty to remember the poor. Every Monday, he volunteered at the Charite to provide medical care to indigent patients. After their discharge from the hospital, he continued to treat these people free of charge at his clinic.

Under the direction of Dr. Becker and his wife, his practice expanded and flourished, as did Thea, who discovered she was pregnant. Both were thrilled with the prospect of their new baby. In the last trimester of her pregnancy, Wilhelm went with Thea to her obstetrician, whose office was at the hospital. As they walked along the hospital corridor, the screams of the woman inside the labor and delivery room frightened her. When she asked Wilhelm why the woman screamed, he took her hand in his and said, "Only hysterical women scream."

The Birth of Marian

Throughout her pregnancy, she never missed a day at the clinic, and in the evening, they usually took a walk. One night, late in the pregnancy, she couldn't go out with him, because she was too tired. She told him that she just wanted to stay home and go to bed. He made her a sandwich, but she was already half asleep. At 5 that morning, on December 3, 1930, she had the first contraction. At 7, she had another slight contraction; at 9:30 the water broke, and at 11, the baby was born.

"She was a beautiful baby... My husband had a terrible toothache... During the delivery, his pain was worse than mine. Then I had trouble with my breasts. Right from the start they started to bleed. The baby, whom we named Marian refused to drink from the right breast. I said, she must be a social democrat, very much to the left... He went to buy me a watch, but I threw the watch on the floor. I didn't want the watch, and I didn't want to breast feed. It hurt me so terribly. He insisted I breast feed so the baby would be healthier... I was so happy when they brought her to me. I wanted to hold her but she hurt me so terribly. I took her along to the office. The nanny would take Marian to the park, and when they came back, I would breast feed her. Later, I made her formula. Then I went back to the office and we

worked together until the evening." The baby thrived and began to walk and talk before her first birthday. Marian was a quiet child. Like her father, she didn't talk much. Thea usually had to talk for both of them, and she gladly obliged.

Marian and her Father in Garmisch, Germany in the Winter of 1936

Marian was affectionate with her mother when the two were alone together. As soon as her father came home, the child gravitated toward him exclusively and reveled in his attention and affection. Thea admitted to feeling left out, but she said that she was happy that father and daughter got along so well.

As a proud wife and mother, Thea attended her first class reunion after she left the Luisen Lyceum. She had remained close to her best friends Ilse and Rita, but many of her other classmates and teachers appeared as characters from a distant past. She laughed when Mr. Borg asked, "How is my little mother-in-law?" "Your little mother-in-law has become a mother." When her teachers and classmates heard the news, they all congratulated her.

Her former music teacher responded differently. Nodding at Rita who had recently received a degree from the conservatory of music, he asked, "Aren't you sorry you didn't go on to the university?" "No, I'm not the least bit sorry," she declared as she reached into her purse for a photograph of Marian. "I have my baby."

Marian and her Mother in Gross Glienicke, Germany

This unpleasant encounter with the music teacher brought to mind memories of Mr. Katzorke, who had become the principal of a boys' school. Hitler's victory in 1933 resulted in a promotion for Mr. Katzorke. For the Jews, Hitler's victory also resulted in their being expelled from all government hospitals and universities on April 4, 1933. Signs were posted in every German town and city proclaiming: "Jews Not Wanted, and "Anyone Who Buys From Jews Is A Traitor To His People." Josef Goebbels wrote in the January 21, 1929 issue of the "Angriff," "The Jew is negative and this negation has to be eradicated from the German picture. Whoever spares the Jews commits a sin against his own people."[3]

During the early 1930s, many of Thea's closest friends became engaged and married. Her friend and former nanny, Mitze, invited Thea and Wilhelm to her wedding. When the Beckers heard that a cousin of the bridegroom planned to appear at the reception in full Nazi uniform, they declined the invitation.

A former classmate invited Thea to attend her wedding ceremony at the church. Thea took Marian with her to see the wedding pageantry. In front of the church, Thea met some of her friends from elementary school. One of Thea's former classmates had brought her five-year old nephew with her.

When the boy saw Marian, he threw his arms around her and kissed her. Marian kissed him back. The classmate darted towards her nephew, snatched him away from Marian and warned, "You better not say "Heil Hitler" to her unless you want to get hit." Marian got scared and began to cry.

Increasingly more Germans openly professed their support of Hitler despite the street violence that the Nazi SA, (Hitler's paramilitary group) staged against communists, immigrants, gypsies, homosexuals, Jehovah Witnesses and Jews. To Thea's horror and dismay, her best friend, Ilse, had become engaged to Hans, an unabashed Nazi. Hitler's intense opposition to the Treaty of Versailles had convinced Hans to join the SA at the age of 14.

Hans, who had majored in foreign languages and education, was unable to find a teaching position until he became a Nazi. After several years, he was promoted to the Ministry of Propaganda, where he worked directly under Josef Goebbels, the propaganda minister.

One morning, Thea spotted a newspaper article which quoted excerpts from a speech Hans had made at a Nazi rally. The writer praised Hans for urging the Germans not to relent until the last Jew could be seen hanging from a lamp post. Shocked and horrified, she could not believe such vicious venom could come from the mouth of her best friend's fiancee, considering Hans and Ilse ate dinner at the Beckers's home at least once or twice a week. Thea couldn't understand how Ilse could hope to marry this Nazi?

While Thea was considering this question, Ilse called to ask if she and Hans could stop by for a visit later that evening. "Absolutely not," shrieked Thea. Ilse asked why she was so angry. "Did you read today's newspaper? Hans was quoted as saying he would not rest until the last Jew had been hung from the highest lamp post." Ilse had not read the article, but insisted she could explain everything during a visit that evening.

She tried to assure Thea that Hans had not intended his comments for the educated German Jews. His message was directed against the uneducated Polish Jews. Thea informed her, "They are people like we are, and we are Jews like they are."

Attempting to change the subject, Ilse reminded Thea of their friendship that dated back to first grade. Both Hans and she valued their friendship. He certainly did not include them among the type of Jews he would like to eliminate from the country. Rising to her full height Thea opened the door: "Please leave, and don't ever come back." Thea stood by her word. She never saw Ilse again.

Since the onset of the depression, about 20,000 Polish Jews had emigrated to Germany. The Jewish Aid Society (Hilfverein Der Deutschen Juden) tried to help the impoverished Jews from Eastern Europe for whom Berlin was a port of entry. Some Jewish families like the Westmanns felt sorry for the impoverished immigrants from eastern Europe and took a chance on loaning money to needy Polish families. Most of them usually repaid the money on time. Others promised to repay the loan but were never seen or heard from again. The Jewish Aid Society helped many refugees emigrate to Palestine or the United States.

Those who remained in Germany obtained financial support while they looked for work as farm hands, as tradesmen or as peddlers. Wilhelm took care of many refugees who lived at a subsistence level in a dilapidated section of Berlin called the "Scheunen Viertel." (Scheunen means barn or stable). To the embarrassment of many German Jews, their Polish compatriots spoke a broken German, wore the black hat and coat of the orthodox, and avoided secular education.

Over a century ago, Napolean had unlocked the doors of the Jewish ghettos in Germany. The German Jews had made a concerted effort to discard their ghetto mentality. They had been assimilated, acquired middle class standing, and had fought and died for the fatherland. But the anti-Jewish propaganda only got worse, especially during periods of high unemployment. Many

German Jews feared that the large influx of Polish Jews would result in even more propaganda, restrictions and violence.

Wilhelm and Thea were not affected personally when on September 15, 1935, the Nuremberg Laws deprived Jews of German citizenship. Wilhelm was assured that he could continue to practice medicine because he had fought at the front during World War I. In Berlin, the Jews could still go to the restaurants, the cabarets and theaters. The Beckers had started to build their house in 1934, one year after Hitler came to power. They believed that he would soon be ousted from office. However, by 1935, Hitler had seized control of every aspect of German life, and most of the Beckers' Jewish friends had already lost their jobs.

The government had declared a boycott on all Jewish stores, but Jews and Gentiles alike continued to flock to Dr. Becker's clinic. Observing proper German etiquette, clients usually addressed the wife of a doctor as "Frau Doctor." To Thea's surprise, one of the patients of about her husband's age had the nerve to call her "Gretchen." With a wink of playful disrespect, he called to mind the blue-eyed, blond-haired Gretchen of Goethe's "Faust" whenever he saw her at the clinic.

Obviously irritated, she asked Wilhelm, "Who is that idiot?" "That is Leo Hartman," he answered. He teases and jokes despite the fact that he lost the fingers of both his hands while making a fireworks display for his daughter. He is always optimistic, even though he was removed from his position as director of the second largest pharmaceutical company in Germany - thanks to the "Race Laws".

Leo and Lissy Hartman

Wilhelm respected Leo Hartman and liked his humor as much as his intelligence. He came to the clinic frequently with the hope of maintaining maximum flexibility in the remaining stumps of his fingers. Because he called her "Gretchen," Thea called him "Max." A few office visits later, she met his beautiful wife, Lissy. She was nearly as old as her mother, but her trim, graceful figure made her look years younger. Thea admired the more mature woman's acceptance of her husband's crushing misfortune.

Lissy, Leo and Steffie Hartman cartooned on one of Steffie's drawings.

The Hartmans and the Beckers went together to the opening night of every operetta that premiered in Berlin. Both had young daughters, even though Steffie was six years older than Marian. Despite the loss of Mr. Hartman's job and despite the "Race Laws," the Hartmans, like the Beckers, went ahead with plans to build a house.

As late as 1934, the Beckers bought a piece of property in Gross Glienicke, an affluent suburb of Berlin. The Hartmans bought the adjacent lot, and both families began to build their homes at the same time. Unlike the rest of the houses in Gross Glienicke, the properties of the Beckers and the Hartmans were not separated by the usual high iron fence which read,"Keep Out."

A friend and Marian on the porch of the Becker Berlin Home, Jan 1, 1936

The Beckers and the Hartmans always had a joint New Year's party. Days in advance, they prepared the food, Leo pushed the furniture back to make space for dancing; Wilhelm made a punch that delivered a real punch, and Thea welcomed the guests. She dimmed the lights as people danced to the waltzes of Strauss and Waldteufel. After a few glasses of punch, people began to swing to the more contemporary beat of Kurt Weil's "Mack the Knife."

In the cabarets of Berlin, they had heard Lotte Lenya, the wife of Kurt Weil

67

sing the songs her husband wrote to expose the plight of the working classes. Their favorite cabaret singer was Claire Waldoff, who dared to poke fun at top Nazis such as Hermann Goering. The music, art, theater and literature that had flourished in the liberating air of the Weimar Republic was frowned upon by the Nazis and other conservatives. They began to burn books and shut down theaters owned by Jews, and they banned any music, pop songs, plays - anything produced by Jews. And most of it was produced by Jews."[4]

Max Wolf

At the height of Wilhelm's professional success, some of their closest friends and relatives suffered not only the loss of their jobs, but were brutally beaten and burned by the Nazis. Their psychiatrist friend, Dr. Bernard, was ousted from his office; his physician wife, who was Christian, divorced him. Max Wolf, a mutual friend of the Beckers and the Hartmans, suffered a more tragic ending. As the proprietor and director of a movie theater in Berlin, Max Wolf had made his wife, who was Christian, the sole owner of their theater. Shortly after he had signed the theater over to her, she died. The sudden death of his wife left him with no source of income. He was destitute and did not have the money to buy food or pay his rent.

The Beckers let Max Wolf stay at their apartment in Berlin, and the Hartmans gave him money for food. On the weekends, he stayed with the Hartmans in Gross Glienicke but returned to the Becker apartment in Berlin during the week. He arranged to have his mail sent to Wilhelm's clinic. Every day he stopped at the clinic to inquire if a letter had arrived from his brother in Chile. His brother had promised to send him an affidavit that would enable him to emigrate to Chile. He had agreed to send the affidavit on the condition that Max would never reveal his Jewish identity. His brother wrote that he hoped Max would not look Jewish. Fortunately, Max had blue eyes. He wasn't sure, however, if he would approve of his nose. The nose wasn't big or crooked, but it wasn't a pug nose either!

When he had not received the affidavit within a year, his hopes dwindled. He became despondent and began to call Mr. Hartman daily to express his deep appreciation to the Hartmans and the Beckers for everything they had done to help him. Before putting down the receiver, he told them not to worry in case they did not hear from him again because he was seriously thinking of doing away with himself.

Neither the Beckers nor the Hartmans payed much attention to his preoccupation with suicide because during the past year he had called them so many times - to talk to them and to thank them, one last time.

Mr. Hartman, however, became more concerned about the deepening despair in Max Wolf's voice, and he feared that if Max would harm himself in the Beckers' apartment, the Nazis would accuse the Beckers of criminal activity.

Max Wolf understood the situation and would never do anything to endanger the lives of Thea and Wilhelm. Once again he thanked his loyal friends and generous benefactors. That was the last time Max Wolf called. Several days later, he was found hanging from a tree in an isolated section of the Grunewald Forest outside Berlin.

Escalating anti-semitism forced Mrs. Hartman to transfer their daughter

Steffie from a public school to a school for Jewish children. The principal of the school she was attending had asked Mrs. Hartman to visit the school immediately for a conference. She said they needed to discuss a grave matter that involved Steffie. The principal reported that Steffie had slapped a classmate but hardly mentioned that the girl had taunted Steffie about being Jewish.

All of the girls in the class except Steffie belonged to the Hitler Youth, which sponsored weekend trips. The girls talked exclusively about the food they would bring to the picnic, and Steffie felt painfully excluded from the group. When she said, " I wish I could go along on the trip," a girl standing next to her scoffed, "Jews can't go on the outing." That's when Steffie slapped her across the face. Because of the temper outburst, Steffie was not allowed to return to the school.

Stunned by this drastic decision, Mrs. Hartman asked if the other girl's racial taunts were not as wrong as Steffie's aggressive response? The principal expressed regret, but advised Mrs. Hartman to take Steffie out of the school before more complaints from parents would result in worse consequences. Thea told Mrs. Hartman, "I still admire Steffie for slapping that girl. She got what she deserved."

Most painful of all was the complete social isolation the Jews experienced, especially in the small towns of Germany. People crossed the street or averted their eyes whenever they passed a Jewish person on the street. Former friends and neighbors never called or stopped to visit anymore. Unlike most of their Jewish friends, the Beckers led an active social life, and Wilhelm continued to work in his profession unhampered by the tyranny surrounding them.

Threats Closer to Home

One evening a middle-aged man walked into Dr. Becker's office. He saluted Thea with a strident, "Heil Hitler." She answered calmly, "Good evening." He repeated, "Heil Hitler." Again she replied, "Good evening." "Don't you know the official German greeting?," he barked. Thea didn't flinch and said, "I know it, but I don't use it." "Did I perhaps come to the office of a Jewish doctor?" "Yes you did," Thea assured him and added, "If you like, you can cancel the appointment and see another doctor."

He warned her that in a short while, a German Fraulein like herself wouldn't be able to work in the office of a Jewish doctor. "Yes I will be able to work here because I'm Mrs. Becker, the doctor's wife. I'm also proud to be Jewish." He looked surprised as he inspected the blond, fair-skinned Thea more closely. "I don't believe you're Jewish. Jews can never be proud. You are free to see another doctor if you like," she said again.

The man then explained that Dr. Becker had performed knee surgery on his best friend's son. He thought that his own son had a similar problem and that he would like Dr. Becker to at least examine the boy. Dr. Becker examined the son and agreed with the father. The boy and his friend's son clearly had a similar orthopedic condition and surgery would be required to correct his gait.

"Perhaps the gentleman would prefer to have another doctor perform the surgery," Thea interjected. Wilhelm looked puzzled, and didn't understand why his wife encouraged the father to consult another surgeon. He agreed, however, that every patient is entitled to get a second opinion, before making a final decision. The father helped his son put on his socks and shoes, left the office without saying a word and never came back.

Later that evening another patient entered the office with an enthusiastic, "Heil Hitler." "Good evening," replied Thea, expecting another angry reprimand. Instead, he smiled kindly at her and said, "How refreshing to hear someone say 'good evening'."

After the last client had left the office, Thea told Wilhelm of her encounter with the two men who had greeted her with an enthusiastic, "Heil Hitler." He didn't seem surprised. Several of his doctor friends had told him of an increasing number of Jewish patients who had sustained severe injuries as a result of brutal assaults by the SA. "We have to get out of Germany," Wilhelm told the astonished Thea. "And leave my mother, father, Kurt and Hilde? Never!" While the police looked the other way, the SA and the SS flaunted their brutality to impress and intimidate the ordinary citizen. Consequently, the majority of Germans stood by passively as their neighbors were beaten, abducted and murdered. By this time, they were too afraid to stage any resistance.

With bruises and cigarette burns all over his body, Fritz Westmann, Thea's cousin, appeared at their clinic. Several days earlier, while driving home, Fritz and one of his Christian friends, were hit by a car. Regular Berlin police officers arrived at the scene of the accident. They asked to see Fritz's driver's license. After they had filled out their reports, one of the police men asked if they were Jews.

Fritz answered, "Yes, I am Jewish, but my friend is Christian." They had strict orders to refer every accident involving a Jew to the Gestapo (the secret police). Two Gestapo officers arrived in full uniform, grabbed Fritz and his friend by the hair, and repeatedly knocked their heads together.

"You should know better than to associate with Jews," they told the friend and let him go. They warned him, "If you're ever found in the company of Jews again, you'll be killed." They arrested Fritz. At the police station they beat him and inflicted cigarette burns all over his body. Thea's face turned ashen as she listened to Wilhelm describe the excruciating pain Fritz endured as a result of the second-degree burns on his penis.

"Is this what you want to happen to me?" he asked as he enfolded the sobbing Thea in his arms. Uncle Ike had already sent them their affidavits and their passports were up to date. She gained her composure and replied, "We'll go to the consulate tomorrow to apply for our visas. Then we'll buy our tickets for America."

A few days later persistent ringing of the doorbell interrupted their dinner hour. When Thea opened the door, two men dressed in the brown SA uniforms asked for a donation to the Nazi party. Disgusted, she slammed the door in their faces. " A couple of Nazis had the nerve to ask me for a donation," she grumbled.

They resumed eating, when the phone rang. She feared the Gestapo had been informed of her disrespect to the two Nazis. During home invasions and searches, the Gestapo customarily captured the men first. She feared for Wilhelm's life and pleaded with him to run to the neighbors for safety. "Absolutely not." Wilhelm wouldn't hear of leaving her alone in the event of a break in by the police. Both froze in terror when the phone rang again. Finally she answered. It was the delivery man from the cleaners. She beamed a smile of relief at Wilhelm. He had called several times before and had wanted to make sure someone was home before he delivered Dr. Becker's suits.

They considered their luck as they finished their supper, but could not shake the lingering panic that had gripped them. The thought of losing their home, the clinic and their possessions seemed insignificant in contrast with the constant fear for their lives. They had no other alternative but to leave Berlin, the city Thea loved and the homeland Wilhelm had defended.

Despite the dangers and threats, many people refused to believe they would be subjected to serious harm. Journalists and radio commentators were prohibited from mentioning any human rights violations, and many people did not know the extent of the atrocities. Others wanted to emigrate, but could not afford to buy visas, or they didn't have the foreign contacts needed to obtain the affidavits.

Fortunately, the consulate sent the Beckers their visas after several weeks of anxious waiting. The Hartmans were lucky as well, and thanked their close friends in Italy who agreed to sponsor them. Eventually both families hoped to emigrate to the United States. To celebrate their hopes for a reunion in the U.S., Thea invited relatives and mutual friends to a farewell party for the Hartmans.

The earth would dance in its orbit on the day they would be neighbors again in their new country. While the two women shared their dreams for the future, Wilhelm and a group of his men friends became entrenched in war stories. Most of them had volunteered to fight for the fatherland at the outbreak of World War I. Some had received the Iron Cross for valor; others had lost their fathers and brothers in that war. They had learned to live with their war injuries, but how could they comprehend the irony of being chased out of Germany only 20 years later?

They reminisced - fighting to hold back their tears - as the evening drew to an end, and the moment of parting arrived. Despite their hopes for the future, the possibility of never seeing one another again resembled the finality of death. Forming an intimate circle, they sought to comfort one another as Thea began to hum one of the most popular melodies of the 1930s. Their voices harmonized softly as they sang, "Gibt es auch kein Wiedersehen, einmal war es doch schoen." ("Though we may never see each other again, once upon a time life was beautiful.")

Most of the Becker's physician friends had left Germany months ago. After their best friends, the Hartmans, fled Germany, Thea and Wilhelm began to prepare for their own departure. In June, 1937, they sold their house. They packed their personal belongings and arranged to have a moving company ship some of their furniture to America. They took their sofa with matching lounge chairs, their dining room set, several antique cabinets and the cocktail table. The rest of the furniture from their Berlin apartment they gave to a former employee.

Before they were allowed to leave the country, they had to pay an emigration tax which amounted to 60 per cent of their total assets. This large sum, which had to be paid immediately, nearly stripped them of their savings. Every month the bank agreed to send them six percent of the balance from their account. The monthly payments stopped one year later, when the government seized all Jewish-owned bank accounts.

The only way Thea was able to broach the subject of their departure was to tell her parents that they were taking a trip to Hamburg. Sharing their daughter's pain, her parents understood Thea's inability to tell them openly that they were taking the train to Hamburg to board an American ocean-liner. Holding Thea in a close embrace, Mrs. Westmann told her daughter, "I'm happy you are leaving for America. I was so worried for your safety." Her father kissed her and told her how much he loved her since the moment he had lifted her out of her crib. Wiping a tear from her cheek he whispered, "No one smiles like my Thea."

Thea knew that once they reached America, she would have a better chance of convincing her parents to leave Berlin. With that glimmer of hope, she waved from her seat by the window, praying that they would be reunited again soon.

Thea's brother, Kurt and Marian's kindergarten teacher, Ellen Sandman, accompanied the Beckers on the train ride from Berlin to Hamburg. Her former teacher had told Marian that her new teacher in Chicago would be happy to have a smart girl like Marian in her class. The six-year old Marian held onto her father's hand tightly, moving in unison with him. Even when he went to the washroom, she waited patiently outside the door, making sure not to lose him.

Marian and her Father

Every time a train official asked to see their passports, they feared for their lives. Thea's heart leaped to her throat when one inspector questioned the validity of one of their documents. They had been stripped of their citizenship; they had no rights. No lawyer would plead their case. If they would be accused of disobeying the emigration law, any German court would automatically find them guilty. Their fate would be the concentration camps.

The Germans telephoned the visa office and double checked every document. Thea felt like the death sentence had been lifted when the inspector finally put his stamp of approval on their papers. When they heard the conductor's gruff voice shout, "Hamburg," they hurried to the harbor where their boat was waiting. Then Thea told her brother, Kurt and Marian's kindergarten teacher, Ellen, who hoped to emigrate to America with their families, "We'll pick you up from the train station when you arrive in Chicago."

As soon as they stepped aboard the American ocean-liner, Thea felt safe for the first time in years. She worried about her parents, Kurt and his wife Hilde and hoped they would soon be reunited in America. The fog horns announced the time of departure as the enormous boat slipped away effortlessly to the sound of, "Farewell My Beloved Fatherland." As a child, it had been one of her favorite songs, but she couldn't stand to listen to it now. The once "Beloved Fatherland" had become despicable to her.

5

AMERICA - "AMERICA THE BEAUTIFUL"

The Beckers, along with hundreds of other passengers stood on deck, mesmerized by the Statue of Liberty. They didn't feel poor, hungry or tired, but they were yearning to be safe. "Miss Liberty" not only welcomed the oppressed immigrants but challenged each of them to give allegiance to the "land of the free." Wilhelm gave voice to this realization when he resolved never to belittle the strange and possibly unpleasant customs they might encounter in their new country.

Wilhelm's brother, Richard Becker, and his wife Thea were waiting with Uncle Ike for the Beckers to disembark. Both Richard and Wilhelm had married women with the name "Thea." Marian clung to her father as they hurried to embrace their Americanized relatives. Thea couldn't thank Uncle Ike enough for sending them the affidavits. She hoped that her parents, Kurt and Hilde, would soon be able to leave for America as well.

Right now Thea and Wilhelm wanted to freshen up at their hotel, which was not far from Richard's apartment. Then Richard and Thea would give them a tour of New York City. The Beckers were used to the crowds of Berlin, that city's modern department stores, its spacious parks and vibrant night life, but the youthful energy and fast pace of this American city exhilarated and exhausted them. They never tired of going to Manhattan everyday to look at the skyscrapers. They would have preferred to keep their feet on the ground, but they tried to stay calm when Ike suggested they have dinner at a restaurant on the 46th floor.

On October 24, 1937 - Thea's 27th birthday - the Beckers and Uncle Ike boarded the train for Chicago. At the Northwestern Station, the entire Becker clan from Chicago was waiting to welcome the newcomers from Berlin. Ike introduced the Beckers from Berlin to his brother Adolf Becker and his wife, Addie, and their daughter, son-in-law and their two grand-children. Thea felt honored that three generations of Beckers had come to the station to welcome them. However, not one of them remembered to wish her a happy birthday.

Three generations of Beckers plus Uncle Ike lived in a large stately man-sion in Hyde Park. The cook had prepared an all-American turkey dinner, including a sweet potato casserole which they loved. They repeatedly raised their glasses to toast Thea, Bill and Marian. But again, no one mentioned Thea's birthday!

Suddenly, Corinne burst through the swinging doors holding a large birth-day cake aglow with 27 candles. Then the group sang "Happy Birthday" to Thea and showered her with wishes for a happy new beginning. She thanked her Aunt politely for the gaudy earrings she gave her and made a mental note not to criticize her new found relatives' rather strange taste.

They could have slept 'till noon, but at exactly 9 a.m., Addie knocked on the door of the Becker's hotel room. Addie had made plans to take Thea to the Loop, Chicago's city center. But first, Ike drove Wilhelm to Michael Reese Hospital where he hoped to do a year-long internship, which was required before he could take the state board examination.

Addie took Thea to Marshall Field's first. They rode the escalator up to the ninth floor and back down again. Upon leaving the store, Addie told Thea, "You won't be able to shop here, it's too expensive." They went up and down the escalators at Carson's, and on the way out, Addie said, "This store also is too expensive for you." When they left Mandel Brothers, Addie warned, "You won't be able to shop here either." Their last stop was the Fair's bargain basement. "You'll be able to find some nice clothes here," commented Addie.

Stranded at the south end of the Loop, they decided to ride the bus to the Palmer House, where they had agreed to meet Ike and Wilhelm for lunch. Handing her a nickel, Addie told Thea, "I'll pay your bus fare today, but in the future you'll have to assume that responsibility yourself." Thea felt like she was five years old and wondered if Addie routinely humiliated people or if she reserved that treatment only for immigrants. Before they met Ike and Wilhelm for lunch, Addie warned, "I hope you won't ruin our name! We Beckers have an excellent reputation." "So do we," Thea promptly assured her.

In the afternoon, they went to Temple Sinai's Community Center. Thea was surprised how proud Addie was to introduce her to the members of the sisterhood. She told them, "She is the wife of a famous orthopedic surgeon from Berlin." Thea heard one of the women comment in a barely audible voice, "How renowned can he be with such a young wife."

Most of the women at the Sisterhood welcomed Thea, and after several months, wanted her to become the director of their social program. Sinai's Emil Hirsch Center began to direct its religious services and social programs to the needs of the growing number of German immigrants. People flocked to the services on Friday evenings. Both the American and the foreign members of the Sinai Congregation respected the learned Rabbi Bamberger but many had difficulty understanding his abstract sermons. When an assistant rabbi tried to bring this problem to Rabbi Bamberger's attention, he said that he had enough trouble preparing his sermons without worrying if people understood them.

Rabbi Bamberger was followed by the equally erudite Rabbi Mann, but people understood his sermons without using a dictionary. Rabbi Mann welcomed the refugees because he thought that their well-behaved children set a good example for their children. He encouraged Thea to become active in the social programs at Sinai. In fact, the following week, Thea received a letter informing her that Sinai's Social Committee would like her to be the chairperson of their Programs Committee. Thea was surprised because she and Wilhelm weren't members of the Temple yet, but she accepted the position and promptly set plans in motion for a Saturday evening dance.

However, their first priority was to look for an apartment. They found a two-bedroom apartment on Woodlawn and Hyde Park Boulevard. Because they were still receiving the monthly interest from their bank account in Berlin, they were able to pay the monthly rent of $97 dollars. Most of her friends each paid $42 dollars for their apartments, and they usually rented out one room for extra income. Their new living room overlooked Madison Park, which reminded Thea of their backyard in Gross Glienicke. She didn't really miss their former house in Germany - perhaps because she was so grateful to be in America.

When a big truck pulled up in front of their apartment building, the familiar furniture from Germany transformed their apartment into a home. The oak dining room set that Wilhelm and Thea had picked out together would serve generations of Beckers for years to come. They especially valued their sofa and arm chairs, a wedding gift from Wilhelm's father. The wrought iron cocktail table and antique desk and chests added old world craftsmanship to their new apartment. After months of sleeping on strange mattresses, they relished the comfort of their own beds. Thea felt fortunate to have such a beautiful apartment - and privileged not to have to work like most of the other immigrant women.

While taking the garbage out one morning, Thea met a woman shaking out her dust mop over the railing of their back porch. When she greeted her with a friendly "good morning," the woman answered in her best English, "Guten morning." "Are you from Germany?" Thea asked. "Of course," Dora Stern replied in flawless German. She and her husband, a physician, had recently come to Chicago from Germany. She felt grateful to the two teachers who had hired her to do housework "Why don't you stop by after work for a cup of coffee?", suggested Thea.

Thea's invitation brought tears to the cleaning woman's eyes. Dora, who had been raised in a wealthy family knew little about cooking and cleaning. The two teachers knew she worked hard, but only paid her a pittance. Like most of the immigrant women, she worked long hours for little money. Several years later, Dora found a better paying job at the Stevens Department Store, while her husband continued the struggle to build his medical practice.

Another woman Thea met during her first months in Chicago became one of her dearest friends. Her name was Ella Rothschild, a petite woman with sparkling eyes, whom she met in the citizenship class at the YMCA. As soon as Thea arrived in Chicago, she began to study for the citizenship exam, and by the end of that first year, she knew the Preamble to the Constitution by heart. She wanted to improve her English as well.

Ella convinced Thea to go with her to a gathering of the Chicago Women's Aid Society downtown. This group of American-born Jewish women welcomed the immigrants to their social gatherings, and taught English free of charge. Members of the Women's Aid Society met to discuss books, plays and movies. Above all, they liked to socialize. They mingled with the refugees and were as interested in their customs as the German women were eager to learn the American way of life.

Instead of demeaning the immigrants, they recognized the hardships they faced, and helped them whenever possible. To the delight of the Americans, once the German women learned English, they provided the entertainment at their social gatherings. Thea wrote a play with scenes which showed her searching for the word "hen." She finally gave up and asked the butcher for a lady chicken. On another occasion, she saw an advertisement for pie and thought it was a public toilet.

Changing Thea to Dorothy and Wilhelm to Bill

Because most American women thought of a nice cup of tea whenever they heard the name, "Thea," she decided to change her name to Dorothy. In a show of support, Wilhelm changed his name to Bill. Her friends at the Women's Aid Society liked the name, "Dorothy," and so did Marian. She liked the cadence of Bill and Dorothy Becker because it sounded American.

Leo and Lissy Hartman had finally arrived safely from Europe and Dorothy invited them and her cousin, Ernst Vogel, to celebrate a real American Thanksgiving. She hoped that her parents would be with them as well the following year. In the meantime, Mrs. Altschuler, one of her friends from the Women's Aid Society, insisted on having the Beckers over for Thanksgiving at her home. When Thea explained that she had already invited people, Mrs. Altschuler insisted, "I want you and your friends to celebrate Thanksgiving with us."

On Thanksgiving day, the Altschuler's chauffeur picked up the Beckers, the Hartmans and cousin Vogel. Twenty guests gathered around the festive table, decorated with bouquets of mums and maple leaf branches. Mrs. Altschuler looked directly at Dorothy when she expressed her gratitude for being able to celebrate this Thanksgiving with her German friends who, like the Pilgrims, had suffered persecution in their native country. Over hot apple pie and ice cream, their hostess shared her late father's family tradition with them. Every year he had celebrated the real spirit of Thanksgiving by inviting people without family, as well as those who had recently come to America.

These words continued to resonate with Dorothy throughout the years as scores of solitary refugees gathered around her table on Thanksgiving. Other American holidays, like the Fourth of July, they celebrated with equal gusto. Many immigrants suffered from home sickness, compounded by relentless longing - that bitter sweet indulgence of German Romanticism. Not so Bill and Dorothy. They only had praise for their newly-adopted country. In fact, Dorothy claimed to hate everything German: " I probably hate Germany because I loved it so much." She never wanted to return to Germany, nor did she care to speak the language.

Bill, who had studied Latin and Greek, had no knowledge of English. To prepare for the Illinois State Board Examination, he decided to take private lessons from Mrs. Brinkman, a certified English teacher of German ancestry. The Beckers agreed to take lessons from her only if she agreed to let them pay her. Mrs. Brinkman knew it was futile to argue with the Beckers, but she discovered another way she could be of help to them. Bill, who depended on referrals from other doctors, needed more opportunities to meet his colleagues socially. So, Mrs. Brinkman staged a party at her home, inviting doctors from Michael Reese, whom she introduced to Dr. and Mrs. Becker.

At the party, they became friends with a psychiatrist and his wife, who invited Bill and Dorothy to a New Year's reception. Elated with their expanding circle of friends, Dorothy told Addie they had recently met a psychiatrist and his wife who had invited them to an open house party on New Year's Day. "Certainly you're not going to that man's home," sniffed Addie. "Why not?" Addie explained, "We Beckers don't associate with people of his East European background." Rabbi Mann is German and he thinks highly of him," countered Dorothy.

Dorothy was appalled that her aunt harbored as much prejudice against the Jews from East Europe as her friend, Ilse, who was married to a Nazi. She informed Addie that she and Bill valued his friendship regardless of his ethnic background. Besides, they also appreciated the opportunity to meet other doctors. Or did Addie expect Bill to refuse patients referred by doctors from Poland or Russia?

Bill did have difficulty with the practice of giving a doctor a commission for referring patients to him. Dorothy explained later: *"My husband didn't like the practice of having to pay the referring doctor $1 dollar when he got $3 dollars. My husband said, "I'm not doing that!" The doctor responded, 'Then I'm sending my patients to another doctor.' "But not all did. I don't know of any German doctors who did this. My husband considered the practice very unprofessional. It was horrible. Absolutely."*

Bill had two offices, one on the south side and a second one downtown. Because he specialized in orthopedic surgery, he depended on referrals from general practitioners. Competition among the doctors was stiff and some may have objected to foreign doctors who were encroaching on their territory. Dorothy would get mad when doctors would ask Bill for advice over the phone. Others came to their house to have Bill interpret X-rays for them. They'd stay for dinner, but they rarely referred patients to him. Only after trying their own remedies and finding they didn't work would they send the patients to Bill.

"In Berlin, we did everything together, we left home together in the morning, we worked together, and at 9 in the evening we took a walk together." The Wilhelm Becker Clinic in Berlin, could accommodate 168 patients and a staff of 12 professionals. Now, her husband's Chicago offices barely provided enough space for the doctor and the patient. In

Berlin, to have been an integral part of her husband's work had been one of the most rewarding experiences of Dorothy's life. Bill's Chicago office was much smaller, and besides, it was not customary in America for the doctor's wife to work at his office.

Jenny Wolf. Photos on the wall: Alfred Wolf and Bertha Pappenheim.

For Dorothy, not being able to work alongside her husband again remained one of the greatest disappointments of her life. She loved her Bill and Marian, but from the onset of their marriage, Dorothy knew that the role of housewife and mother alone would not satisfy her. She loved people and parties, but not just for diversion. She liked bringing people together to lift their spirits, to relieve some of their loneliness, and to work for a common cause. She remembered being alone only once, and that was one of the worst experiences of her life.

Dorothy once again found herself with lots of time on her hands. Bill usually had to be at the hospital by 8 a.m. Marian had adjusted well to her new school. She made friends and the teacher reported excellent progress. Except for the noon hour when she ate lunch with Marian, Dorothy was home alone until late in the afternoon. She recalled, *"We came in October of 1937, and Jenny Wolf started the Women's Group in 1938. That's the story of Selfhelp, the most beautiful story of all."*

The gatherings at the Chicago Women's Aid Society on Wednesday afternoons became the highlight of her week. These meetings began to hold an even greater interest for Dorothy after she and Ella Rothshild met Jenny Wolf, a woman who had worked to help poor families in Frankfurt. The regal, but compassionate Jenny Wolf was 18 years older than Dorothy. She shared Dorothy's concern for the plight of immigrant families and spoke from first-hand experience about her work with underprivileged women and girls. At Neu Isenburg, outside of Frankfurt, she had spent years volunteering at the acclaimed home for unwed mothers, a home founded by Bertha Pappenheim, the woman Freud immortalized in his case study of Anna O.

According to the German census of 1917, the League of Jewish Women, (Der Judische Frauen Bund) founded by Bertha Pappenheim, claimed a membership of 44,000 women. Groups of women throughout Germany worked relentlessly to alleviate conditions that lured impoverished girls into prostitution. Jenny Wolf had the League of Jewish Women in mind when she told a handful of women that they should organize and help other immigrant women who couldn't afford baby-sitters when they were ill.

The Women's Neighborhood Group

After the Wednesday gatherings at the Women's Aid Society, Dorothy Becker, Jenny Wolf and Ella Rothshild usually stopped at Hillmans where a cup of coffee cost only a nickel. Groceries were also less expensive at Hillmans, a supermarket on Washington Street between State and Dearborn. None of the women ordered sweet rolls, because with the dime they saved they could ride the streetcar both ways. Dorothy thought that the people who ordered cake with their coffee were millionaires.

Dorothy told her companions about her encounter with Dora Stern, her neighbor's cleaning woman, who worked 50 hours a week to help support her two children. When the children were sick, she couldn't afford to take time off, nor could she afford to hire a baby-sitter. She hardly made enough money to pay the rent and grocery bills.

Jenny Wolf compared the plight of the immigrants to the destitute families she had worked with in Germany during the Depression. Dorothy felt sorry for Dora because she had only a half day off per week - on Thursday afternoons - and hardly got to see her husband and children. She told Jenny that many women in Chicago are alone, without family or friends. "It's horrible!" For Dorothy, life in a lonely apartment was worse than a jail sentence. It was "solitary confinement."

"We have to help them, we have to form a women's group!", declared Jenny Wolf. Dorothy, who felt very privileged, wanted to do everything to help. Both Dorothy and Ella agreed that they had an obligation to help their compatriots. That afternoon at Hillmans, their resolve to assist the immigrant

women and their families fired their imagination and set their hearts aflame.

Jenny Wolf proclaimed, "We have to organize to help our people." She was the chairperson and gave her phone number to the women coming to the meetings. A handful of women began to meet at each others' apartments to divide the work and to draw up weekly schedules. Dorothy volunteered to work from 9 a.m. to noon and from 1 to 3 p.m. Mondays through Fridays. Bill wanted her home on the weekends and also wanted her there when he got home in the evenings.

Marian recalled that many times just as they sat down for supper the phone would ring. The call was not for her father, who was the doctor, but for her mother. Dorothy explained: *"Everyday we went somewhere to clean or to take care of children. A friend of the Rabbi called and asked if I would help a woman who had just delivered twins. He told me, 'I'm sure she'll like you.' The mother had phlebitis and had to keep her legs elevated. She asked me to cook some spinach, but she only had one pot which I had to use for the baby bottles. The following day I went back with a pot under each arm."*

Dorothy learned how to cook spinach that day. She put a big package of spinach in a pot, filled it with water, and went back to the bedroom to talk with the mother. The next time she checked, the whole kitchen was green with spinach. While she was scrubbing spinach off the stove, the walls and the floor, the unsuspecting mother asked, "Is anything wrong?" Dorothy told her that she had to make supper for her husband and Marian that night and had to get some things from the store. She went to the super market and asked the produce man how to make spinach. She followed his instructions exactly and it was a big success. A few days later she made spinach for her own family and even Marian liked it!

Dorothy Becker was one of the five women who started the Women's Group in 1938. In a few weeks, five more members joined. There were then 15, and pretty soon 35. Within three months, 40 women had joined the Women's Group. Jenny Wolf was very choosy and wanted only educated women to join. Dorothy explained that Jenny, like many people from Frankfurt, was a little snobbish. Then she added with a wink, "After all, Goethe was from Frankfurt, and not from Berlin." At times, Jenny implied that Dorothy wasn't quite up to par because she was from Berlin or because she was too young. "I was 27!" In the beginning Dorothy had a hard time with these put downs, but later when people specifically asked for Dorothy, she realized that Dorothy could work most effectively with all types of people, even those from Frankfurt.

"Later, when Jenny moved north, I became chairman. I took anyone who wanted to work for Selfhelp, which I think was much better. People were so proud to belong to Selfhelp. We made more friends this way, and we recruited more workers from among our friends. This enabled us to do more. Everybody helped and we helped everybody!"

The Loewengart family offered to let the women open a "Clothes Closet," in their basement. Mr. Loewengart installed the rods for hanging the garments. Karl Levy, who had been in charge of a large clothing factory in Germany, developed a file card system to keep track of each article by gender and size. Then he'd call people, "I think I have a winter coat for your

92

son." Elsa Hofman, wife of Dr. Paul Hofman and their son, worked in the Loewengart's basement - collecting clothes. People got the clothes they needed. It worked beautifully!

Any emergency request for food was handled by one of the women who set aside half of her pantry to store the canned goods, rice, beans and flour we collected. The network of volunteers provided the immigrants with all types of information and services. People called Jenny Wolf or Dorothy Becker if they heard of job openings at department stores like Mandel Brothers and Goldblatts. The volunteers gave people the names of carpenters, upholsterers and dressmakers who were looking for work. At the same time, Dorothy kept an eye out for lonely ladies who might be interested in equally lonely bachelors.

The reputation of the Women's Group spread and attracted more members. Others, who could not spare the time, supported the volunteers with whatever money they could spare. With the financial contributions, Jenny Wolf suggested that they rent a small apartment for those Jewish immigrants who had just arrived in Chicago and were looking for jobs. The women furnished it with donated furniture, drapes and linen. The family could stay in the apartment until one of the parents found work.

The Women's Neighborhood Group Joins Selfhelp

The Women's Neighborhood Group had been in operation only several months when Jenny Wolf got a call from Dr. Walter Friedlander, a sociologist from the University of Chicago. "I heard you started a women's group

93

here in Chicago." he said, and Jenny Wolf told him she had. He was a member of "Selfhelp of Immigres of Central Europe," which was based in New York. He explained that the Selfhelp organization was founded by Paul Tillich, a Protestant theologian, to provide social services to Jewish and non-Jewish immigrants alike, who have had to flee Nazi oppression and persecution. Apart from the president Paul Tillich, Einstein, James Franck and many other great people were members of Selfhelp. "They asked me to establish a branch in Chicago," said Dr. Friedlander, "but then I heard about your group."

Dr. Friedlander told Jenny Wolf that it would be better to work together and have one group. Since both groups had the same objectives, he thought that the Women's Group would benefit from a merger with Selfhelp. Jenny Wolf wanted to talk it over with the members of her Group first. The Selfhelp organization had prestige and power and they joined as a Women's Group at first. Dr Friedlander was the first president of Chicago Selfhelp. He asked Jenny Wolf to be on the Board. Dorothy recalled, *"Dr. Friedlander liked me so much that he said, " you and Ernst Block have to be on the Board too."*

After the Women's Group merged with Selfhelp, they officially became a non-sectarian organization and remained so until after the Second World War. The Women's Group had to pay Selfhelp of New York 25 cents membership dues every month. This came to about $3 dollars a year. Later they paid 75 cents every month. It was hard for the women to save this money. What they got in return was an affiliation with the University of Chicago and lots of prestige.

By the time the name of the Women's Group changed to the Selfhelp Neighborhood Group, Mrs. Irma Monarch and Mrs. Elsa Franks organized a Selfhelp Neighborhood Group on the north side. Mrs. Franks' son, Gerry Franks, who served on the Board of Selfhelp throughout his life, started a Youth Group when he was only 16. Dorothy beamed, *"The young Selfhelpers shopped for people who couldn't go out.. Everyone was involved. It was beautiful. The whole thing was beautiful. The Neighborhood Groups touched the life of nearly every immigrant. Then I invented our Bachelor Parties in 1938."*

The Bachelor Parties

Dorothy who knew most of the Jewish newcomers in Hyde Park by name, reached out - especially to those people who had come to this country alone. Shortly after Dorothy joined Sinai's Community Center, she became chairperson of the Program Committee. What better way for people to meet than at a dance? Many more men than women attended their Saturday evening dance on the roof garden of the Sinai Temple.

Dorothy discovered later that most of the single women worked as housekeepers and weren't off on Saturday evenings. Several young men approached Dorothy and asked her to dance. Dorothy replied: *"I only dance with my husband!"*

"Most people danced with others, but I never did. My husband was a better dancer than I, but he never danced with other women either. He never suspected me and I never suspected him. He knew I only loved him and I knew he only loved me. We didn't dance with other people, unmarried or married."

Several of the men left early complaining, "There are no women to dance with." At the next meeting of the Selfhelp Neighborhood Group, Dorothy told the women that the dance had been disappointing and quipped, "We almost had a stag party." Not to be deterred, Dorothy offered to host a party on a Sunday afternoon when most women would be off from work.

She recalled: The first Bachelor Party was held in the Becker apartment. Dorothy called it, "Bachelor Party" because she didn't invite any married people. Everyone teased her and said that she has a wedding promotion club. She wanted to give the women an opportunity to meet other women as well because she thought it was horrible for them to work as maids all the time. The women who worked as maids only got every Thursday afternoon and every other Sunday off. At the Bachelor Parties, they could meet and make friends and some marriages did have their start at her parties. Dorothy's cousin told her, "In 25 years you'll either be shot or they'll erect a monument to you."

Forty-five people came. People sat at little tables with candles. It was a tremendous amount of work, but Bill helped make the punch, and Jenny Wolf, a great cook, made potato salad and roast beef. Marian always admired Mrs. Wolf because she could make the potato salad while she was on the phone. I made some tongue and bought the paper plates. One man turned them over and said, "Ah Rosenthal china ."

"People baked cakes and everybody helped. That was the Selfhelp spirit!" Professor James Franck came. I didn't want people to think I was only in the marriage making business. Besides Bill, he was the only other mar-

ried man there. After all, he was a Nobel Prize winner, one of the most famous people in the world. He brought along all of his non-Jewish assistants who worked at the University of Chicago's Fermi Lab. Hitler hadn't wanted him to leave Germany, but he left with his entire staff. Otherwise Germany already would have had the atomic bomb. James Franck did not want his grandchildren to know that he was Jewish. I was so upset about that. He was the nicest, best-looking man I've ever met in my life. He had beautiful eyes, like those of a German Shepherd. He was such a fine, nice man... Dr. Walter Friedlander came to my Bachelor Party too. He was a small man with a big heart." [Appendix C]

Walter Friedlander, who was the first president of Selfhelp, was not jewish, but had been forced to flee Germany because he spoke out against the Nazis. He took a personal interest in everyone. People knew they could call Dr. Fiedlander for advice, for a letter of recommendation or for a small loan in an emergency. One woman, struggling to support her family, became a successful sales-woman, selling Fuller brushes to all of Dr. Friedlander's friends. It seemed they bought enough brushes to last a lifetime!

A circle of people gathered around the friendly Walter Fiedlander and the unassuming James Franck. The young man standing across from them laughed when Dr. Friedlander told him that his mother was beginning to speak English like a native. She had waited on him at the 53rd Street bakery last Saturday.

Suddenly, all the lights went out just as Walter Friedlander finally sat down to savor the succulent slices of tongue. People suspected the Beckers of having pulled a prank. What could be more romantic than turned off lights at a bachelor party?

The guests joked and laughed, while Dorothy frantically tried to contact their janitor. Bill checked the fuse box and called Commonwealth Edison, but darkness prevailed. Dorothy laughed nervously and asked, "Who needs electricity?" as she searched for candles and matches.

Before leaving, one woman expressed a sentiment shared by many. She confided to Dorothy, "All week I worked as a maid, but at your party I felt like a human being again." The party gave people a brief respite from the worries and struggles of life, an opportunity to meet other people, to talk and to dance. Popular request persuaded the Beckers to host a Bachelor Party every second Sunday of the month. The following year, the small Becker apartment became too small a gathering place for the ever-increasing crowds of single people.

But Henny Molten came to the rescue: She had a large enough house to be able to take in some boarders. Henny's house was located across the street from the Beckers and she offered to host the parties at her home.

Fundraising

The Selfhelp Neighborhood Group had to devise some creative fundraising strategies to meet the growing number of requests for all types of help. The women met at Jenny Wolf's apartment to discuss how best to serve the needs of the large number of refugees entering the community. They didn't have enough money to meet the increasing requests for food, clothing, housing and furniture.

The Jewish community, especially at this time in their history, wanted to demonstrate that they could take care of their people without asking for government assistance. They feared that Congress might reduce the number of refugees that would be allowed to enter the country. Jenny Wolf convinced the women that they needed to become as actively involved in fundraising as in community service.

Ella Rothschild, who had been a member of the Jewish Women's Group in Germany, offered to make collection boxes out of blue cardboard. Traditionally, the collection box for the poor held a prominent position in every Jewish household. Some people could only afford to each drop a penny, nickel or dime in their weekly collection box; others would each give a quarter.

Every two months, 40 Selfhelp volunteers climbed two or three flights of stairs, and knocked on back doors to collect the contents of the collection boxes. Some people complained that the volunteers woke them up too early on Sunday mornings.

Hedy Strauss and her husband were on their honeymoon when they heard someone knocking on the door. Selfhelp volunteers did not give up easily. Hedy and her husband finally rolled out of bed reluctantly, put their wall unit bed away and unlocked the back door. Hedy handed the volunteer the contents of the collection box and vowed not to renew her Selfhelp membership again. Had anyone told Hedy that she would volunteer for the Selfhelp organization, non-stop, for the next 50 years, she would not have believed it! However, as it turned out, Hedy Strauss, would go on to volunteer as treasurer of the Selfhelp Home for half a century and became one of Dorothy Becker's most loyal friends.

Dorothy was always thinking of ways to make a few dollars for Selfhelp. She discovered that they could earn money at a food-tasting party. Forty women went with her to try an assortment of cheeses, which she thought would have tasted even better with a sampling of wine. They gave their verdict, were paid 35 cents each and together made $14 dollars for Selfhelp. Dorothy, who couldn't negotiate a decent salary for herself, took charge of fund raising like a professional.

"I was always collecting money and I still collect money now. Rolf Weil, who worked for Selfhelp since he was a teenager, and who later became President of Selfhelp's Board, always said that I had a 'bringing-in' personality. I brought in lots of people and money."

The success of Dorothy's parties and her involvement in Selfhelp and fund raising did not diminish her constant fear for the safety of her parents, her brother, Kurt, and his wife, Hilde. It was on Sunday, June 19, 1938, while Bill was playing golf, that Dorothy happened to glance at the morning edition of the "Chicago Tribune." Struck with panic, she stared at the photo on the newspaper's front page, depicting the nearly-demolished Westmann store on Grosse Frankfurter Street in Berlin. (Today it's the "Karl Marx Street.") Nazi Storm Troops had posted a sign on the door. "Don't buy from Jews." They smashed the windows and lamps, pulled the merchandise off the racks, and hurled it to the jeering mobs. The "Tribune" reported that a group of Nazis had severely beaten a Jewish man on Grosse Frankfurter Street. The reporter estimated that at least 1000 Jews had been arrested in Berlin during the past three weeks. [Appendix D]

Terror in Berlin

Dorothy was waiting anxiously for a telegram from her parents when Addie rang her doorbell. Accounts of beatings and deportations raced through Dorothy's mind as she paced the floor. Finally, she heard from her parents. The telegram read, "All is well. Send affidavits." Dorothy sighed, "What a relief! I was so worried." Addie asked, "You're not thinking of sending affidavits, are you?" The question stunned her. "Of course we'll send them affidavits." But Addie persisted, "I knew a man who came to this country when he was as old as your parents and all he could talk about was the magnificent peach tree he had left behind in Germany."

Dorothy demanded to know how she could compare a peach tree with the danger threatening the lives of her family. How dared she be flippant when their lives were at stake? Dorothy never could understand or forgive Addie's disdain for her parents' survival.

The following day, Mr. and Mrs. Westmann went with Kurt to their vandalized store in Berlin. Cabinets and shelves had been smashed, and glass littered the floor. He was about to pick up a piece of glass from one of the lamps when a policeman, standing nearby, held him back. "Don't touch anything," he warned. "They will use your fingerprints as proof that you destroyed the property yourself."

The clothing store that had been built by three generations of Westmanns had been demolished in one afternoon. The policeman, observing the shocked expression on Mrs. Westmann's face tried to console her. "Don't worry, after every storm the sun appears again." Looking around to make sure no one was in hearing distance, he leaned toward her, and in a barely audible voice gave her these instructions: "In the future, whenever your phone rings and an anonymous caller talks exclusively about the weather, send your husband and son into hiding immediately."

Several weeks later, on a rainy afternoon, the phone rang. A voice she didn't recognize said, "Rainy weather today," and hung up. It had been raining for days. Why would anyone belabor the obvious. Her heart began to pound fiercely as soon as she remembered what the policeman had told her the day they had inspected their demolished store. She urged her husband and Kurt to go into hiding at once. Hilde's Christian friends, Kurt and Waltraut Schilde, who lived in a suburb of Berlin, agreed to open their home to the Westmanns anytime they were threatened. The husband was officially a member of the Nazi party, but neither he nor his wife refused to help their Jewish friends - despite the risk to their own lives.

Several hours after the mysterious phone call, Dorothy's mother heard a loud knock on the door. Two men in Nazi uniforms commanded her to open the door immediately. "Where is your husband?" they yelled as they opened closets, and pulled the drapes off the rods. Their attempt to deport Mr. Westmann and Kurt had failed.

Two weeks later, the phone rang again. The voice announced, "Beautiful weather today," and hung up. Immediately, Mr. Westmann, Kurt and his wife

Hilde again fled to the home of their undaunted friends, Hans and Waltraut. The same routine: the phone call, the escape and searches of the Westmann home. This scenario occurred four more times. If the Nazis had discovered their hiding place, all of them, including Kurt and Waltraut Schilde, would have been deported to concentration camps.

While the Westmanns waited for their affidavits to arrive from America, Hitler seized the opportunity to stage a massive pogrom or massacre on the night of November 9, 1938. Two days earlier, Herschel Greenspan, the son of Polish Jewish immigrants living in Germany, had shot a German diplomat in Paris. He shot the Nazi official in an attempt to bring to the attention of the world Germany's plan to deport 20,000 Polish Jews, including his parents.

Imagining the worst, Dorothy couldn't sleep. She had read that Heydrich, the head of the Gestapo, ordered the police in every part of Germany to watch passively while Nazi troops broke into Jewish homes, stores and synagogues. In Berlin, twelve thousand Jews were captured and sent to concentration camps. Jewish stores were demolished and 40 of the 50 Berlin synagogues were set aflame. The name "Kristall Nacht," (Crystal Night), refers to the broken glass which covered the streets of every town and city in Germany.

From their hiding place, Kurt ventured outside once on that fateful night and saw the flames engulf the Fasanen Street Synagogue. He and Hilde as well as Bill and Dorothy had been married at that Synagogue. They were worried sick about Dorothy's mother, who was alone in their apartment in Berlin. While her son and husband remained in hiding, she stayed at their apartment because strangers were quickly seizing and occupying abandoned apartments.

Hilde and Kurt received their affidavits from relatives in Texas and left for America before year's end. Dorothy's parents received theirs from Bill and Dorothy. As soon as her parents obtained their visas, they purchased their tickets for a ship scheduled to leave for America from Denmark. They left everything behind, but they felt so lucky to have made it out of Germany at a time when thousands of Jews were being deported to concentration camps. They breathed freely for the first time in years when the cheerful lights of Copenhagen came into view.

They had been stripped of their livelihood, but German law required them to compensate each former employee with a large severance pay. In addition, the Westmanns were ordered to pay their former staff, many of whom had worked at the store more than 20 years, a monthly salary for one year. Each person was allowed to take 10 marks out of the country. They weren't bothered by the fact that they couldn't even buy a loaf of bread with the 20 marks they had between them. They could live without bread, but they would have lost their lives if they hadn't been able to get the necessary documents to leave Germany.

Many Jews, stripped of their livelihood and their savings, had neither the money for transportation nor the foreign contacts needed to obtain the affidavits. Most people didn't make it past the stalling tactics of the bureaucrats, especially in Germany's small towns. Dorothy's parents never looked back; they looked forward to building a new life in America.

Marian's Confirmation, May, 1945 - Front: 3rd from left - Marian Becker in a white dress with cousins Edith and Margo. - Back: Ernst Vogel, Hilda Westmann, Adolf Becker, Wilhelm Becker, Joe Lazor, Thea Becker, Addie Becker, Leo Hartman, Natalie Mottek Westmann, Lizzy Hartman, Richard Becker and Ike Becker

Reunited with Family and Friends

For Dorothy and Bill, their first New Year's Eve in America was unforgettable because Lissy and Leo Hartman, the Becker's best friends and former neighbors, had arrived to celebrate with them. The year "1939" was one of their luckiest years because they were reunited with their parents as well as with Kurt and Hilde.

That year, the German government confiscated Bill and Dorothy's bank account just when they had to pay rent for their own apartment plus the rent for Bill's two offices in addition to the apartment of their parents. They struggled financially for some time, but managed to stay out of debt. Despite the difficulty, Dorothy's parents liked their apartment - especially after they managed to eliminate the bed bugs. Kurt and Hilde found a room for $5 dollars a week, not far from where Mr. and Mrs. Westmann lived. Hilde was a hat designer and got a job at Bes Ben, the Mad Hatter on north Michigan Avenue, while Kurt continued to look for work.

The Hartmans in America

Lissy Hartman, the sole breadwinner of the family, went from door to door selling the chocolates she made in her kitchen. Mr. Hartman had difficulty finding work, despite the excellent references he presented to prospective employers. When Dorothy told Mrs. Brinkman, their English teacher, about Mr. Hartman's struggle to find a job, she offered to speak to a friend of hers, a top administrator at the Eli Lilly Pharmaceutical Company.

The friend got Mrs. Brinkman an appointment with the director of Eli Lilly, telling him that Mr. Hartman had years of experience as director of one of the largest pharmaceutical companies in Germany. The director of Eli Lilly did not hesitate to inform Mrs. Brinkman that his company did not place Jews in any administrative positions. "They only bring in more Jews." On the other hand, he did not want to insult the man by offering him a job as a sales clerk.

Denying themselves any extras, they saved their money until they were able to open a small delicatessen on La Salle Street and Elm. At 6 a.m., the store opened to serve coffee and fresh rolls to commuters. Until late in the evening, Mrs. Hartman made mounds of sandwiches. Her husband, who had learned to use the stubs of his fingers, stocked the shelves, ordered supplies, balanced the books and made signs.

The humorous Leo Hartman and his wife Lissy

Mr. Hartman's original signs admonishing customer to, "Squeeze your husband - and not my tomatoes," succeeded to coax smiles from the most disgruntled customers.

The deli was open seven days a week, unless Mrs. Hartman was called to school for a conference with their daughter's teacher. Some of the white parents had called the principal to complain about Steffie.

Lissy Hartman asked Dorothy to go with her to Waller High School (Lincoln Park High School) on Armitage near Halsted Street. In the early 40's, a few black students attended Waller High School. Dorothy recalled, "At home, Steffie was great but at school, she was impossible." Steffie told her parents, "The blacks in America are treated the same way we were treated in Germany." In Germany, her classmates had rejected Steffie because she was Jewish. Now, Steffie rejected her white classmates and was a friend of the blacks only.

At Waller, the white students were scheduled to swim on Wednesdays and the black students on Thursdays. Steffie insisted on swimming with her black friends on Thursdays. On the weekends, she drew angry stares from the mostly white crowd, whenever she went swimming at the Oak Street Beach with her black friends. Many white parents complained to the principal about Steffie's black friends.

The principal asked Mrs. Hartman and Dorothy to come to his office. Before broaching the problem, he assured them of his concern for their safety. Several people had called to complain about Steffie's habit of bringing her black friends to the Oak Street Beach. He worried, he said, because the callers threatened to throw stones at Steffie if she didn't stop bringing her black friends to the beach with her.

Dorothy tried to explain to Steffie that the whites in the neighborhood might even break the windows of her parents' store on LaSalle and Elm. She explained the danger of overstepping racial boundaries but to no avail. The problem was one of principle. Dorothy agreed with Steffie and opposed racial injustice as much as the rebellious teenager. In fact, Dorothy confided to Lissy Hartman, "I'm still glad that Steffie slapped that girl in Germany. That took courage!"

Dorothy's Parents in America

Dorothy's parents, who were completely dependent on their children for financial support, liked the less formal manners and dress codes. They adopted the American way of life with the eagerness of teenagers.

Mrs. Westmann, who had a teaching degree in English, spoke the language fluently. She taught her husband to say a few words, but his pronunciation sounded more like Chinese. Words he could pronounce he got mixed up and whenever his wife asked him to get some potatoes, he'd come back with tomatoes. He waited patiently for his wife to finish reading the comics while eager to find out if war had broken out in Europe. When Dorothy asked her mother how she could read trash like the comic strips, Mrs. Westmann replied, "If they're good enough for Eleanor Roosevelt, they're good enough for me!"

The English teacher at the YMCA asked Mrs. Westmann if she would be willing to help foreigners prepare for their citizenship exam. For the first time in her life, she would be able to teach, even though she wouldn't get paid. Her students not only passed the citizenship exam, but joined her book club.

The women took turns hosting the book groups, but liked going to Dorothy's apartment best of all. They told her, "You seem to enjoy our get-togethers as much as we do. You must *like* older people."

For the first time in his life, Dorothy's father had the opportunity to enjoy some leisure time. In Germany, he had worked long hours even on Sundays. Now he looked forward to talking with the men who gathered at their favorite bench near the totem pole in Lincoln Park. Whenever one of the women pushing a baby buggy would stop to ask him how he liked his new country, he would smile and answer, "America is beautiful!"

On that bench in the park, lively discussions ensued among him and a few of the German-speaking men. Each one of them held unshakable opinions about world politics, the state of the economy, and the scarcity of jobs for their children.

He spoke with pride of Kurt who had obtained a position as foreman at a factory. Shortly after he had accepted the job, Kurt discovered that the company had hired him instead of a man with a large family. Kurt spoke with his boss and told him he would resign from his job to make it available for the man with the wife and five children. Kurt explained, "He needs the job more than I do." The entire Westmann family was mad at him.

His mother had trouble understanding this act of self-sacrificing kindness at a time when he'd have trouble finding another job. His father confided to Kurt, "I would have done the same thing." Eventually, he found another job but it paid much less than the one he had relinquished.

That first summer in America, Dorothy's father, who had always been in good health, celebrated his 67th birthday. The entire family - Mrs. Westmann, Dorothy, Bill, Marian, Kurt and Hilde - prepared picnic baskets for a gala birthday celebration. The day was exceptionally hot and humid. On their way to a shady alcove of the forest preserve, Bill noticed that his father-in-law was walking much slower than usual. He checked Mr. Westmann's pulse, and became concerned about the irregularity of his heart-beat. In his calm, confident manner, he suggested they go back to the car and celebrate Mr. Westmann's birthday in the comfort of his home.

The following day, the family gathered at the doctor's office to wait for the outcome of the physical examination. Dorothy became concerned when she saw the serious expression on the doctor's face. He ordered complete bed rest, the standard treatment at that time for people with heart problems. Dorothy's father had to stay in bed except to go to the bathroom or to occasionally enjoy the evening breeze on their balcony.

Dorothy's mother stayed by his side day and night. Dorothy kept him company by day, while Kurt stopped to see his father after work. Dorothy urged her mother to get some rest while she stayed with her father, but Mrs. Westmann would not hear of sleeping when she had an opportunity to be with her daughter.

One golden day in October, when the trees wore their brightest colors, Mr. Westmann asked his wife, Thea and Kurt to come into his room because he wanted to say the "Shema," the prayer which glorifies the oneness of God, the central concept of Judaism. He called Kurt to his bedside and told him how much he loved him and how deeply he respected his son's goodness and decency.

Dorothy, who had never doubted her father's love for her, now realized for the first time how much her father loved Kurt as well. Her father beckoned her to his side. Her smile had been the sunshine of his life. From the moment of her birth, when he had first held her in his arms, she had only been a joy to him. He repeated what she never tired of hearing, "No one smiles like my Thea."

He stretched his arms out to embrace his wife. "For me you have always been the most beautiful woman on earth," he whispered. He disclosed what she had always known. Throughout their life together, he had always been faithful to her. He had loved her since the day they met and would love her forever. He rested a few minutes to gather his waning strength before he bestowed his blessing on each of them. Fixing his eyes on the Bible on top of his dresser he said:

"Shema Yisroael, Adonaoy Elohaynu, Adonoy echod.
Hear O Israel! The Lord Our God, the Lord is One!
Booruoch shaym, Kivod Malchusoh, Li Olom Vo-Ed
Praised be His Name Whose Glorious Kingdom is Forever and Ever."

At peace with his God, he reclined his head on the pillow and died on the harvest feast of Zukkos on October 20, 1940.

6

THE NEIGHBORHOOD GROUPS

After her husband died, Mrs. Westmann stayed at the Becker home for awhile. The two women comforted each other. After several months, Mrs. Westmann found an apartment not far from the Beckers. Every week, they said "Kaddish" together, the prayer for the dead which never mentions death, but affirms God and life.

Immersion in the work of the Selfhelp Neighborhood Group was the best remedy for Dorothy. The fund raising continued. Dorothy suggested that they could invite famous speakers like James Franck and Mahogy-Nagy, the designer from the Bauhaus, to conduct lectures at the Sinai Social Center; and they could charge 50 cents to raise money for Selfhelp. Not only did Mahogy-Nagy agree to speak, but he designed greeting cards exclusively for Selfhelp of Chicago.

Following her father's death, Dorothy discontinued the Bachelor Parties for awhile. When the year of mourning was over, she and Jenny Wolf planned to have a party at the larger home of Henny Molten - *on December 7, 1941.*

On the morning of the party, Dorothy walked three blocks to the Molten residence carrying shopping bags of crepe paper and other party decorations. By early afternoon, balloons were swaying to the sound of the steam from the radiators. Platters of cold cuts, large chunks of cheese, and bowls of coleslaw and potato salad filled the refrigerator. Several women were just arriving with home-baked cakes and Jell-O molds when Dorothy decided to go home and rest for a few hours. However, as soon as Marian saw her mother enter their courtyard, she rushed into the hallway, shouting, "Mom, Mom, we're at war. There's a war going on!"

Dorothy ran upstairs, turned on the radio and listened with wide-eyed disbelief. President Roosevelt had addressed the nation earlier that day. America had declared war on Japan in response to the Japanese attack on Pearl Harbor. The stunned Dorothy discovered America had entered the Second World War two hours before their first guests were to arrive. Jenny Wolf called to ask, "Should we have the party or call it off?"

They decided not to change their plans at the last minute. About 60 guests spent most of the evening huddled around the radio. People hardly talked, nor did anyone dance. Some expressed regret that the U.S. had declared war solely on Japan. They were convinced that only America could destroy the Nazi Regime.

Most of the men planned to enlist in the Army the following day. They expressed their apprehension with their silence as they continued to eat. Only three or four years ago, they had left their families and friends to escape Nazi tyranny. Now they prepared to fight Hitler's troops to the death. They embraced and said "good-bye," realizing they might never see one another again.

In a show of support for America's war effort, the Selfhelp volunteers, in conjunction with the synagogues, decided to hold a special "Loyalty Drive" to help fund a fighter plane. [Appendix E]. Instead of using the money they had saved to buy new shoes, people gave three or even five dollars to the

"Loyalty Drive." Elated with people's unprecedented generosity, Dorothy rang the doorbell of the Schaaf family. The wife answered and said, "Before I can give you anything, I have to ask my husband first, and he isn't home. I'll know tomorrow."

It was the middle of summer, and Mrs. Schaaf most likely didn't expect Dorothy to come back in that heat. In 90 degree humidity, Dorothy again climbed the three flights of stairs, only to hear the woman repeat the same alibi, "I forgot to ask my husband, and he isn't home right now."

Two rebuffs didn't deter Dorothy Becker. For the third consecutive day she trudged up the stairs. Without saying a word, Mrs. Schaaf handed Dorothy a dollar. Dorothy couldn't hide her disappointment.

"What's the matter?... Won't you get your commission?", Mrs. Schaaf asked with a smirk. She felt like slapping the woman. "I had expected a little more for the Loyalty Drive," answered Dorothy.

In later years, when Mrs. Schaaf's husband became successful in his profession, he contributed generously to Selfhelp, but his wife remained a miser. Except for a few laggards, the immigrant community was exceptionally generous. That year, Dr. Bamberger, their Board President, received a letter of appreciation from the U.S. government thanking the members of Selfhelp for their generous support of the war effort.

As the fighting spread throughout the world, more women began to work outside the home. Like many of her women friends, Dorothy's mother began to scan the employment section of the "Tribune."

One day she told Dorothy that she had gotten a job at Marshall Fields.

Dorothy exploded: "Under no circumstances! Absolutely not! I will not let you do this. It's impossible. I don't work and you work? It would be shameful. You're too old to work."

"Marshall Fields doesn't think I'm too old," replied her mother who was 57. Dorothy suggested, "you take care of Marian and the household and I will go to work." When Dorothy found a job her mother moved to the south side and took care of the Becker household. When Steve, her grandson was born in 1945, Mrs. Westmann moved in with Kurt and Hilde. Years later Dorothy regretted the pressure she had placed on her mother not to work.

"I'm sorry that I did everything wrong. I usually understood old people, but I couldn't understand my own mother. She wanted so much to be independent, but she had to ask Bill and Kurt for every penny. If she had worked she would have gotten social security. She told me that she wanted to work because she needed more money for Marian's birthday and for Chanukah. I told her that she had always taken care of her children and now her children would take care of her. Her mother replied, 'There's a big difference.' " When I told her that I couldn't see the difference, she responded simply," 'I hope you'll never find out'."

Mandel Brothers

Dorothy, who looked much younger than 29, had been hired for a position in the billing department at Mandel Brothers. To alleviate the monotony of the job, she invented an innovative method for tallying the checks, which impressed her boss. After several months, he promoted her to a supervisory position. She would have to train Margaret, a new employee, before she could transfer to her new position. Dorothy taught Margaret all the details of her job; and on the last day of the orientation period, the two women went out to lunch.

Margaret, who thought Dorothy was Gentile, told her that for $3 she had ordered a book from a Jewish-owned mail order house. In a loud, indignant voice, she declared that she had no intention of paying the $3 because, "Those Jews make money wherever they can!"

Later that day, Dorothy and Margaret overheard two department heads arguing furiously. Nodding in the direction of the two wrangling department heads, Margaret scoffed, "Look how those Jews fight. You can pour water on a pig, but it will always remain a pig."

"Why do you work here?" asked Dorothy. "Mandel Brothers is a Jewish-owned store. My entire family and I had to flee from the Nazis." Surprised and embarrassed, Margaret insisted she liked Jews and had many Jewish friends. "But I don't want to have anything to do with you," Dorothy told her. When Margaret didn't come to work the following day, Dorothy's boss asked why Margaret had quit. Dorothy repeated some of Margaret's anti-Semitic remarks to him. "Try to keep politics out of the job," he admonished.

After Christmas, people formed long lines to see Mrs. Becker, who listened patiently to each customer's complaint and refunded their money with a smile. "Why don't you serve them cake and coffee, too" snarled the department head. She calmly informed him that it was much better to have a satisfied customer buy something on the way out, than an angry one who might never shop at Mandel Brothers again.

Dorothy took a special interest in Evelyn Redel, a teenage girl who had started working to help her mother take care of her younger son. Evelyn had graduated from Jones Commercial High School at 16 and she could take shorthand and type with exceptional speed and accuracy. She confided to Dorothy that she liked her secretarial job at Mandel Brothers, but that her mother could barely pay the bills on her meager salary. In the near future, she would have to look for a better-paying job.

Shortly thereafter, another company offered Evelyn a bookkeeping position with a significant increase in salary. On her last day at Mandel Brothers, Dorothy took Evelyn to lunch and gave her a small farewell gift. She would miss her and knew the competent young girl would be difficult to replace. Ten days later, Evelyn visited Dorothy at the department store. Dorothy was delighted to see her, but wondered what had happened. Despite the higher salary, Evelyn did not like her new job. She wanted to come back to Mandel Brothers.

Dorothy decided to speak to the head of her department on behalf of her protege. "Evelyn is exceptionally capable and deserving of a more responsible, higher-paying job," she told her boss. "She works to help her mother take care of the family," Dorothy explained. Her boss agreed to speak with the director of the store, who said that he could use a good secretary. Evelyn Redel Heidke, wrote in her letter of 2/16/2000:

"My life was enriched by knowing Dorothy from the time I started working for her as a 15-year old high school student. Nine months after graduation - during a visit with her - I mentioned to Dorothy that I was not pleased with the hours I was required to work at the CPA firm. She then spoke to my boss, and I was hired to work in the Executive Offices. Eventually I was appointed Advertising Controller. Both my husbands were Mandel Brothers' employees. My first husband passed away when he was 46. Clarence, my second husband and I have been married almost 25 years. My two marriages (two children from the first) were all a result of Dorothy's speaking out for me in 1946." [Appendix F]

"Yellow Dog Accounts"

Dorothy remained in charge of the Customer Control Department and worked in the Claims Department until 1947. At that time, Mandel Brothers had a policy of not returning over-payments on accounts of customers who lived in predominantly black neighborhoods. These accounts were coded with the initials YD (Yellow Dog) accounts. Dorothy noticed that one of these YD accounts had been credited with an over-payment of $187 dollars. It turned out to be the account of a very nice black man. She called the owner of the account, who was pleased to hear he would be reimbursed the excess amount of money his wife had sent Mandel Brothers by mistake. He explained that they had bought furniture at another store. Instead of sending the monthly payments to the furniture store, his wife had mistakenly sent the payments to Mandel Brothers. Dorothy told the customer he would have to pick up the check for the $187 dollars from the Claims Department in person.

The following day, the African American customer thanked Dorothy profusely for notifying him about the overpayment on their account. After he received the check for $187 dollars, he asked to speak with Dorothy's boss and thanked him for enforcing fair and honest practices in his department.

As soon as the grateful customer had left the store, the head of the Claims Department called Dorothy into his office and reprimanded her for not following company policy. He explained that the store consistently lost money on the accounts of black customers who reneged on their payments. To compensate for this loss, Mandel Brothers did not refund overpayments on accounts of people living in predominantly black neighborhoods.

"Why do you punish decent black people?" asked Dorothy. "We have to obey company policy," her boss answered flatly. "I don't want to work for a company that penalizes innocent people." She submitted her resignation and walked out of Mandel Brothers for good. "My husband didn't want me to work anyway."

Years later, the Wieboldt Store took over Mandel Brothers and continued the same discriminatory practices. To her satisfaction, she read in the paper that Wieboldt had been involved in a lawsuit and had been ordered to refund hundreds of thousands of dollars to minority customers.

As soon as she had more time to devote to Selfhelp again, mothers called to ask if she could watch their children for them. Erika, a German immigrant mother with two boys, needed to visit her husband at the Dunning Psychiatric Hospital. The boys only wanted Dorothy and cried if someone else came. For the next two years, Dorothy watched Erika's boys whenever their mother had to visit her husband at the hospital. The doctors didn't expect him to recover because he continued to withdraw deeper into his psychosis. Erika continued to visit him regularly even though he hardly recognized her. According to state law, a person is able to obtain a divorce after a separation of seven years.

After the divorce, Erika went back to school and obtained a diploma in a health services career. While her boys were still in grammar school, she met a man who asked her to marry him. She agreed to get married if he promised to pay for her boys' college education.

Erika never forgot how Dorothy had stood by her throughout the most difficult years of her life. Shortly after the wedding, she called to tell Dorothy that her husband had not only promised to send her boys through college, but he had given her the tuition money in advance. "Are you happy?" asked Dorothy. After a pause, Erika replied, "Happiness is feeling secure." For most of the refugees, obtaining American citizenship offered the hope of finding that measure of security.

American Citizenship

After five years in the U.S., Bill and Dorothy applied for *their* citizenship papers. Dorothy, who had memorized the Declaration of Independence and the Gettysburg Address, probably broke the record for getting the highest grade since the founding of the country. When the judge pronounced the long-awaited words, "You are now a citizen of the United States of America," Dorothy could not hold back her tears. The judge noticed that

Dorothy was crying and said in a consoling voice, "You'll still be able to read Goethe and listen to Beethoven." Surprised by his misinterpretation, she replied, *"I'm crying because I'm so happy to be an American citizen."*

Dorothy Becker in 1945

Dorothy worried because Bill was detained an exceptionally long period of time in the examination room. During the five years they had been in America, he had become proficient in English and he had passed his medical boards, but he hadn't had enough time to prepare for the citizenship exam.

Dr. William Becker in 1945

Finally, Bill emerged with a triumphant smile. After he handed in his test, the examiner detained him to ask him about an orthopedic problem affecting his hands. Bill, who had become engrossed in the examiner's medical problem, nearly forgot to ask if he had passed the citizenship exam. "You passed, no doubt about that," exclaimed the examiner, eager to return Bill's attention to the contracted fingers of his right hand. That evening, the entire family gathered to celebrate not only their U.S. citizenship but also their official name changes to *"William and Dorothy Becker."*

Dorothy helped many of the Jewish families find apartments when they first arrived in Chicago. As soon as they arrived in the city, they already expressed the hope that she would go to court with them when they would become citizens. She went with so many immigrants to court that the judge asked her if she got paid for being a witness. When he retired, this judge invited her to his retirement party.

On one occasion, the judge called Dorothy into his private chambers to ask what she knew about the woman she had accompanied to citizenship court that day. Dorothy told the judge that the woman and her husband were decent people who worked long hours at Mount Sinai Hospital - she as a nurses' aid and he as an elevator operator.

When the judge finished questioning Dorothy, two officers of the court questioned the woman again, and asked if she had ever committed adultery. After Dorothy received permission from the judge to explain the word "adultery," the woman vehemently denied she had ever been unfaithful to her husband. Leaving the courtroom shaken but relieved to have obtained her citizenship papers, she invited Dorothy to lunch.

At the restaurant, the woman explained that the judge might have been informed about a male boarder who had shared their apartment when she and her husband lived in Shanghai. They were forced to sublet a room in their apartment to be able to buy milk for their son who had a calcium deficiency disease of the bones called "rickets." For additional money that enabled them to buy the needed milk, her husband had agreed to permit the boarder to sleep with his wife. Evidently, rumors of this unusual living arrangement of many years ago, had come to the attention of the judge. He felt obligated to question possible character defects before granting her the citizenship papers. During the 1940's, issues such as adultery or divorce were considered character flaws which could be sufficient ground for denying American citizenship.

By the end of World War II, most of the refugees including many of Dorothy's childhood friends became citizens and were proud to be self-supporting members of American society. Dorothy's childhood friends and neighbors, Margo and Herbert Kainer, were living in New York. Margo was married, while Herbert had established a medical practice. Margo and Dorothy called each other every Sunday.

Marian's kindergarten teacher, Ellen Sandmann, lived in Hyde Park, near the Beckers. She worked as a teacher at a Hebrew school. Only Gerda Israel Karrfunkel, one of Dorothy's closest friends, had remained in Europe with her mother and brother throughout the War. They had become estranged in Wildbad when Dorothy met Bill. Gerda never congratulated Dorothy when Marian was born. Twenty years later, Gerda visited Dorothy in Chicago and told her what had happened to her and her family after Hitler came to power.

Dorothy's Friend, Gerda Israel Karrfunkel

Since adolescence, Gerda knew she wanted to become a judge. Her entry into law school in the early 1930s was a feat in itself, considering she was *a woman and Jewish*. Neither her gender nor her religion deterred Gerda from pursuing a law degree. After Hitler came to power in 1933, the German universities were banned from granting Jews any type of academic degrees. However, because her father had been killed fighting at the front during the First World War, the university made an exception and awarded Gerda a law degree in 1934. But she still had to take the bar examination, which included an oral exam. One of the questions on the oral exam, designed to trap her, dealt with the burning of the Reichstag building, the German house of congress. In an attempt to implicate the communists, the Nazis falsely accused Marinus van der Lubbe of setting the Reichstag fire. They tried and executed van der Lubbe, even though the evidence indicated that the SA and the SS, on orders of Reinhard Heydrich, were responsible for the Reichstag fire.[5]

When Gerda took her oral exam, the Nazi examiner had asked her if the execution of van der Lubbe was legal. If she said "no," the execution was illegal, she would be jailed for questioning Hitler's orders. If she said "yes," the execution was legal, the examiner would have questioned her knowledge of German law. Instead, she chose her words carefully and answered, "At this particular time in history, the execution of van der Lubbe is legal." She had given a politically correct answer, and passed the bar examination.

Before she graduated from law school, Gerda married a physician named Victor Karrfunkel. Nazi administrators accused Victor of illegal and negligent medical practices, forcing him to resign from his position at the hospital. In the small town of Konigwusterhausen, where they lived, a group of SA thugs grabbed him and beat him brutally. Gerda and her husband had no other choice but to flee for their lives.

Several weeks earlier, Victor had received an invitation to set up a medical practice in Tientsin, a city in China with a shortage of doctors. The Tientsin officials had sent them their affidavits and they had obtained their visas, when Gerda's mother intervened. She objected fiercely to their plan to emi-

126

grate to China, and succeeded in convincing Gerda to stay in Germany. Victor went to China alone.

Shortly after Victor's departure, a German woman entered Mrs. Israel's millinery store with an ultimatum. She wanted to buy Mrs. Israel's millinery store for 2000 German marks, a pittance even in 1936. Gerda's mother did not want to sell her store, which was her only means of supporting herself. She realized she had no choice but to hand over her millinery business after the German woman insisted. The woman's son, a member of the SA, wanted her to have the store.

Already as early as 1932, the SA, a paramilitary group of Hitler's Nazi party, had a membership of well over a million men. Mrs. Israel knew their tactics. They had demoralized her son-in-law, closed his medical practice, and beaten him. She had no choice but to give up her store. The SA son's mother smirked triumphantly as she pointed Mrs. Israel to the back door.

Having lost the business, Mrs. Israel and her son James fled to Holland, where each went into hiding with a different family. Hannah, the gentile woman who had been the manager at Mrs. Israel's store, insisted on going to Holland with them. She could work in Holland only if she obtained Dutch citizenship papers. At great risk to herself, she changed her name and identity by buying Dutch identification papers. She worked and brought food to Mrs. Israel and James throughout the duration of the war.

After Mrs. Israel and James fled to Holland, and her husband emigrated to China, Gerda was cut off from her family for nine years. In 1937, Jews could still leave Germany if they had the necessary affidavits, visas and money.

Gerda had been one of the lucky ones to have obtained an affidavit from people in England. She had been assured of shelter at an English detention camp. She arrived at her safe haven with hundreds of other refugees, despairing of ever seeing her family again.

Lying on top of her bunk bed in the crowded detention camp, Gerda wondered if her mother and James had found a hiding place in Holland or if they had been deported to a concentration camp. She could not eat or sleep, but stayed on top of her bed day and night just staring at the ceiling. The woman in the bunk beneath Gerda's befriended her. She knew Gerda would only get more depressed the longer she remained isolated and inactive. She insisted Gerda get up and nearly dragged her into the kitchen, where she and a group of women peeled potatoes all day.

For several weeks, Gerda sat mute as a statue amidst a circle of women who talked nearly as fast as they peeled the mountain of potatoes in front of them. One morning, the women in the circle stopped peeling, raised their heads, and smiled at each other because they had heard Gerda talk for the first time in weeks. Several days passed before she signed up for kitchen duty and joined the circle of potato peelers. Day in and day out, she peeled hundreds of potatoes, and in the process discovered a new talent. In her spare time, she began to carve a few potatoes into faces, vases and animals.

If any of the supervisors would see her wasting food, she would be punished severely. One day, while engrossed in her sculpting, a camp supervisor did see her carve a potato. He watched with fascination as she transformed a drab potato into a ferocious lion. Himself an artist, he marveled at her talent and offered to give her lessons in sculpting - but not potatoes. This newly-discovered talent helped her survive the detention camp and remained her lifelong avocation.

In 1945, when the war ended, Gerda knew she couldn't earn a living sculpting, and she had lost faith in the legal profession. Hitler had made a travesty of constitutional law. With financial help from her brother James, she studied accounting in England, which enabled her to find a job immediately when she came to the United States.

Gerda's husband, who had lost contact with her, thought she had not survived the war, and eventually married a Chinese lawyer. Seven years later, he discovered that Gerda was living in New York. Not wanting to disrupt his marriage, Gerda agreed to give him a divorce. Victor and his wife moved to Israel, where Gerda visited them almost every year. When Gerda became sick, Victor came to New York to be by her side.

In 1947, Mrs. Israel began legal proceedings to get her store back. Because she had never sold the store, her business had remained officially in her name. In 1950, she returned to Berlin to repossess her property. She entered her former millinery shop and ordered the Nazi woman to leave - through the back door. With the money Mrs. Israel received from the sale of the store, she bought a chicken farm near New York.

James had fallen in love with Hannah, the woman who had remained faithful to them while they were in hiding in Holland. The couple married and helped Mrs. Israel run the chicken farm. When Mrs. Israel became infirm, Hannah tended to her mother-in-law's every need until she died. After James and Hannah died, Gerda transformed the chicken farm into an artists' colony for painters and sculptors.

During the last years of her life, Gerda fought a valiant battle against cancer. Before her death she arranged to leave the chicken farm to her colony of artist friends and willed a sum of money to Selfhelp, in honor of Dorothy Becker.

Dorothy's Childhood Friend, Ilse

After the war, Dorothy's estranged relationship with Ilse, her friend since first grade, ended permanently. Dorothy had left Germany without saying "good-bye" to Ilse, who had married a high-ranking Nazi from Goebbels' propaganda office. Just after the War ended, Dorothy received a letter from Ilse's mother, who addressed her in the most endearing terms. She wrote Dorothy about her daughter's plight. Ilse was living with her three sons in Ohnhausen, while her husband was in jail for his participation in Nazi propaganda. The mother begged Dorothy to send food and clothing to Ilse and her three young sons.

When Dorothy received the letter, she immediately sent Ilse a large food package, including some clothing and chocolate for the boys. The packages briefly renewed the correspondence between Dorothy and Ilse. However, Dorothy could not forget that Ilse's husband had been an unabashed Nazi, responsible for the murder of 6,000,000 Jews. Ilse glibly brushed aside these atrocities, and spoke with pride about her husband's promotions in Goebbel's propaganda machine. She accused Dorothy of being unsympathetic to the loss she and the German people had suffered during the War and insisted that the thousands of Germans who lost their lives during the bombing raids had suffered just as much as the Jews in the extermination camps.

Ilse continued to deny the facts, and rejected any appeal to reason. In the last letter Dorothy wrote Ilse, she conceded: "The Germans have suffered as a result of two world wars that they started themselves. Yes, you suffered a lot, but you asked for it! This ends our friendship."

She had also told Ilse about Kurt and Waltraut Schilde, the couple who, at the risk of their own lives, had given shelter to her father, Kurt and Hilde. Several years after the war, Waltraut visited Kurt and Hilde in Chicago and Dorothy took the opportunity to host a party in her honor.

After dinner, Dorothy recounted how her father, brother and sister-in-law had repeatedly fled to the home of Waltraut and her husband, in a Berlin suburb. At the risk of being sent to a concentration camp, they had given shelter to her family every time SS searches of the Westmann home were imminent. Waltraut looked embarrassed while Dorothy told the spellbound guests about her heroic deeds. She and her husband had helped their Jewish friends, as a matter of course, without any discussions about the risks involved. Waltraut returned to Berlin pleased to know that her friends in Chicago had begun to rebuild their lives, successfully.

7

SELFHELP CHANGES ITS FOCUS

By the time the war ended in 1945, most of the refugees had become citizens and had found better jobs. Those who had worked as stock boys initially, were department heads by the late 1950s. Some people with academic degrees held teaching positions at universities. The majority of women who had worked as maids now were sales ladies at large department stores. People were still calling the Neighborhood Groups for advice and assistance, but not as much as before the War.

Dorothy Becker and Richard Emanuel.1947

In 1946, Richard Emanuel, the Board President, suggested closing Selfhelp. For Dorothy that was a let down, and Bill said, "We can't dissolve Selfhelp because we have to do something for the old people," and that's what they did. After Richard Emanuel retired, Bill Becker became president of the Selfhelp Board, and Dorothy its secretary. From the onset, the Beckers placed the welfare of the aging German Jewish immigrants at the top of their agenda. Rolf Weil, who already served on the Board when Bill was president, maintained that Bill Becker was as committed to building a home for the older people as his wife, but it was Dorothy who sold the idea to the Selfhelp Board and the Neighborhood Groups.

Dorothy realized that they had to continue the Jewish tradition of being independent from the government, especially after the War when more Holocaust survivors hoped to come to America. She considered it her mission to help the people who were the sole survivors of their families. Dorothy and the Neighborhood volunteers would not only help them find apartments and jobs, but she invited every newcomer to join the Selfhelp family. She knew every person was needed in order to make their dream of a retirement home a reality. She reiterated, "My strength is to bring people in," and by 1947, Selfhelp had a membership of 2,000 people.

The Becker's dream of building a retirement home spread throughout the German Jewish community. As Bill and Dorothy were packing to go on a vacation in Wisconsin, a German-speaking woman residing at another retirement home rang their door bell. She was carrying a small suitcase, Dorothy recalled, "This lady started to cry and said, *'Mrs. Becker, I brought a suit case, I want to stay with you; I'll sleep on the floor. I heard you are such nice people.'* She said that people at her retirement home didn't like it when she spoke German. She had trouble learning English. At breakfast that morning, *she had asked one of the women at the table to pass her the sugar - in German. The woman told her, 'Why don't you go back to your Hitler.' She begged me to let her stay with us that night. I told her that when we open our retirement home, she would be one of our first residents."*

The following day Dorothy and Bill drove to Wisconsin with Alfred and Jenny Wolf. She shared with the Wolfs her encounter with the forlorn woman who had asked to let her sleep in a corner on the floor. "Instead of finding a little joy and peace during old age," Dorothy lamented, "this woman and many others like her feel rejected and lonely." The encounter with the woman from the other retirement home made her even more convinced that, *"We have to do something; we have to build a home for our people."*

Dorothy envisioned a home encircled by a southern style porch, where at least 30 people could gather on a balmy afternoon for coffee and cake. Her dream house would have a large garden with flowers for the birthday parties. She imagined the song of birds waking the residents from their sleep, when suddenly, hordes of chirping crickets roused her from her dreams.

Dorothy wondered, "How would they be able to afford a home for the elderly?" Selfhelp's treasury had a total of $300 dollars, designated exclusively for helping families and children. Bill agreed: This money could not be used as seed money for constructing the home. The Board would have to establish a separate fund for the home.

At the next Board meeting, Bill began his address by recounting Selfhelp's tradition of service to the community. Since 1938 and throughout the Second World War, a core group of mostly female volunteers had gone directly into the homes to help working women and their families. He pointed to the young people who had been able to go to school because their parents had found better jobs. But the people who needed their help now were the elderly - especially those recent immigrants who had survived the concentration camps. A few had survived the camps, others escaped before the War, but all had lost relatives, friends, their homes and their communities.

He told them, "Many of us have elderly parents, aunts, uncles and friends who live in lonely apartments, struggling to pay the rent. Our old people have trouble learning the language and won't be able to find jobs. Many of these elderly refugees would welcome the opportunity to live in a safe, affordable home with people who speak the same language." Bill paused momentarily, and then he concluded, "We need to build a retirement home for our people." The Board members jumped to their feet and applauded. Bill told them that first they would have to set up a separate retirement home fund.

Selfhelp of Chicago, Inc. and
Selfhelp Home for the Aged Immigrants, Inc.

One of the first changes Bill Becker made was to separate from Selfhelp of New York. He said, "We can remain friends with New York, but we are capable of having our own "Selfhelp of Chicago," without having to send dues to New York. As a result, the original "Selfhelp of Emigres of Central Europe" was officially changed to "Selfhelp of Chicago" in 1949. At the same time, they established "The Selfhelp Home for the Aged Immigrants," which later was called, the "Selfhelp Home." Each of the two branches of

Selfhelp had its own separate fund. With unswerving resolve, the Selfhelp Board never dipped into one fund to make up for a deficit in the other one. The fund, which supported "Selfhelp of Chicago," could only be used to finance the work of the Neighborhood Groups. It also made scholarships available to needy students and provided financial assistance to people with physical and mental disabilities.

The Selfhelp Home for the Aged also had its own fund. On July 20, 1949, the "Chicago Home for the Aged" was officially incorporated under the General Not For Profit Corporation Act of Illinois.[6] The problem was that the newly-established fund, which would support the "Selfhelp Home," didn't contain even one penny.

Before they could begin to look for a residence that could house the 20 people on their admissions list, they would have to raise at least $10,000 for a down payment. In a show of support, each Board member handed Bill a check or gave him money. By the end of that historic meeting, Dorothy announced they had raised their first $225 for the building fund. The Selfhelp Home of Chicago actually began its work with the elderly with only $200 dollars in its treasury.

Inspired by this small, but significant contribution, Dorothy, Jenny Wolf, Guttie Hirschfeld, Rolf Weil, Burton Strauss, Ella Rothschild and Ewald Kamp began one of the most intensive fund-raising drives in the history of Selfhelp. They knew they would need to contact hundreds of people to reach their goal. In addition to the 80 active members in the organization, they planned to con-tact another 2000 people who had previously supported Selfhelp.

Just finding phone numbers and updating addresses took several weeks. Dorothy could still see Guttie Hirschfeld typing the letters late into the night, with the tail of her black cat wrapped around her neck. The letters informed people of Selfhelp's plan to build a retirement home and asked for a donation to make this dream come true. The photocopying machine was still a dream as well. They decided to spend a little more money in order to use a fresh piece of carbon paper for each copy they made. For a period of two years, the women took shopping bags of letters to the post office every three months.

Their efforts were not in vain. Most of the members gave whatever amount they could afford. Some returned the envelopes with two or three dollars, others included checks for $10 or $15 and the wealthier people gave $25. They were proud to be part of Selfhelp and people marked their calendars so they wouldn't miss the socials Dorothy and Jenny organized.

About 400 people attended the afternoon get-togethers which were held either at a Jewish organization on 12 West Roosevelt or at Jones Commercial High School, where they reserved a room for free or for a small fee. For these gatherings, a number of women baked tortes, cakes and cookies. Platters of open-faced sandwiches, and deviled eggs preceded the desserts. Dorothy was always trying to get a pianist or a speaker, but the people said they didn't want any entertainment; they just wanted to talk. With an admission fee of $1.50 per person, the women usually cleared $550-$800 at each gathering for the building fund.

Every day, women of the Neighborhood Groups went from door to door asking for donations. One evening, Dorothy received a call from Justin Wetzler, an engineer who helped the elderly by repairing their appliances free of charge. He told Dorothy, "You walk up and downstairs everyday knocking on peoples' doors. This evening, I'll stop by your apartment to give you our contribution." Later that evening, Mr. Wetzler handed her a $50 check, which was the equivalent of $800 today. Peoples' support and generosity energized the women to think of ever more creative ways to raise money.

They started a "tea chain," which was a misnomer because none of them drank tea. It began when one woman would serve five women coffee and cake for the price of one dollar each. The original five guests would each invite five other women, and raise $25. In this way, the money multiplied until they raised $1,000 dollars.

"We had the first "May Party" in 1947. The cakes were all homemade for the "May Party." I asked 30 women to bake cakes, and each one baked one or two cakes. I said everyone who wants to help should come to our Neighborhood Group. They all volunteered. I got a woman with a beautiful voice to sing for us, free of charge! Mahogy-Nagy, a prominent designer and architect from the Bauhaus, was one of our people. He talked about art and architecture on a very high level. We used to have the musical program at intermission but it didn't work out because people were always talking. Now we have coffee and cake first so people can talk all they want. About 70 people would come. The admission was $1.50 and we were happy if we made $100 dollars.

"Since the 90s, the "May Party" was held at Temple Immanuel. People said it was outdated but we were always successful. Marliese Katzenstein, a Selfhelp volunteer for decades, was the chairman. Eventually, Dr. Baum took over but Marliese was still behind it. About 90 women baked cakes. A few people said they didn't bake anymore, and wanted to give money instead. We charged $10 dollars for admission and all the cake they could eat. The "May Party" was for the people who didn't want to spend $75 dollars for the Fall Dinner Banquet."

"In 1947, Agnes Strauss started the "Fall Dinner Banquet" with 400 people attending. We rented a room at a Jewish organization on Michigan Avenue and Roosevelt Road. About 100 people cooked. The woman who was in charge of the dinner parties was absolutely fantastic, but she didn't like to keep strictly kosher. There was always discussion about the word "strictly." People said it's either kosher or it isn't. It was like being a little pregnant. In later years, about as many people attended the Fall Banquet either

at the Drake Hotel or at the Skokie Hilton. It was our biggest fund raiser."

The proceeds from their first "Fall Dinner Party" contributed several thousand dollars to the building fund. By 1949, the combined efforts of the Neighborhood Groups, the volunteers and the membership had succeeded in raising the $10,000 dollars needed for a down payment on a home large enough for 20 people. Dorothy recalled, "We felt like millionaires." At the next Board meeting, Bill announced that they could begin looking at properties for sale, even though they needed to continue their fund raising efforts.

Agnes and Burton Strauss, Ilse and Max Ries, Dorothy Becker,
Gerry Franks and Jenny Wolf.

The Search for a Home

Every Sunday, Dorothy and Jenny looked in the "Chicago Tribune" at the list of houses for sale. The women, including Agnes Strauss and Henny Molten, took the bus to look at various properties for sale in Hyde

Park. They kept a record of each house, noting its size, and the number of bedrooms, as well as the condition of the kitchen and bathrooms. They looked for houses with shade trees and porches overlooking gardens. The homes not meeting their specifications were simply scratched from their list. On Sundays they took their husbands to look at those houses they thought their prospective residents would like best. One Sunday, Jenny and Alfred Wolf and Agnes and Burton Strauss went with the Beckers to look at houses.

The three couples and six-year old Steven Strauss, the son of Agnes and Burton, saw a "For Sale" sign in front of a large mansion. They admired its winding staircase, its modern kitchen and bathrooms. "Daddy, this is beautiful. Why don't you buy it for Selfhelp?" asked the boy. "It's too expensive," his father told him. "Why don't you charge it?", the first grader asked his astonished parents.

Dorothy, Jenny and Henny Molten continued their search for weeks. *"Finally, we found the house on Drexel and 49th Street. This was such a nice experience. It had a beautiful terrace. Forty to 50 people could comfortably sit on the terrace."* The three women admired the hand-carved staircase, the flawless oak of the parquet floors and the Italian marble in the large bathrooms. They visualized their people sitting beneath the canopy of shade trees in the backyard. They called the owner and arranged to meet him at the mansion.

Chicago's streets were covered with ice on the day they had the appointment with the real estate agent. Dorothy rang the bell. A man who looked like he hadn't shaven in days opened the door. Dorothy told him that they had an appointment to see the house. He grabbed her arm and said, "I have an appointment to meet my girl friend, but I'll take you any day." She got such a shock that she told him they would wait outside. But Ella Rothschild and Jenny Wolf informed her that they were not going to wait outside in the cold.

The man apologized and said that he hadn't been very polite. He told them that his father, one of the meat packing barons, had built the mansion at the turn of the century. Both of his parents had escaped the potato famine in Ireland to make their fortune in Chicago. His mother's religious faith had given her the strength to withstand her husband's drunken outbursts. After his parents died, he and his brother inherited the house. His account of the family saga came to an abrupt end when the real estate agent arrived. The outside of the house looked beautiful, but it was so neglected. However, Dorothy figured they could fix it up and couldn't wait for "our people" to move in and sit around the fire place.

"Eight of our people looked at the house the following Sunday. Everyone said the house had possibilities. They liked it. Gerry Franks brought a young architect along who said that we'd need $8,000 to remodel it."

The owners were asking $25,000 dollars for the property. Considering the size of the house, terrace and garden, the price seemed right, though perhaps somewhat high. They had the $10,000 dollars for the down payment. Bill hoped that they would not have to take out a loan to pay for the renovation. On January 30, 1950, "Chicago Home for the Aged Inc." obtained title to the property at 4941 South Drexel Boulevard.[7]

Plans to Remodel the Mansion

Thirty Board members came to Selfhelp's first meeting at their recently acquired property. They roamed from floor to floor through its spacious rooms, and up to a full-length gymnasium on the top floor. They liked its location in the heart of the German Jewish community. The size seemed adequate and they thought they had agreed on a fair price. Just as they were commenting on the extensive remodeling they would have to do, they heard a crash that made the building tremble.

Had there been a shooting? they wondered. The young Gerry Franks, who had been swinging on the rings in the gymnasium, had sailed to the floor with a thump. Gerry looked embarrassed, but was unharmed. He had jumped up to grasp the rings when a large part of the ceiling crashed to the floor. Luckily, none of the plaster had hit him. Bill concluded that the Olympic gymnast had survived the emergency landing uninjured.

When Bill resumed the meeting, one of the men asked if they had gotten a zoning permit. Bill didn't think that they needed a zoning permit since they were opening a home not a business.

Dr. Ernest Turk, a lawyer and an active member of Selfhelp, spoke with every person on the block to obtain their signatures. Some people said that they didn't want a retirement home because of all of the ambulances. Dr. Turk explained that they planned to open a retirement home, not a nursing home. When people got sick, they would either go to the hospital or to a nursing home. He got signatures from all the people on the block but to get construction permits from City Hall became a problem.

Before Dr. Turk could get the permits, an inspector from the fire department came out. He said that the home was a fire hazard and had to be fireproofed. Dorothy recalled: *"They had to tear down and throw out that gorgeous mahogany staircase. The rooms had the same wood paneling, and that had to come down. The marble had to be taken out of the bathrooms because it was too slippery. My heart still aches every time I think of it."*

He estimated that it would cost $29,000 dollars to bring the home into compliance with fire regulations. Bill felt sick. The cost of remodeling the home exceeded the price of the property by $4,000 dollars.

After Bill had given the Board members a breakdown of the real cost of bringing the home into compliance with city ordinances, some felt betrayed and began to shout questions at Bill. Why hadn't they been told about this exorbitant expense before they had put a down payment on the house? Bill, a surgeon, not a contractor, had not known of the need to obtain permits from the various housing departments at City Hall. He assured them that he hadn't intentionally misled them. Some of the members said that they didn't want to be responsible for a "white elephant" and walked out of the meeting.

That day, 20 of the 30 people resigned from their positions on the Board of Selfhelp. The remaining members considered the possibility of selling the property they had just bought. Dr. Becker, with the solid support of Dorothy, remained steadfast. He convinced the remaining members not to abandon their plan to open a home for the aged. He admonished, "Only children get mad, refuse to play and walk away."

Bill called a membership meeting. After an emotional discussion of their options, they voted to keep the mansion and to begin renovation as soon as possible. Elated over the outcome of the vote, Bill used a quote from "Jonathan Livingston Seagull" to predict: "From castles in the air come cottages on the sand."

The people in the community were relieved to hear that Selfhelp was not going to abandon plans to construct a home for the aged. Dorothy, feeling personally pressured to vindicate her husband's oversight, galvanized the women of the Neighborhood Groups to double their efforts. Their goal was to raise the $15,000 needed to set the crew of construction workers in motion. It took forever to remodel the home, because construction stopped whenever they ran out of money. Anytime they had raised $100 dollars, the men could work for another two days. They resumed the fund drive in 1949, but some people didn't believe they'd ever finish remodeling the home. Dorothy exclaimed, "It took two years to renovate the home, but it was gorgeous. Gorgeous!"

Dorothy recalled that one successful business man had given her $25 toward the building fund and told her to come to his office in two months when he would give her another $25. When Dorothy arrived at his office two months later, he began to shout at her. Evidently someone had told him that the cost of renovating the home would be higher than the purchase price. Instead of giving her another donation as he had promised, he demanded she give him back the money he had given her earlier. He had changed his mind about Selfhelp. He told her that the people working for the Neighborhood Groups were "swindlers and showoffs," who had no intention of building a home.

145

The stunned Dorothy staunchly defended the motives of the Selfhelp volunteers, but she couldn't convince him. Twenty years later, this same man arrived at the Selfhelp Home and asked to see Mrs. Dorothy Becker. "Do you remember me?" he asked, smiling broadly. She replied, "How could I forget?" He muttered sheepishly, "You have a beautiful home." She rose, pointed to the door, and ordered him to get out of her office.

She harbored resentment toward the handful of people who had accused her husband of false motives when he had simply made a mistake in judgment. Nor could Dorothy understand the people who had received help from Selfhelp but refused to support the organization when they could afford to do so.

One Viennese woman had called the Neighborhood Group because she couldn't afford a baby sitter for her sick child. For a period of six weeks, Dorothy went to their apartment everyday to take care of the child. Throughout the years, the mother repeatedly expressed her gratitude to Dorothy and to Selfhelp, but in words only. Not even after she had become quite wealthy, did she ever make a single contribution to Selfhelp. On the other hand, Dorothy never forgot the majority of refugees who supported Selfhelp wholeheartedly with their time, talents and whatever money they could spare.

Marian's Wedding

During this exciting time in the history of Selfhelp, another momentous event occurred in the Beckers' personal lives: Marian's wedding. Initially, Bill and Dorothy questioned their daughter's wish to get married because she and her fiance, Phil, were not quite 18 yet. Despite her reservations, the wedding preparations strengthened the bond between mother and daughter. Dorothy, who had gotten married when she was 18, readily identified with her daughter. [Appendix G]

Mother and daughter planned the wedding ceremony and decided what food to serve at the reception. Unfortunately, a few weeks before the wedding, Dorothy fell and hurt her back while walking down the front steps with her dog in her arms. Her back was hurting terribly and throughout the marriage ceremony, she had to remain seated beneath the chupa, the traditional canopy used at orthodox weddings.

Dorothy missed not having Marian at home, but the newlyweds found an apartment five blocks from her parents' home. She didn't see her daughter very often, because both Marian and Phil were busy with work, school and housekeeping. Dorothy waited five years, eagerly anticipating news of a prospective grandchild and her heart brimmed with joy when she was finally able to hold her first grandson, Ronny, in her arms. The Becker family had regrouped and grown.

Mr. and Mrs. Marian and Phil Shaffer

By June, 1951, the first Selfhelp Home had been completely renovated to the satisfaction of every inspector at City Hall and the Board of Health. As the construction workers loaded their equipment onto their truck, and placed the last pieces of debris into the dumpster, Dorothy and a group of 80 women arrived to transform the 25 room house into a home. They admired the modern kitchen and bathrooms, but Dorothy still mourned the loss of the mahogany staircase.

Before they could begin to think of color schemes and furniture, they had to scrub, clean and polish every corner of the three-story building. Dorothy

148

knew that a different color for each room helped older people to find the room they were looking for. After several men installed the curtain rods, the drapes were sewn, pressed and hung.

Dorothy received a call from a woman who had recently inherited a large Persian rug from her mother. She asked if Selfhelp could use the rug. Its brilliant red, gold and blue floral designs gave the home's large living room a palatial look. Another benefactor, donated the hand-carved dining room set. A ceiling lamp with fringes was destined to spread its warm glow across the faces of 19 residents gathered in the dining room. Dorothy took joy in seeing everyone gathered around the long oak table at meal time.

July 4th, 1951 remained the happiest Independence Day of Dorothy's life. The women continued to work that entire day. With special care, they placed the Delft plates and Dresden figurines that people had donated in a curio cabinet in the living room. Dorothy watched Bill carry a table on top of his head before he placed it near a window overlooking the garden.

The cookie jar on the coffee table would soon be filled with chocolate chip cookies to the delight of the grandchildren who would visit the Home. Newly upholstered sofas were placed across from each other in front of the fire place. A small table and chairs, illuminated by a swivel lamp, invited conversation or a game of cards. Upstairs, new mattresses and down pillows, covered with soft linen, awaited the arrival of its first homemakers.

On July 8th, 1951, the original Selfhelp Home at 4941 Drexel Boulevard opened its doors to six people, most of whom had survived the concentration camps. Unfortunately, the woman who had asked to stay at Dorothy's home had died. Selfhelp's 200 active members, its volunteers and benefactors - a total of 600 people - attended the opening ceremony.

The Selfhelp of Chicago Home - South 1951 - 1973

Three rabbis, representing the predominantly German Jewish congregations of Chicago, asked God to bless the Home, as well as the people who had worked to make it a reality and the people who would eventually reside there. One of the rabbis attached Mezuzahs to the door post of the entrance to the Selfhelp Home and to all bedroom doors. Dorothy beamed! Yes, there had been glitches, but the dream had come true. [Appendix H]

"They all sent flowers. It looked like a villa in Germany. That's how it looked. Our Southside Home was our most beautiful Home!"

150

8

THE SOUTHSIDE HOME - "THE MANSION"

Within two weeks, 19 residents moved into the Selfhelp Home. From the onset, the Board's policy had been to give priority to those Jewish people who had suffered persecution after the Nazis had seized power in 1933. There was no room for further considerations. Once the Board adopted a rule, they upheld it with iron determination. Dorothy had submitted the applications of a man who had left Germany already in 1929, years before Hitler came to power. His German supervisor at the pharmacy where he worked was a Nazi who had fired him because he was Jewish. Dorothy, who hoped they would bend the rules for hardship cases, presented his situation to the Board, but they didn't think he was eligible for admission to the home. He had lost his job *before* 1933, and therefore they didn't consider him a victim of Nazi persecution. Dorothy, the lone dissenter at the Board meeting, asked, "If he isn't a victim of Nazi persecution, who is?" She admitted, " I got very upset because people didn't go along with me."

After the Board approved people for admission to the Home, Selfhelp's policy was to ask for a donation of $200 dollars, but no one was refused admission because of inability to pay the admission fee. In 1951, the residents paid $50 dollars per month for a single or a double room, including meals, linen and maid service.

Originally, Selfhelp had been a non-sectarian organization. Christians like Dr. Walter Friedlander, Selfhelp's first president, had fled Germany because he opposed the Nazis. By the time the Selfhelp Home opened its doors, only a small number of Selfhelp's members were Christians. Dorothy wanted the Selfhelp Home to be a Jewish retirement home. She argued passionately on behalf of the survivors who she believed would feel most at home with people who spoke their language, practiced the same religion and who were united by their culture and history. At Board meetings she made it clear that she wanted a kosher kitchen at the Selfhelp Home, "so that all of our people can eat at the same table." This time, she succeeded in convincing the Board to make Selfhelp a predominantly German Jewish retirement home because *they* were the ones who had put the nickels and dimes into the collection boxes.

Some argued that the German refugees who where Christian and those married to Jewish spouses would not like to eat strictly kosher food. "In a kosher home we'll never be able to eat shrimp," lamented Mrs. Zekel, who was married to a Christian. "You'll have to eat that at a restaurant," Dorothy told her. " Besides, we couldn't afford to serve shrimp."

Neither she nor Bill had been raised in an orthodox household, nor did they themselves keep a kosher kitchen. Her vision of a family seated all of its members around one table. She wanted, "all of our people," the orthodox as well as the reformed Jews, to be able eat in Selfhelp's dining room. The debate ended when the members of the Board finally voted in favor of serving kosher food at the Selfhelp Home.

When Dorothy told Mrs. Oschitzke, "The name is impossible; you have to change it," she changed it to Oschatzke. The first director of the Home, Mrs. Hannah Oschatzke, had been the housemother of a home for difficult girls.

She welcomed the chance to work with the contented people who lived at the Selfhelp Home. Dorothy described her as a very talented, nice person, who lived with her husband in an apartment on the premises. The Southside Home did not have an infirmary. So, when one of the residents would get sick, Mrs. Oschatzke went with the person to the hospital. Dorothy Becker thought it was important to be there for people especially when they became ill at night and had to go to the hospital. This was especially true for people who had lost their relatives in the concentration camps, according to John Bowlby:

"In sickness and calamity, sudden danger or disaster, a person will almost certainly seek proximity to another known and trusted person. It is misleading for the epithet 'regressive' to be applied to every manifestation of attachment behavior in adult life, as is so often done in psychoanalytic writing where the term carries connotations pathological or at least undesirable."[8]

Lotte Aufrecht, a member of the Board, disagreed. She thought that the policy of having the director accompany the elderly to the hospital infantilized them. These debates prompted Lotte Aufrecht, a member of the Board to say, "Mrs. Oschatzke may have been the director of the Home, but Dorothy Becker and Jenny Wolf ran it."

The employees worked at the Home for decades and were part of the Selfhelp family. The staff consisted of a cook, a maid, and a house-man named "Cliff." The mother of Mitzi Marx was one of the first residents at the South Side Home. Mitzi, one of the pioneers of the Neighborhood Group, wrote a letter to the editor of the "Chicago Tribune" about Cliff. Her letter read: "Cliff is an educated man, shows wonderful understanding for the old people, has always a kind word to say, and is beloved by all." Cliff, an African American man, told Mrs. Becker that he appreciated the fair treatment he received at Selfhelp years before Congress passed the equal employment laws.

Visiting in the Southside Home Garden

Every Thursday, when the cook had a day off, Jenny Wolf, a fabulous cook, made the meals at the Home. She arrived at 5 a.m. to make breakfast; they ate dinner at noon, and had sandwiches in the evening. They loved cold cuts, and no one, including their doctors, had heard of cholesterol. One morning, Jenny couldn't come and asked Dorothy to make breakfast. *"One wanted chocolate milk; another one wanted hot cocoa; the next one wanted*

coffee (several drank it decaffeinated); one woman drank tea, and another,

milk. For 19 people, I made ten different types of eggs and then I collapsed."

Every afternoon, Dorothy and Jenny visited the Home to chat with the people either on the porch or in the garden, while the grandchildren raided the cookie jar. The Home purred with contentment except for a few minor incidents.

As soon as Lillie Kaufmann and Mrs. Mansbach - the first two residents - had moved in, the furnace broke. The service man did his best to repair it, but finally conceded that they needed a new furnace. Dorothy, told Else Bonem that Selfhelp didn't have enough money to pay for such an expensive item. Else suggested talking to her brother-in-law, a successful accountant.

Else and Dorothy met Mr. Bonem at his office. Dorothy, nearly in tears, explained that Selfhelp couldn't afford to buy a new furnace. After a few minutes, he handed Dorothy a check explaining, "I can't stand to see women cry." The amount of the check gave them most of the money they needed to buy a new furnace. Max and Ilse Ries gave them the balance they needed to install a new heating system.

No sooner had the furnace man left the premises, then the man who had come to install the TV antenna on the roof, got his leg stuck in the ceiling of one of the bedrooms. By the time several excited residents rushed to tell Mrs. Oschatzke that a man's leg was stuck in the ceiling of their bedroom, the TV installer had extracted himself from the gap between the sagging boards. Mrs. Oschatzke and the house-man rushed upstairs to find him humming with satisfaction while adjusting the clarity of the picture on their new TV.

He apologized for having upset some of the ladies and conceded this had been the first such experience for him. Mrs. Oschatzke asked how he was feeling. Luckily he had not sustained any injuries.

One more relatively minor snag had to be corrected before some visitors from the Jewish Federation were scheduled to visit their new Selfhelp Home. Dorothy expected the experts to criticize their use of the large banquet table, even though people liked to sit together at one table. Every book on the elderly recommended seating not more than four to six people at smaller tables to facilitate conversation. Dorothy knew that neither the beautiful oak table nor any other table would stop her people from talking. Nevertheless she worried that the visitors from the Jewish Federation would criticize their use of the large table.

Dorothy raised the topic at the next Board meeting, but Burton Strauss, the treasurer, considered buying new tables, an extravagance they could not afford. Dorothy confessed, "I cried because I wanted that table. Sometimes it helps." That evening, Bill and Dorothy met their friends, Carol and Hugo Mayer at a restaurant for dinner. Noticing the worried look on Dorothy's face, Carol asked, "What's the matter, Dorothy? You look worried. Is anything the matter?"

Dorothy explained that a group of professionals scheduled to visit the Home would probably criticize their use of one large table in the dining room. "Selfhelp can't afford to buy the smaller tables right now. If we at least had one small table, I could say additional tables will be delivered next week." Hugo Mayer, who had been listening to Dorothy, said he wished that all problems could be solved as easily as this one. He took out his check book and handed Dorothy a check for the table she needed.

The table was delivered one day prior to the arrival of the visitors. Mrs. Becker met them at the door, and invited them into the sun parlor. The consultants were captivated by the trees, shrubs and flowers blooming in the garden. They admired the colorful bedspreads and handmade throw pillows on the beds. One of the women brushed her hand across the smooth surface of the dining room table. She noticed the one small table standing in a corner of the dining room, and presumed additional tables had been ordered. They thanked Mrs. Becker for the home-baked treats and the impressive tour. One of the women from the Jewish Federation left with this backhanded offer of assistance, "Call us if the administration of the Home gets too much for you to handle. We'll be glad to take it over." Dorothy told the Board, "The woman was not joking."

By the end of that first year, generous contributors replaced the family style table in the dining room with six smaller tables. *"People got used to the change. They were in very good shape. It was different then. Most of the people were in their 60's. One woman came from Russia, and spoke English and German very well. She was in her 90's. A darling woman who didn't want to live much longer, just long enough to attend her great-grandson's Bar Mitzvah. Then she said, 'I don't mind dying but I would like to see my great-granddaughter become a bride.' Most people don't live long enough to see their own golden anniversary, but she lived to celebrate her daughter's golden anniversary. She was such a sweet, nice and very intelligent woman. Her* son was a doctor, and when he died, she died a few months later.

"I loved the people. They liked Mrs. Oschatzke too, but they loved me. I always found the good side in people. Lotte Aufrecht didn't think this was normal, but my brother was like this too, and so was my father. My husband liked people too, but he always told me, "You can't love people as much as you do, because you'll be disappointed." I never was.

"I was at the South Side Home everyday. I saw Selfhelp cases there. Not applicants for the Home, but people from the neighborhood, German immigrants who needed money or some other type of help from the Neighborhood Group. If they needed financial help, I'd call Leni Weil, the Treasurer of Selfhelp, Inc. She and her husband Rolf Weil had worked for Selfhelp since they were teenagers.

"If women needed help from the Neighborhood Group, I'd call Mitzi Marx. I loved Mitzi and her husband Martin. Mitzi, who had three children, had been a volunteer since we started the Neighborhood Group. She would cook an extra portion and would bring the food to the people the following day. Several women took turns to cook for families who needed help. We would do this for as long as a person was sick. Today, people still come to my office even though their requests have nothing to do with the Home.

"After we opened the South Side Home, I began to see people at the Home instead of my apartment. Mrs. Oschatzke didn't like it. She thought that the Home was not the place for seeing the people from the neighborhood, who needed help, but I thought it was the right place to see them!"

When the Board of Selfhelp received some restitution money from

Germany in 1958, Dorothy formed the South Side Senior Group and transformed the basement of the South Side Home into a recreation room. The Senior Group started with five people who met every Monday from 12:30 to 4:30 in the afternoons. After a few weeks, the number had almost doubled and by the end of two months, 25 people had joined.

Dorothy Becker and Mitzi Marx

People who lived north asked Dorothy to start a Senior Group closer to where they lived. She spoke with the rabbi at Temple Ezra on Winthrop Street who agreed to let the women meet in their recreation room every Thursday. "We had a kitchen so we had lunch first. The women from the temple complained that we didn't clean the kitchen well enough." Dorothy laughed, "But the rabbi took our side."

Pretty soon, about 200 people came to the Senior Group gatherings at

Temple Ezra. They celebrated everybody's birthday. Alice Adler, one of Dorothy's favorite people, was in charge of the women who signed up to bake cakes. Dorothy was trying to get entertainment, but one woman told Dorothy, "Please don't have any entertainment I would prefer to just talk." She said that when her daughter comes home from work, she doesn't feel like talking. Her son-in-law, who is a salesman, tells her the same thing.

Southside Senior Group

When Dorothy related this story to the director of a nearby nursing home, she exclaimed, "Are you lucky. We all break our heads to get people to talk." Dorothy fostered the interaction between the residents of the Selfhelp Home and the members of the Senior Groups, to the benefit of both groups. Many of the people who belonged to the Senior Groups became residents of the Home or placed their names on Selfhelp's admission list.

The original Selfhelp Home did not just *look* beautiful, it *felt* like home. The Selfhelp Home didn't need a public relations person; the Senior Group was its own best advertisement. Within a period of four years, 150 people were awaiting admission to the Home.

The Annex

Under the leadership of the Beckers, the members of the Selfhelp Board voted to build an extension to the original retirement home. They discussed the architect's drawing of the addition or annex at their next Board meeting.

Thanks to previous hard-earned experiences, their dealings with fire inspectors and safety regulators proceeded without a hitch. The majority of Selfhelp members supported the Board's decision to enlarge the Home, and contributed generously to the flurry of building drives. In 1957, the Annex opened its doors to accommodate an additional 25 residents. [Appendix I]

The Becker Wing

On opening day, Dorothy returned to the social room with scores of visitors she had taken on tours of the new addition. Most of these people were active members of Selfhelp who shared in the organization's pride of accomplishment. Four rabbis from the Hyde Park community blessed the home, the residents and the entire Selfhelp family. [Appendix J]

When Max Ries, a member of the Board, took the microphone, Dorothy worried that people wouldn't be able to stand much longer. He paid tribute to those people who had worked for Selfhelp, but who had died in recent years.

Their former president, Richard Emanuel, and deceased Board member, Alfred Wolf, would always be remembered for their invaluable contributions to Selfhelp. Moved by the tribute to her late husband, Jenny Wolf whispered to Dorothy, "I wish Alfred could hear these words of appreciation."

While offering words of consolation to her friend, Dorothy had not heard Mr. Ries ask Bill and Dorothy to please step to the front of the room. By the time she took her place by her husband's side, Mr. Ries had already handed Bill the gold, engraved plaque dedicated to Dr. William and Dorothy Becker with the following inscription: "This building is dedicated as the Becker wing in honor of Dr. William F. and Dorothy Becker." (The plaque now hangs near the east entrance of the Selfhelp Home - North at 908 West Argyle Street in Chicago, IL).

When the applause subsided, Max Ries pointed to the achievements of Selfhelp under the leadership of the dynamic Becker team. Raising his voice he concluded the ceremony with this incantation: "Es lebe das Alte und das

Neue daneben," which means: "Long live the old alongside the new."

Bill and Dorothy could hardly grasp the unexpected honor and outpouring of love people had shown them. Bill thanked the people on behalf of his wife and himself, but acknowledged that without the cooperation of the Board, the Neighborhood Groups, and the support of its members, they could never have achieved their goals. [Appendix K]

go Daily Tribune
nday, May 28, 1956   F*   Part 1—Page 17

Cornerstone at Home for Aged

U.S. Rep. Barratt O'Hara (D-Ill.) helps Dr. William F. Becker (right), president of Selfhelp Home for the Aged, place a cornerstone for home's $100,000 annex at 4941 Drexel Blvd. The home was established in 1950 by immigrants from Europe, all victims of Nazi persecution. (Sun-Times Photo)

Dr. William F. Becker, president of the Self-Help Home for the Aged, Inc., 4941 Drexel blvd., laid the cornerstone for a $100,000 annex to the home sterday. The corporation was established in 1950 by a group of German immigrants who remodeled a home at the Drexel blvd. address and recently collected funds for the annex.

Several weeks earlier, Dorothy had invited about 20 of their friends to the South Shore Country Club to celebrate the opening of the Annex. When she had called to invite the people, most of them had prior engagements and wouldn't be able to attend the celebration. She wondered why most of their friends had accepted invitations to weddings and Bar Mitzvahs on the opening night of the Annex.

What Bill and Dorothy did not know was that for the first time in its history, the Selfhelp Board had met without the Beckers. [Appendix L]

At that meeting, they voted unanimously to name the Annex, "The Becker Wing," and in addition, the usually frugal Board members planned to surprise the Beckers with a party at the South Shore Country Club. Days before Dorothy called to invite them to celebrate the opening of the Annex, they had made reservations for 70 people at the same country club. A member of the Board had taken the maitre d' in her confidence and explained they wanted to surprise the Beckers with a party. She asked him to cancel the reservation Mrs. Becker had made, and to reserve the room for the Selfhelp Board instead.

Just as the Beckers were ready to leave for the South Shore Country Club, Martin and Iby Mainzer asked Dorothy to show them the new addition. Dorothy said she had people waiting for them at the restaurant, and they were in a hurry to leave. The Mainzers had come all the way from Winnetka and had been stuck in traffic. She could hardly refuse since, at that time, Martin did all the accounting work for Selfhelp. To make matters worse, he asked lots of questions. After she showed them one bedroom with its adjoining bath, she returned them to the sweets table and made a quick exit with Bill.

Dorothy and William Becker on their way to the country club

By the time the Beckers arrived at the restaurant, all of the people who had accepted their invitation, plus those who had given Dorothy phony excuses, shouted, "Surprise! Surprise! We're all here." Even Fred Weissman, Executive Secretary of Selfhelp of New York had flown in for the Beckers' surprise party [Appendix M]. Dorothy was elated:

"Dr. Arlsberg gave a speech. His wife was very active in Selfhelp. He said, 'I always admired the Selfhelp people. They never talked about any of the people they helped. They didn't talk about who got money, who didn't get money. It is rare for women not to talk about what they're doing and for

whom they're doing it. What is even more unusual is that Dorothy Becker didn't know about this party. It's beyond belief.' [Appendix N]

"Other parties were just as good as this one. The South Side Group made a birthday party for my 50th birthday. Then the North Side Senior Group made a birthday party for me. I didn't want it, but they said if they couldn't do this for me, then I couldn't make birthday parties for them anymore. Everyday we had parties. Every year they gave me a surprise party at the Southside Home. It was just beautiful!"

Two Unforgettable Birthday Parties

Mrs. Oschatzke and her enterprising group of residents put their bid in early to host Dorothy's 50th birthday party. According to Bill, Dorothy loved the element of surprise almost as much as the party itself. That year, her birthday fell on a Monday, but to surprise her, the seniors decided to have the party on Wednesday.

To avoid arousing her suspicion, Bill had suggested they invite their friends, the Blumhofs, to go out to dinner with them that Wednesday evening. Mr. and Mrs. Blumhof, a fashionable couple who lived in New York, were visiting Chicago. Bill expected that an engagement with the Blumhofs would prompt Dorothy to get her hair done that Wednesday morning, the day of the party.

Bill asked casually, "why don't you make a hair appointment for Wednesday morning?" "I'm having my hair done Friday; I want to look nice for my birthday on Monday." "Can't you look nice for me on Wednesday too?", teased Bill. "Besides, appearance means everything to the fashionable Blumhofs." Dorothy did get her hair done that Wednesday morning.

She wore Bill's favorite red dress that evening. For some unexpected reason, the Blumhofs were not able to meet the Beckers for dinner that Wednesday evening. Instead, Bill arranged to have dinner with their friends, Lotte and Fred Aufrecht at the Berghoff Restaurant, famous for its sauerbraten and creamed spinach. Bill knew that since their "Morgenthau wedding," Lotte and Fred ate any type of food except Chinese.

Henry Morgenthau, who was the secretary of the treasury under Roosevelt, had given Lotte her affidavit, and was their witness when Lotte and Fred got married. The Morgenthaus gave the newly weds a card with five gold dollars. After the wedding, the Morgenthaus invited Lotte, Fred and his brother-in-law for dinner. They landed at a Chinese restaurant. Lotte and Fred had never eaten Chinese food before, and didn't like anything except the fortune cookies. After dinner, Fred thanked the Morgenthaus for all they had done for them and parted. When they got out of the restaurant, Fred said to his brother-in-law, "We don't have much money, but now let's go and eat at the Berghoff."

The "Morgenthau Wedding," was one of Dorothy's favorite stories. They had finished dinner, and it was time to tell Dorothy another story. Bill said that he had promised to check a patient who lived in Hyde Park and suggested that Dorothy wait for him at the Selfhelp Home while he made the house call. Having said "good-bye" to Lotte and Fred, they drove south.

As they approached the Home, Dorothy commented on the hordes of cars lining the streets there. She speculated that the cars belonged to people attending services at the KAM Temple, next door to the Selfhelp Home. Bill double parked, walked Dorothy to the entrance of the Home, and returned to his car. "Is there a power outage?", she asked Jenny Wolf who met her in the pitch dark vestibule.

Dorothy Becker on her Birthday with Edith Gross

Suddenly, the Home lit up, and a sea of people shouted, "Surprise! Surprise!" The Home was filled with hundreds of people who shouted, "Happy Birthday Dorothy." Every one was there. Her mother, Marian and Phil were all there. Dorothy couldn't get a word out. Then she turned to her mother and said, "I wish Bill were here." "I'm right behind you," Bill whispered as he clasped her shoulders with his hands.

"We were entertained the whole evening. Mrs. Oschatzki and Mrs. Lumly, the cook, read a skid. People recited poems. There were many educated peo-

ple and they could make nice speeches. I was so excited. The following Monday was my birthday and the Northside Senior Group had another party for me. I was just in heaven." [Appendix O]

People understood that to Dorothy Becker's parties were a celebration of love and life, especially since she and her people had come so close to losing their lives. Several poets in residence at the Home had written these verses for Dorothy:

Mrs. Gertrud Rawraway's poem ended her poem with these lines:
"Dass Sie als rettender Engel kamen zur Zeit
Zu lindern Not und schweres Herzeleid."
Like an angel of healing she imparts
The words that heal our broken hearts.

Mrs. Jenny Burin concluded her poem with these words:
"Ihr Name allen wohlbekannt
Wird mit Liebe und Ehrfurcht genannt."
Her name which everyone can recall,
Is uttered with love and respect by all.

Dr. Otto Koechoner quoted from Fiedrich Schiller:
"Schoener find ich nichts wie lang ich auch waehle,
Als in der schoenen Form die schoene Seele."
The search for perfection by any standard or norm
Can't surpass the beautiful soul in a beautiful form."

For the grand finale, Mrs. Oschatzke and Mrs. Lillie Kaufmann had written a play, which was read by Mrs. Lumley and Mrs. Saphir. In 1960, three years after the Russians launched Sputnik, the first satellite went into orbit and the race to the moon inspired scientists and poets alike. The play was:

"This Is Your Life"

With advances in space exploration, the moon expected many earthlings would want to retire in outer space in the near future. To make adequate preparations for the seniors who would want to settle on the moon, their director of senior affairs needed to consult Dorothy Becker, the earth's expert on the elderly.

The chief of planet earth, unwilling to lose Dorothy, advised the moon to invite a gerontologist from another planet. The moon's director of seniors insisted that he had to consult Dorothy Becker. Bill convinced Dorothy to accept the moon's speaking engagement, and the following week she left in a luxurious space ship. Retirement home administrators on the moon took extensive notes while Dorothy spoke. They toasted her with moonbeam punch, and before she returned to earth aboard the "Lunar Express," they gave her a generous contribution of moon gold for Selfhelp's building fund.

A flurry of parties followed, until one guest brought the week long celebration to a sobering halt. Before leaving, this woman wished Dorothy the best of happiness for the future, but she worried that an opposite scenario might occur. From her own experience she generalized that if the first part of a person's life was blessed with happiness and good fortune, tragedy would strike during later years. She believed the reverse to be true as well. If tragedy marked a person's first years of life, then happy years would follow. She explained: "My first years were wonderful. Then my husband died, and I had to raise my two children by myself."

Dorothy pondered these words; the possibility of losing Bill or her mother made her shudder.

Mrs. Westmann, noticing the frown on her daughter's face, asked Dorothy what was the matter. Dorothy repeated what the woman had predicted, and wondered if she could be right? Her mother asked, "Do you believe in fairy tales?" Her mother had reassured her, but worries remained in the back of her mind. The Board's plans to build a new Selfhelp Center on the north side helped to distract Dorothy from her vague apprehensions.

Plans to Build Selfhelp Center - North

By 1960, over 300 people waited for admission to the Southside Home, even though many refugees had moved from Hyde Park to the north side of Chicago. With the support of its membership, the Board of Selfhelp voted to build a new retirement home on the north side of the city. Bill Becker and Fred Aufrecht, went to Washington twice before they succeeded in obtaining a loan for $600,000 dollars from the Housing for Seniors Program.[9]

Assured of the federal loan, the Selfhelp Board voted to buy the property at 908 West Argyle Street. Selfhelp bought the property for $658,000 dollars. The organization received an additional loan for

$25,000 dollars from United Help, New York, the parent organization of Selfhelp of Chicago.[10] The remaining $33,000 dollars had to be raised by the enterprising Neighborhood Groups.

Busy throughout the year and preoccupied with raising funds to jump start the construction of Selfhelp - North, the year had flown by and Dorothy had nearly forgotten that her birthday was once again approaching. This year, she anticipated celebrating her 51st birthday with a small, intimate group of friends. But the Northside Senior Group objected. Dorothy tried to dissuade them, but they insisted that if they couldn't celebrate her 51st birthday, they wouldn't allow her to plan anymore parties for them. Confronted by their impossible ultimatum, Dorothy relented, and began to look forward to October 24, 1961.

Mr. Josef Gruen, a former cantor at Temple Ezra, was determined to attend the celebration with his wife Meta, even though he hadn't been feeling well for several months. He had confided to Dorothy that he did not think he would live long enough to see the opening of the new Selfhelp Center on Argyle Street and had asked Dorothy to look after his wife in the event of his death.

Mrs. Gruen, who had been his student before they were married, was much younger than her husband. "She is totally dependent on me," he told Dorothy. He would appreciate it so much if Dorothy would look after her since he did not expect to live much longer. The new medication the doctor had prescribed hadn't helped much, but he would be there for Dorothy's birthday.

Dorothy's 51st Birthday

Ever since her 17th birthday, Bill had given Dorothy a bouquet of roses on her birthday with the number of roses equaling her age. Earlier that morning, he carefully arranged the 51 red roses he bought for her. Every year, the bouquet, like their love, added another dimension. "Some day, I'll present you with a small bunch of 70 roses," he teased before he left to go to his office.

Before lunch, 200 people filed into the social room of Temple Ezra to celebrate Dorothy's birthday. Women from the North-Side Senior Group had set the tables with decorative tablecloths and napkins. Bouquets of chrysanthemums harmonized with the plates and cups. Mr. Gruen sat at the head of the table next to Dorothy. He looked tired and pale, but appreciated the honor Dorothy had shown him by seating him next to her.

Before lunch, a few people stood up to publicly congratulate Dorothy. Others read poems they had written for her. Mr. Levy, who liked speaking to large audiences, could be counted on to end his speech with his original twist of a familiar invocation. Instead of prefacing his last sentence with, "God willing," he said, "If God remains impartial, we'll meet again one year from now to celebrate Dorothy's 52 birthday."

The laughter subsided when Mr. Josef Gruen slowly rose to his feet. Attempting to harness enough strength to give volume to his voice, he began by making a reference to America's race to send a man into space. He compared the astronaut's dream of exploring the heavens with "our hope of building an earthly paradise." He stopped momentarily to take a deep breath, and continued, "We at Selfhelp don't have to search the skies for an angel, we have our own Mrs. B e e e cker." His voice wavered, rose momentarily, and drifted away on the last letter of her name. With those final words, Mr. Gruen sank into Mrs. Becker's arms and died.

The Family of Josef and Meta Gruen
Drs. Dolores and Dieter Gruen with son Dr. Jeff Gruen

A hush fell over the audience. Most people thought Mr. Gruen had suffered a heart attack, but Dorothy knew Mr. Gruen had died even before the ambulance arrived. One of the people sitting at the head table explained to the guests that an emergency had occurred, and asked them to cooperate by leaving the premises quickly and quietly. After the stunned crowd filed out of Temple Ezra, the engineer turned off the lights.

Dorothy went with Mrs. Meta Gruen to the hospital where her husband was pronounced dead on arrival. We frequently respond to the sudden death of a loved one with denial. This common reaction may explain why Mrs. Gruen, at the time, could only talk about how sorry she was to have ruined Dorothy's birthday party.

Mrs. Gruen missed her husband terribly. As soon as the new building was completed, she moved into an apartment next to the new Selfhelp Center and ate all her meals there. To Dorothy's surprise, Mrs. Gruen managed her life very efficiently. Dorothy, who had never made out a check, admired Mrs. Gruen's ability to manage her own finances. Contrary to Mr. Gruen's expectations, his wife Meta became quite independent.

The Beckers Move North

The Beckers found it impossible to get a good night's sleep with the noisy new tenants who had moved into their building. When Dorothy asked Bill to complain to the owner about the noise, he answered, "It won't be necessary. We're moving!"

She knew Bill had made the right decision, but the prospect of moving out of Hyde Park felt like leaving home for the second time. She was born and raised in Germany's largest city, but she loved the village atmosphere of the immigrant community on the south side of Chicago. She had helped Jenny launch the Neighborhood Group 20 years ago. She knew the people; they were her extended family. She could never abandon the Neighborhood Group, the Senior Group and certainly not the residents. She and Bill might move north, but she promised to visit her people at the Selfhelp Home everyday.

For six years, Dorothy made the daily pilgrimage to the Southside Home on public transportation. Sometimes, she and Jenny Wolf visited the old neighborhood together. Occasionally, Lotte Aufrecht, who was active on the House Committee, accompanied Dorothy. In the afternoons, the same residents sat by the window to catch the first glimpse of their daily visitor. Over a cup of coffee, they shared their worries with her as well as any good news about the children and grandchildren. She returned home in half the time because she took the train to Bill's office downtown, and rode home with him.

Mitzi Marx Heads the Southside Neighborhood Group

For years, Bill had asked his wife to train another person to take charge of the Southside Neighborhood Group. This may have been the only time she refused to honor his request. She maintained she could not find anyone willing to accept responsibility for the Neighborhood Group. After years of prodding from Bill, Dorothy finally asked Mitzi Marx to take the leadership position at the Southside Neighborhood Group.

Dorothy called Mitzi Marx, "the born volunteer." She was also the woman who reminded her most of her closest friend, Lissy Hartman. She could rely on Mitzi at any time of the day or night. Mitzi had an educated heart and a great sense of humor.

One day, Mitzi's phone had rung just as she was rushing out the door to the dentist. Dorothy had called to ask if Mitzi would go to the hospital to give support to a mother who sat day and night by the bedside of her sick child, after the mother was told that her seven-year old Matilde had cancer. The woman hadn't eaten anything for days. Dorothy's dictum, "When someone is in need you can't disappoint them," convinced Mitzi to cancel her dental appointment and Mitzi took time to sit with the frantic mother a few hours everyday as the woman began to eat some of the fruit Mitzi brought her. After the child died, Mitzi continued to help the bereaved mother with her housework.

Tragedy struck this family twice. Within two years after the child's death, the husband died. The grief stricken mother was determined to salvage her family by working two jobs to educate her other children. Mitzi wrote a letter to Dr. Schwerin requesting financial assistance from Selfhelp's scholarship committee. Selfhelp of Chicago agreed to pay for their tuition, enabling both children to finish college. Years after the children graduated and married, Mitzi and her husband, Martin, remained close friends of the family.

With Mitzi in charge of the Southside Neighborhood Group, Dorothy reduced her visits to the Southside Home from everyday to once a month. In the late 1950s, the waiting list for admission to the Selfhelp Home grew steadily despite the fact that many German Jewish families had moved to Chicago's north side. For several years, Dorothy again galvanized the Selfhelp community to raise the $35,000 they needed to complete the construction of Selfhelp Center - North.

9

UNITED FOREVER

The Selfhelp Board met in the winter of 1962, to review the final draft submitted by the architects from the firm of Friedman, Altschuler and Sincere. The three story, air-conditioned building provided ample space for 35 studio apartments. At least half of the apartments featured kitchenettes, a component seldom included in the design of retirement homes, built during the 1960's. From the onset, the Board's top priority was to give seniors the opportunity to live as independently as possible. The building was designed to provide safe, affordable housing for at least 70 people.

The intercom system, linking the front desk to every apartment, would provide security beyond that required by law. Seventy people could eat comfortably in the spacious, bright dining room. The southern exposure of the dining room and lounge opened the building to natural light and sunshine. The small lobby led directly to the elevators, the dining room and lounge. The administrative office, with its small waiting room, was conveniently located right across from the lobby.

The architect proposed surrounding the benches in the garden with trees and flower beds. Having carefully reviewed every detail of the blueprints, Bill called for a vote and the Board gave its unanimous approval. For the next year, the rumble of bulldozers before the break of dawn sounded like music to Bill and Dorothy. Since all of the building plans so far had gone according to schedule, Bill and Dorothy decided to take a vacation.

It was bitter cold in Chicago that February of 1962. Bill's brother, Richard, and his wife Thea, lived in Florida and joined Bill and Dorothy mainly to spend some time with them. Dorothy liked spending winter vacations in Florida with Richard and Thea, although the two women didn't have much in common. Selfhelp held no interest for Thea, but she liked to race Dorothy across the length of the pool while their husbands played golf. They strolled for miles along the white beach until the ruffles of white foam swept the sand from their feet.

On the last night of their vacation, they went out for dinner and dancing. The two couples met in the dining room, elegantly attired in cocktail dresses and dinner jackets. The moon hung like an orange lantern above the Atlantic as they danced to the Caribbean rhythms. Dancing to a live band reminded Richard of the Widbad Spa where 33 years earlier he had prodded Bill to ask Dorothy for a dance. He liked to remind his brother that he had "discovered" Dorothy. "You certainly did," Bill conceded, "but it still took me a whole week to convince her to marry me." Their easy banter continued as they said "farewell" to the moonlit beach.

Their plane landed in Chicago at 2 a.m. They arrived home exhausted, but before Dorothy could go to bed, she had to make a few Jell-O molds for the Senior Groups' party the following day. By the time she went to bed, Bill was already sound asleep. He had appointments to start seeing patients at 8.

Shortly after Bill left the house, Lotte Loewenstein drove Dorothy and her Jell-O molds to the KAM Temple. The Senior Group had reserved the large social room at KAM because they expected over 200 people to attend the combined gathering of the North- and Southside Senior Groups. Fatigued from the jet lag and the lack of sleep, she brewed a strong cup of coffee, delivered the Jell-O molds and fell into bed as soon as she got home.

A few days later, a gold-engraved invitation, addressed to Dr. and Mrs. William Becker, arrived in the mail from the Society of Industrial Surgeons. This group of physicians wished to honor the couple at a dinner in recognition of Dr. Becker's scholarly article on the "Prevention of Back Injuries." Dressed in tuxedos and long evening gowns, about 70 physicians and their wives attended the dinner at the National Surgeons Club on Lake Shore Drive.

After dinner, the president of the orthopedic surgeons rose to speak. The paper Bill had written contributed significantly to the diagnosis, treatment and prevention of back injuries. He reviewed the main concepts of the article and invited questions from the audience. Bill welcomed the questions asked by doctors in other specialties, but he especially valued the orthopedic surgeons' positive responses.

The festive dinner and holiday parties faded in the glow of a stellar event in their lives - the birth of their third grandchild! Bobby, barely 10 months old, would attend his first Seder at his grandparents' home. While Dorothy was preparing the chicken soup and matzoh balls, Marian called. Four-year old Lori, their only granddaughter, had a sore throat, and would have to stay home with a baby sitter, but Marian, Phil, Ronny and Bobby were looking forward to celebrating the Seder with them.

"Can I bring anything?" asked Marian as seven-year old Ronny tugged at her skirt, impatiently waiting to talk with Grandma Dorothy. As soon as his mother handed him the receiver, he asked: "Is great grandma coming tomorrow?" "Great grandma is coming and she'll be so happy to see you." "Grandma, what will we have for dessert?" "I'm making the honey cake you liked so well last year. But first we'll have soup, chicken and noodle kugel." "I like the honey cake best of all," he told her. "After dinner," Dorothy added, "you'll have to find the missing pieces of matzoh called the 'afikomen'." "Now I remember," exclaimed Ronnie, "we played that game before." Grandma laughed and couldn't wait to see him. The kiss he sent Grandma echoed through the phone as his mother pried the receiver from his hand.

Dorothy returned quickly to the kitchen to prepare the charosis, the sweet mixture of apples, raisins and walnuts, which symbolizes the healing sweetness of work even during the time of slavery in Egypt. To Dorothy, the Passover Seder was the holiday of holidays. Her love of parties and birthdays, the celebration of life, originated at the large family Seder celebrations of her childhood. The scene of 40 aunts, uncles and her favorite cousins gathered around one long table that stretched through two rooms at her grandparents' house, was indelibly etched in her mind. At Passover, every person relived his or her own struggle to be free from internal or external jail wardens.

Dorothy had shed tears, symbolized by the salt water on the Seder table; she had eaten the bitter herbs of slavery during the Nazi era. Most of her aunts, uncles and cousins had perished during the Holocaust, but she found sufficient reason to focus on the sprigs of parsley and the egg, the symbols of Spring and renewal. Every member of her immediate family and their closest friends, the Hartmans, had survived the war. Above all, she was grateful for their three darling grandchildren, Ronny, Lori and Bobby.

When the family arrived, Lori was better, but she still had a slight temperature. Dorothy filled the water glasses and poured enough wine for four joyful sips. Earlier that morning, she had polished the tall silver candelabras. Bill hid the broken pieces of the afikomen that Ronny was expected to find later.

Ronny began to look for the missing pieces of afikomen as soon as he entered his grandparents' apartment. Everyone was already seated at the Seder table when the disappointed Ronny emerged from behind the sofa, empty handed. He sat quietly while they recited the story of the Exodus and was waiting patiently for Grandma Dorothy's honey cake.

Dorothy filled their wine glasses and asked Ronny to set the front door slightly ajar, in anticipation of the Prophet Elijah. The candles shed a soft light across the room as they sang, "Elijahu Hanavee," inviting the Prophet to join their Seder celebration. A glass of the Prophet's favorite wine was waiting for him by his place at the head of the table.

After the Prophet entered the room without a sound, Ronny closed the front door and resumed his search for the afikomen. Everyone clapped when he discovered three pieces of afikomen on the window sill behind the drapes. Triumphantly, he handed the found treasure to his grandfather, who reunited the pieces of matzoh into a unified whole, symbolizing the oneness of God and the unity of the entire human family. Ronny told his grandfather that he's got some "crazy glue" at home that would hold the pieces of matzoh together.

Before thanking God for the miracle of the Exodus and for their own escape from Nazi tyranny, Dorothy brought out colorfully wrapped packages for the three grandchildren. Clutching his package, Ronny jumped up to give his grandmother a hug and kiss. She complimented him for sitting quietly throughout the long Exodus story and sang "Dayeinu" with him one more time.

Over one last cup of coffee, Dorothy captured her family's attention when she shared with them her happiness about the industrial surgeons' favorable response to Bill's paper on "The Prevention of Back Injuries." As she spoke, they noticed the happy glow in Bill's eyes and the modest smile that hovered across his face.

They said "good night," and the smile of accomplishment lingered as they fell into a deep sleep. A few hours later, Bill woke up with severe abdominal pains. He told Dorothy not to worry. The pain was probably due to the horseradish sandwich he had eaten at the Seder. He tried to go back to sleep because he was scheduled to perform surgery at Resurrection Hospital that morning. The pain didn't subside, and Bill realized he hadn't slept enough to perform surgery. He asked Dorothy to call the surgical department to cancel Dr. Becker's surgery for that day.

On Dorothy's insistence, they called John Scheid, a general surgeon and one of their closest friends. He drove to their apartment immediately. He shook hands with Bill and told him, "I know what the problem is: You

Jewish people eat a lot of junk on your holidays." He suspected Bill might have appendicitis. His kidding stopped and his silence became ominous, as he proceeded to examine Bill. With studied calm, he advised his friend to go to the hospital admitting department, since surgery might be a consideration.

Marian and Phil had just entered the waiting room when Bill and Dorothy arrived at the hospital. Dr. Scheid ordered some lab work and decided to operate immediately. For several endless hours, Dorothy, Marian and Phil paced the floor of the waiting room, anxiously anticipating Dr. Scheid's report.

Dorothy wondered why the appendectomy was taking so much longer than expected. Dr. Scheid had sent a section of a lymph node for microscopic examination, hoping the pathologist would disprove his suspicion. The generally talkative Dr. Scheid lowered his eyes, waiting in silence while the pathologist studied the tissue from the excised lymph node. When the pathologist read the report, he shook his head at the precariousness of life. His friend had Hodgkins disease, a cancer of the lymph glands. Dr. Scheid informed the surgical team to prepare for closure of the abdomen and told his assistant what kind of cat gut to use for the final sutures.

In a shocked daze, he removed his surgical gown, gloves and mask. Barely able to comprehend that one of his closest friends and colleagues had a virulent form of cancer, he contemplated how best to impart this information to Bill's wife, Marian, and Phil. In times of crisis, he had always depended on his religion to restore his equilibrium. Dr. Scheid, a devout Catholic, believed in telling terminally ill patients their diagnosis. He tried to give his patients some hope without distorting the truth.

He considered different ways of presenting the diagnosis to the family. He knew that Jews as well as Catholics prayed; and he believed in the miracle of prayer. Too much time had elapsed already. Realizing he could not procrastinate any longer, he hurried to the waiting room.

Dorothy's eyes widened with fear as she tried to interpret the ashen pallor of Dr. Scheid's face. She knew he harbored their worst suspicion before he had even uttered a word. In a tone, resigned to the will of God, he told them, "Yes, Bill has cancer of the lymphatic system." He had recognized a surgical emergency when he had examined Bill, but he had not been prepared for this fatal diagnosis. Overcome with emotion, he told Dorothy, Marian and Phil to fall on their knees and pray, for no one with his type of cancer had ever lived more than eight weeks. "Please don't tell Bill his diagnosis," pleaded Dorothy.

After the surgery, Bill remained hospitalized another two weeks. He received the intensive nursing care he needed despite the shortage of staff during the Easter holiday. A group of nurses from Western Electric, the company that had hired Bill shortly after he passed his State Board Exam, took care of him, around the clock. For many years Dr. Becker had been the Chief Industrial Surgeon at the famous Hawthorn plant of Western Electric. The nurses who worked at Western Electric never forgot that Dr. Becker had spoken on their behalf at the company's union meetings. Speaking in his calm, persuasive voice, he had convinced Western Electric to meet some of their demands.

Rosel Stein, one of the dietitians at Resurrection Hospital, prepared special milkshakes Bill liked. Rosel told Dorothy that when the new Selfhelp

Center opened, she would be willing to help set up a kosher kitchen and plan nutritious meals for the people. She kept her promise and volunteered for Selfhelp for decades.

Rosel Stein

Before Bill was discharged from the hospital, his doctor, friends and relatives advised Dorothy to hire nurses to care for him at home. She refused; she wanted to care for her husband herself. Day and night, she answered his feeble call and gave him a teaspoon of water every half hour. Phil offered to stay with his father-in-law a few nights a week to let Dorothy get some rest. Whenever Bill stirred, Dorothy would jump up from the sofa, even if he hadn't asked for anything. Phil, who had taken off from work to help take care of Bill, finally told Dorothy there was no point in both of them staying up all night. Dorothy agreed, "It's no use. I wake up whenever he makes the slightest move. I can't sleep."

In time, Bill had regained his appetite, and planned to go back to work in June. By the end of the summer of 1962, his energy had improved and they started to see their friends again. One summer evening, while sitting in the garden at the home of Jenny Wolf, they recalled that years earlier the Beckers had discussed with Jenny and her late husband, Alfred, a hypothetical situation:

In the event one or the other spouse were to die, would the remaining one consider the possibility of ever marrying again? On controversial issues, Jenny usually sided with Bill, while Alfred and Dorothy generally supported each other's point of view. Bill and Jenny did not object to marrying again, if they would find the right person. Alfred and Dorothy objected strongly to even the thought of marrying another person.

After their hypothetical question became reality when Jenny lost her husband, she changed her mind and never wanted to remarry again. Dorothy declared: *"I didn't marry for life; I married for eternity! Before Bill finds another partner, I expect to receive the seven dozen roses he promised me for my 70th birthday."*

Hoping to keep his fatal disease a secret, Dorothy used the money they received from Germany to buy new furniture for Bill's office. The German government had paid Dr. and Mrs. Becker 50,000 German marks to compensate for the orthopedic clinic he had been forced to abandon during the Hitler regime. In 1962, that amounted to $10,000 dollars. With some of the money, she bought a new desk, chair and medical equipment in a desperate attempt to hide from her husband the seriousness of his illness. In recent days, she had again begged Dr. Scheid not to tell Bill his diagnosis.

Dr. Scheid insisted people had a right to know the truth about their condition. He decided to speak more openly with Bill, who already suspected the severity of his illness. "I asked you not to tell my husband he has cancer," lamented Dorothy. "He has to face his Maker some day, and so do I," answered Dr. Scheid.

Bill, who all his life had faced disappointments with courage and reason, accepted his diagnosis with equanimity. After Dr. Scheid left, he enfolded Dorothy in his arms and consoled her. "Don't be afraid," he whispered, "we'll fight this together." Holding her close, he contained her sobs with his quiet strength.

She dried her tears as she remarked on his renewed surge of energy and his improved appetite. Bill raised the possibility of taking a trip to Germany to visit the graves of his parents. He had wanted to visit the cemetery in Reinfals for years already. But Dorothy wouldn't hear of it.

"I never could go back to Germany. The German consulate invited me to go to Germany three times with all expenses paid. I took care of all the restitution work for our people. This saved the consulate a lot of work. The consulate called to ask me if I couldn't take a week off to go to Germany. I told them I could, but that I would never go to a country that threw me out. They told me that it's a different generation now and they stretch their hand out in friendship. "Die Botschaft hor ich gern aber allein nur fehlt der Glauben." (This message I like to hear, if only I could believe it). I would never go back - not for a million dollars!

"My husband wanted so badly to go to his parents' graves. They lived very

close to the Swiss border. So I said, "I have an idea." We could stay at a hotel in Switzerland. We eat breakfast in Switzerland, we take sandwiches along and a thermos of coffee. But you have to promise me not to talk to anybody. We won't even drink a cup of coffee in Germany. We go there and we'll go right straight to the cemetery. We won't have to stop any place but at the cemetery. That same day we'll go back to Switzerland. But Bill soon became too weak to go.

"My brother-in-law, Richard, went. He showed Bill pictures of their parents' graves. I, however, look down at everyone who goes to Germany. They have no pride whatsoever. One doesn't go where one has been mistreated. I would consider going to Switzerland, but Jackson Hole is just as nice. America is beautiful! You can go to the Adirondack Mountains; you don't have to go to Europe."

That autumn, they decided to take a short vacation closer to home. Bill, who climbed the Alps in Germany and Switzerland, loved the mountain village of Gatlinberg, nestled in the Smoky Mountains of Tennessee. They strolled hand in hand through the pine forest as if they were on their honeymoon. With a degree of satisfaction, they relived each segment of their lives together. Marian and Phil had established a family of their own. Bill's and Dorothy's happiness had soared with the birth of each grandchild.

They found a bench, and sat down awhile to watch the sun lift a veil of mist from the tree-lined slopes. They had spent evenings and weekends on making the Selfhelp Home a success. They had spent a good deal of their own money on the organization. When friends asked Bill which stocks he considered good investments, he told them, "We always invested in Selfhelp."

They spoke of Dr. Weyl, the rabbi who had married them and who had admonished them not to forget the less fortunate people. Would Dr. Weyl have been satisfied with their service to the community? Since they were first married, the pursuit of money had not been their primary goal - but only a means with which to help crippled children, struggling immigrants and the elderly.

The experience of working in her husband's clinic, which had been the source of her greatest happiness, had not been feasible in America. Her immersion in the work of Selfhelp had helped to assuage the disappointment she felt from not being able to work side by side with Bill. As secretary of the Board when Bill was president of the organization, she seized the opportunity to combine her efforts with his in bringing the ideals and goals they shared to fruition.

They had walked a stretch and were ready to rest awhile on a sunny patch of grass just as they had done on their walks through the Black Forest when they had first met. Resting her head on his shoulder, she gazed into the distance and wondered if they had done enough to help others. The sun shone brightly on one side of the sky, while charcoal clouds formed to the east. She sat upright, and vowed, "We've crossed many obstacles; we'll conquer this illness."

They had asked their closest friends not to inform others of Bill's fatal condition. Nothing - not even their personal tragedy - should interfere with the work of Selfhelp. As they talked, her thumb had unwittingly caressed the smooth contours of her wedding band. She recalled Rabbi Weyl's invocation when Bill had placed the ring on her finger, "The ring is without end; so may your love be." Whatever tragedy she might have to face, she knew that their love would unite them forever.

After they returned from Gatlinburg, Bill and Dorothy spent more time at home. One evening, the story line of a television movie, which paralleled their own situation, caught their interest. The movie portrayed a grief-stricken wife who took care of her physician husband as he was dying of a terminal illness. The husband's doctor came to the house several times a week and became enamored with his patient's wife. After the husband died, the doctor, out of respect for the grieving woman, waited several years before he declared his love for her. In time, she became more responsive to his affection and eventually married him. When the movie ended, Bill took Dorothy's hand, and asked, "Is this what you'll do some day?"

She kissed him and said, "You're very much alive and you'll always be my husband."

"After I die," said Bill, "work for Selfhelp. Don't just sit on the sofa and cry. People don't cry for the person who died. They cry for themselves."

Holding back her tears, she went to the kitchen to make some peppermint tea. Her heart ached. Tears flowed endlessly throughout Yom Kippur, the day of atonement, death and rebirth. When the rabbi asked God to inscribe everyone in the "Book of Life," she sobbed uncontrollably. Bill tilted his head toward her and whispered, "I feel so sorry for you."

Having lost an inordinate amount of weight and still tanned from the trip to Getlinberg, he looked like Ghandi. Bill looked forward to seeing all of the members of his immediate family on November 9, 1962, his 66th birthday. Marian, Phil and their children - Ronny eight, Lori five and Bobby two years of age - were the first to arrive at their grandparents' home. For his brother's birthday, Richard and Thea flew in from Florida. Dorothy's mother helped prepare the dinner.

Grandma Dorothy had placed a beautifully-wrapped present alongside the children's plates in honor of their grandpa's birthday. Bill sampled a bite of the brisket and a teaspoon of mashed potatoes, but saved his meager appetite for his mother's cherries jubilee. His mother had given Dorothy the recipe.

Dorothy had covered the large black cherries with an extra portion of "Cointreau," an after dinner liqueur. When she lit the cherries jubilee, the children jumped up as the flame leaped to the ceiling. Everyone tried to blow out the flame, but not even Ronny could extinguish it.

Dorothy ladled the brandied cherries over their ice cream, but the flame continued to spiral and dance with abandon. The guests had departed; Bill was resting, while Dorothy watched the tenacious blue flame flicker, descend, rise once again, rest at the bottom of the crystal bowl, and expire.

During the spring of 1963, Bill became so weak he couldn't get out of bed. The nurses from "Western Electric Company, where Dr. Becker worked took turns caring form him around the clock. When Percy Love, a Western Electric employee visited his friend Bill Becker at the hospital, the chief nurse told him, "He was your friend, but he was a father and advisor to many of us." He had to force himself to eat and hardly had enough strength to speak. Dorothy and Marian stayed with him around the clock, and watched helplessly as he began to gasp for breath. Shortly thereafter, he lapsed into a coma. With his wife and daughter by his side, Bill Becker's suffering came to an end on May 15, 1963.

At the memorial service Percy Love was asked to give the eulogy which he said was not easy for, "I am grief stricken at the loss of my friend. I am not from the Medical Organization but from the factory. There we speak in words and from ideas; when I think of Dr. Becker, I think of ideas, principles, and things of value. Dr. Becker loved his profession because it gave him the privilege to serve his fellow men, and he truly served them. He was attuned to them both as a specialist in his field and as a human being, genuinely interested in them. He loved his company because it gave him a chance to treat his patients like people who needed not only medical attention, but recognition as persons." [Appendix P[1]]

In a letter of May 23, 1963, Percy's wife, Nell wrote Dorothy about the touching scene her husband had been privileged to witness but had forgotten to mention at the memorial service. Nell wrote:

"Dear Dorothy, Shortly after Dr. Becker returned home from the hospital in February, Percy was visiting him one day and he needed to be moved. You went to him to help him, and he put up his hand so that you could assist him and he looked up at you with a look of absolute affection and adoration which you returned in kind. Percy says that he feels privileged to have witnessed that little scene and that he can't erase it from him mind." Signed, Nell Love and also Love from Percy. [Appendix P[2]]

Mr. Ernest A. Turk concluded the ceremony with these thoughts, "During these long years, together with his devoted wife, Mrs. Dorothy Becker, he has set new aims and given outstanding leadership, at the sacrifice of much leisure time and of many - to him less important - pleasures in life. Bill Becker has established one home for the aged, and has been working hard for the establishment of a second one. But - and this is tragic - he was not granted the few more weeks of life which would have permitted him to see the completion, the opening and the dedication of that second home. One is tempted to think of Moses to whom God showed - from far away - the Promised Land, but who, similarly, was not allowed to enter it."

"We all deeply mourn this grave loss to the community, to our organizations and those they serve, to his family, and especially to his brave companion in marriage and Selfhelp work, Dorothy Becker. Bill and Dorothy Becker's devotion and selfless endeavors to help others have been extraordinary, their strength obviously deriving from their true and utter personal happiness." [Appendix Q]

10

A REASON FOR LIVING

After her father died, Dorothy's daughter Marian hired a baby-sitter and stayed with her mother for a week. "For my mother, life without my father had lost its meaning." Marian recalled, "Theirs was a marriage made in heaven, and after my father died, my mother lost the will to live." The thought of suicide crossed Dorothy's mind, but she could never imagine inflicting that kind of pain on Marian and leaving that kind of legacy to her grandchildren.

"Marian is like her father, very quiet. He was 14 years older than I but he was so young. I'm much more old fashioned. Marian and I talk about him all the time. She loved him and was so much like him. My daughter is such a good mother - better than I was. I worry about Marian because her husband is very ill. When his time comes, I don't think I'll be able to do for Marian what my mother did for me."

After Marian left, Dorothy's mother, who usually lived with Kurt and Hilde, stayed with her daughter for a month. For weeks Dorothy couldn't eat and spent most of the days crying. At night, she slept in Bill's bed while her mother slept in the bed next to her. *"My mother was a pillar of strength and so was Marian."*

Dorothy received a letter from a friend. The woman wrote that Dorothy and Bill were the only couple she knew who had a happy marriage. She said, *"You shouldn't complain because you can live on your wonderful memories."* Dorothy wrote back: *"It isn't so. I think you can get over the death of a husband easier if you were not happy."*

Seeing her tear-stained face, the doorman of her building also tried to console her as best he could. He knew that the rent was expensive and confided that he had some savings which he would gladly give her in the event she needed money. She appreciated his kindness and compassion. He made Dorothy laugh one afternoon when he escorted a couple with a heavy German accent to her door. The German-speaking visitors had barely entered the lobby when the doorman stepped from behind the desk and escorted them directly to Dorothy's apartment.

As soon as Dorothy opened her door, the porter realized he had made a mistake. She had never seen this German couple before, and they didn't know her. The doorman apologized profusely, but explained that when he had heard their German accents, he assumed they had come to see Mrs. Becker. The incident made her laugh, and momentarily dispelled the dark cloud that enveloped her.

Guttie Hirschfeld, the woman who with her cat wrapped around her neck had typed hundreds of letters for their fund drives, was one of Dorothy's best friends. Guttie's husband, a good-looking man, had given up his position as director of Blue Cross and Blue Shield in order to work in Africa and India for "Mankind for Peace." He had a wonderful income, and they had an apartment with two grand pianos. However, they decided to sell everything and work for this cause. They tried to convince university professors all over the world to oppose every kind of war and to work for peace.

Guttie came back for a visit. She looked so poor Dorothy almost cried when she saw her. She wore an old blouse that she had bought seven years ago and a threadbare skirt. Dorothy recalled: *"Hedy Strauss and I bought her clothes so she would look decent. It was absolutely horrible!"* When her husband died, Guttie got letters of condolence from all over the world. After Bill died, Guttie told Dorothy: "I'm so jealous of you because you can continue the work you did with your husband." "Why can't you?", asked Dorothy. "I can't do it." But Dorothy insisted, "You're a terrific typist and stenographer. You could type for the professors who believe in 'Mankind for Peace'." Guttie lamented, "I can't even type that much anymore, I can not do anything."

Guttie's husband had told Dorothy: "You shouldn't work for Selfhelp, you should work for 'Mankind for Peace'." "It was a wonderful cause, but it wasn't realistic. I have to believe in a cause and I believe in Selfhelp!"

"Work for Selfhelp"

In September, 1963, Chicago's Selfhelp Center, at 908 West Argyle Street, officially opened its doors. Dorothy liked the word, "Center" because it reflected her vision of the new Home for the elderly as the *social center* of the German Jewish community. She remembered Bill's advice, "Don't just sit on the sofa and cry; work for Selfhelp." She was determined to do just that.

Every morning she walked two blocks from her apartment building to the Selfhelp Center and immersed herself in screening the 70 people who were awaiting admission to the new Center. Mrs. Becker met with the applicants first, before Irmgard Heymann and Maria Ikenberg did the social interviews.

Ethel Goldsmith, Irmgard Heymann and Hanna Goldschmidt

As early as the 50s, Irmgard Heymann, a licensed social worker, had impressed Bill and other members of the Board with the well-written reports she submitted on behalf of prospective applicants. Remembering that Bill had told her that Selfhelp needed a person with Irmgard's excellent writing skills, Dorothy asked Irmgard to become a member of the Selfhelp's Admission Committee. Irmgard became active on the Admissions Committee and later continued serving on the Board of Selfhelp for decades.

Maria Ikenburg, who was the chairperson of the Admissions Committee at that time, thought that Irmgard's interviews were excellent. After Maria left for Florida, Irmgard became the chairperson of the Admissions Committee. Dorothy explained the admission process:

"I saw the people first. If I felt that they would fit in, I gave them an application. They would be placed on a waiting list. Usually it took two years before their numbers came up. I saw them again before their applications were sent to the Admissions Committee. Irmgard Heymann or Maria Ikenburg would interview the people at their homes. The person who did the interview wrote the social report which was then given to the Board. The Board made the final decision. In fact, the Board prided itself on adhering strictly to Selfhelp's admission policies. The hallmark of Selfhelp was to treat everyone equitably."

Neither money, position or power could advance a person's position on the waiting list. People had to wait their turn. The Board members adhered strictly to their policy of considering only those Jewish refugees who had been forced to leave Germany *after* Hitler came to power in 1933. On several occasions, Dorothy spoke out on behalf of applicants who had left Germany because of Nazi persecution before 1933 but to no avail. The Board considered Selfhelp's policies as binding as constitutional law. They didn't need any oversight committees because they policed themselves.

Nor did they need auditors. They adhered to strict fiscal policies by staying within their budget and steering clear of debt. "This was how we were raised," explained Dorothy. "New furniture makes a good impression, but it doesn't make people happy." They were able to keep their prices low through supplements, fund drives, donations from members and benefactors, and hours of service from their large corps of volunteers.

After Dr. Becker's death, Fred Aufrecht, who had been vice president when Bill was president, was elected President of the Selfhelp Board. Dorothy wanted Fred to become President because he had worked so hard for the organization. Jenny Wolf became the President of Selfhelp Inc., but just for one year. The following year, Fred Aufrecht became President of both Selfhelp Inc., and the Selfhelp Home for the Aged, Inc. His wife, Lotte, an active member of the House Committee, became Vice President of the Selfhelp Board when her husband accepted the presidency.

Gertrude Schwerin, Fred and Lotte Aufrecht, Hedy Strauss

Many members on Selfhelp's Board were lawyers, accountants, financiers, social workers and university professors who donated time and expertise to the organization for decades. Dorothy was convinced that the voluntary service done out of love had much more value than that of a paid employee. Her enthusiasm and commitment inspired hundreds of people to volunteer for Selfhelp. She feared however, that some day people would acquire personal wealth from their affiliation with Selfhelp and added, " If that happens, I hope I won't be alive to see it."

Within a period of six weeks, the Board members in conjunction with the people on the Admissions Committee, processed and approved 70 people for admission to the new Selfhelp Center while the House Committee, under the direction of Jenny Wolf and Lotte Aufrecht, worked feverishly to decorate and furnish the Home. Lotte asked her sister-in-law, Mrs. Magda Rebitzer, an interior decorator, to suggest colors and fabrics for the new Center. The first thing Dorothy learned was that each room in a home for the elderly has to be a different color. This is how the people know if they're in the library or the dining room. Dorothy also wanted the Home to be an elegant, comfortable home. She didn't want the public areas to look like hotel lobbies and restaurants.

Mrs. Rebitzer chose a soft white for three walls of the dining room and painted the fourth wall a corn flower blue. It complemented the radiant blue of a hand-loomed wall hanging. Indoor trees and floral arrangements divided the multipurpose lounge into corners for discussion groups, a section around the stereo for music lovers, and an area with tables for bridge players.

Inside the 35 apartments, the earth tones of the carpets highlighted the golden hues of the drapes and sofa beds. The people on the House Committee considered the quality of the sofa beds a top priority. Since the average age of the prospective residents was 76, the sofa beds had to provide solid support, they also had to be comfortable and they needed to open and close easily. Mrs. Rebitzer consulted a German Jewish immigrant who owned a furniture store. He considered the top of the line sofa bed made by Simmons the best choice for the new Selfhelp Center.

When Fred Aufrecht spoke with the owner of the furniture store, he explained that Selfhelp couldn't afford to buy the top of the line sofa beds. One month later, the Simmons truck delivered 30 of their best quality sofa beds to the Selfhelp Center. The sales ticket on the furniture was marked, "Paid in Full." The owner of the furniture store had donated the sofa beds to Selfhelp on one condition: that his name never be disclosed.

The Center had 14 single rooms, but the majority of the apartments had two sofa beds, to accommodate either a couple, two sisters, or two room-mates. In addition, the Selfhelp Center supplied every apartment with a locked cabinet, a table and two chairs. People could bring their own furniture and decorate their apartments to make them as homelike as possible.

The Opening of Selfhelp Center - North

In September, 1963, the Selfhelp Center - North officially opened its doors. Hundreds of Selfhelp members and supporters attended the opening ceremony. The rabbi from Temple Ezra lauded the spirit of Selfhelp, the guiding principle which motivated hundreds of people to give of their energy, talents and resources to the organization. He commended the members of the Board, who under the farsighted leadership of the late Dr. William Becker, decided to build a second Selfhelp Home on the north side. In addition to the

Southside Home, the new Selfhelp Center - North would provide affordable, home-like accommodations for another 70 people, many of whom were survivors of the concentration camps.

Johanna Oschatzke, Dorothy Becker and Dr. Parker . Sep 1963

Many people who had not seen Mrs. Becker since Bill's death expressed their condolences as they discreetly pressed a check into her hand in memory of her late husband. She described to sympathetic visitors the joyful smile that had animated Bill's sunken face as he listened to the welcome clatter of Selfhelp under construction.

Attempting to hold back her tears, she rushed into the privacy of the office, where she encountered Bobby Rebitzer, the six-year old son of Magda.

Racing his miniature cars along the edge of the carpet, the boy looked up at Mrs. Becker and perused her tearful eyes. "Are you the president?" he asked softly. Not recognizing the boy, she asked, "Who are you?" When he told her his name she answered, "Your Uncle Fred is the president." "You must be Mrs. Becker." She nodded yes. "Your husband was real nice. My mother said that he was the best doctor I ever had. He told me that my legs wouldn't hurt when I got older, and they don't."

She felt like kissing the boy. At that moment, Bobby's mother entered the office. "You mustn't disturb Mrs. Becker," she admonished as she led him out of the office. "He didn't disturb me at all," Dorothy assured Magda. Smiling at Bobby, Dorothy confided, "He has been for me what my husband was for him: The best doctor anyone could have."

During the fall of 1963, 70 people, including several couples, moved into the Selfhelp Center. To accommodate as many people as possible, the Board assigned roommates to most of the single residents by drawing numbers out of a box. Amazingly enough, few of the elderly residents voiced complaints, considering the difficulties of a person having to share small living quarters with a stranger.

Dorothy's closest friends, the Hartmans, belonged to the first group of residents to move into the Selfhelp Center. For years, Leo Hartman had struggled to control his diabetes, but eventually one of his legs had to be amputated. Despite his many health problems, or maybe because of them, he kept his wife laughing at his funny rhymes. One of the last signs he made for their deli now hung in their apartment at the Selfhelp Center. It read:

"Sample the grapes, eat your fill, but a double price will appear on your bill." The Hartmans had been at the Selfhelp Center for only three months when Mr. Hartman died.

During most of their adult lives, Dorothy and Mrs. Hartman had shared each other's triumphs and sorrows. They had been neighbors in Berlin and had celebrated the New Years together in Berlin and Chicago. Toward the end of his illness, when Bill pushed most of his food away, he would eat a few bites of the vanilla pudding Mrs. Hartman made for him. When Mr. Hartman was confined to a wheelchair, Dorothy stayed with him whenever his wife had to go shopping. The two women had stood by each other to the end of their husbands' debilitating conditions. The sharing of joys and sorrows since early adulthood forged an inseparable bond between them.

Dorothy, for whom life had lost its meaning after Bill died, found the source of healing in her work with people who had not been fortunate enough to get out of Germany in time. Her fury against the Nazis only strengthened her resolve to bring some happiness into the lives of the survivors. She felt driven to help survivors of the camps and those who had lost families in the Holocaust. She was there for them day and night and her reward was to see them smile when they gathered to celebrate life. The constant celebrations also helped her deal with her personal grief over the loss of her husband. She often felt like a "Pagliaccio," the betrayed clown who made others laugh while his own heart was breaking. Hundreds of people went to Dorothy Becker with their problems, but she found solace only with her mother, Mrs. Hartman, and her daughter.

Dorothy's mother, who encouraged her daughter to work for Selfhelp, had been on Selfhelp's waiting list for many years. When Mrs. Westman expressed a desire to move into Selfhelp Center - North, Dorothy objected at first. She feared people would think she had devoted her life to Selfhelp for the sole purpose of getting her mother into the Home. However, Mrs. Westmann's doctor supported his patient's wish and raised the reverse argument, "People could say, 'Selfhelp is all right for others, but it isn't good enough for Dorothy's mother'." Dorothy relented and in 1963, Mrs. Westmann moved into the Home, and shared an apartment with Mrs. Goldschmidt, a woman she had befriended at the Senior Group. They liked each other from the start.

Appointing a Director

Before Dr. Becker died, he had appointed Lili Wollman to head the new Selfhelp Center. Dr. Becker had chosen Mrs. Wollman because for many years she had been the supervisor of housekeeping at the Shoreland, one of Chicago's finest hotels. He and Lotte Aufrecht, the chairperson of the House Committee, lauded her housekeeping skills and convinced the Selfhelp Board to approve her appointment. As director of the Selfhelp Center, she devoted most of her time to instructing her staff in the details of their housekeeping duties and gladly left the personal welfare of the residents to Dorothy Becker.

The residents, many of whom were members of the Senior Group, knew Dorothy since they first arrived in Chicago. Regardless of who was the director at the new Selfhelp Center, they turned to Dorothy whenever they had a question or needed to discuss a problem. She was half their age, but like a friend and confidant, she cared about them, understood them and was there when they needed her. She knew their families, their personal histories and understood their concerns. Decades ago she had testified on their behalf when they became citizens and she continued to be their advocate on the Selfhelp Board. They could go to her with the complicated papers they had to fill out for restitution from Germany. Many residents consulted Mrs. Becker first when they made out their last wills. They asked her to be there with them when they died and hoped she would think of them once in awhile after they were gone. They trusted her implicitly!

At Board meetings, she spoke persuasively on behalf of the residents and often was the only dissenting voice. She admitted, *"I did get upset when people didn't go along with me, and I cried easily. Burton Strauss said that I'd bring stray dogs into the Center if they'd let me. No one listened to us but I spoke up at Board meetings. The other women sat on the Board for years and never said a word."*

Many of her colleagues on the Board respected Dorothy's power of persuasion, but objected to her unyielding stance on issues she felt strongly about. She was passionate about the welfare of her people and was their most ardent advocate. The Board members too wanted to do what was best for the residents, but their main concern was to keep the organization financially afloat on a limited budget. Her persistence was formidable, her tears upset them and many of the male members of the Board agreed that, "Only Bill could keep Dorothy in check."

Mrs. Rosa Bergmann ON MOTHER'S DAY

Dear Mrs. Becker
wishing you a special
Happy Day, you deserve
it! You are a Mother
to all of us.
You take's care
of us, like a Mother in
dark and in good days.
I am very thankful to you
I feel very secure under
your kindness care.
Stay well and enjoy
the Mother Day
love you
R. B.

After one year, Mrs Wollman resigned because she preferred to find a position as supervisor of housekeeping at one of the large hotels. The new Selfhelp Center was in need of a director but the position was not advertised nor did the Board interview any applicants for the director's position. Even though they maintained that Dorothy was too emotional to be an administrator, they asked her to take charge of the Selfhelp Center. While Bill was alive, she had almost come to believe that she was too emotional for an administrative position. Now, she rejected that assumption and accepted the offer to take charge of the Selfhelp Center even though she had no title, no job description and no salary. It was a vague position, but she knew exactly what needed to be done.

The following day, she received a call from Rolf Weil and Gerry Franks, both officers on the Board of Selfhelp. They wanted to talk with her private-ly. Rolf Weil expressed concern when he asked: "Are you sure you want to become the administrative director?" The question stunned her. "Yes I do," she declared unequivocally.

"People complain and criticize an administrator," he warned. He feared she would get hurt. He maintained that, "Without Bill, you're not *it* anymore."

She had never thought her value as a person could drop overnight, like the stock market.

Dorothy didn't flinch and said, *"Yes! I want to be the director.* Gerry Franks chimed in: "You're still young and too pretty to remain single, " and suggested, "You'll probably get married again in a few years."

Black flashes of anger darted from her eyes. *"No! I'll never marry another man."* She felt outraged that anyone would doubt her loyalty to Bill, the only man she would ever love. She stunned both men when she faced them squarely and said, "Bill would want me to be the director." That least expect-ed assertion abruptly ended their conversation. Rolf Weil was convinced that Dorothy needed a job desperately. He may not have realized that she could have gotten a much better paying job elsewhere. However, she did need Selfhelp, desperately, because she needed a reason for living.

Shortly after this confrontation, Rolf and Leni Weil asked Dorothy to attend their daughter's bat mizvah, and Helga and Gerry Franks invited her to their son's bar mizvah. Since Bill's death, Dorothy had refused all invitations, but she graciously accepted these gestures of conciliation from Rolf Weil and Gerry Franks. But for years she continued to resent Gerry Franks' suggestion that she might marry again.

The Board of Health Inspector

The members of the Selfhelp Board recognized Dorothy's ability to win the confidence and respect of Department of Health officials, who visited the Center regularly. She had a checklist of all of the health and safety features the architects had included in the design of the building. Under Mrs. Wollman's scrutiny, the Home sparkled, and smelled of "4711," the time honored cologne some residents dabbed on their handkerchiefs. Blooming plants basked on the sunny window sills in the dining room and lounge.

The inspector acknowledged the importance of the intercom system, a safety feature the organization had installed voluntarily. The weekly calendar of social events and activities, posted on every floor, caught her attention. "People flock to our current events groups, and many of our residents transform our hallways into art galleries," explained Mrs. Becker, as they stopped to admire the details of an Alpine landscape one of the residents had painted. The inspector admired the well-groomed, friendly group of people who had gathered in the dining room. "Yes," conceded Mrs. Becker, "More than anything, our people love to talk."

Winding their way through the dining room, they stopped to say "hello" to Dorothy's mother, who was surrounded by a group of her lady friends. After she introduced the inspector to Mrs. Westmann and her friends, Mrs. Becker asked each one of the women about their children and grandchildren. Dorothy's mother lamented : "You never ask me about my family." Dorothy assured her mother that she didn't need to ask her that question. "You could be nicer and spend a little more time with me," Dorothy's mother teased.

By the end of the tour, the officious young woman told Mrs. Becker she reminded her of her own mother. Over a cup of coffee, she sat in a quiet corner of the dining room to write a summary of her impressions. She concluded: "The mostly German Jewish people appear comfortable and at home in the friendly atmosphere of the Selfhelp Center."

Having completed her report, she asked Dorothy to sign it. After reading it carefully, Dorothy gave the inspector an approving smile. The inspector handed the report back to Dorothy and instructed her to put her title after her name. "I don't have a title." "What do you do," asked the inspector. Dorothy described her work on the Admissions Committee. She coordinated the daily activities of over 100 volunteers who worked at Selfhelp. Listening to a few of Mrs. Becker's functions, the inspector exclaimed, "You're an administrator. You have to put a title after your name."

Dorothy called the Board President and explained to Fred Aufrecht that she couldn't sign the health commissioner's report without a title. Fred Aufrecht told her definitively, "Selfhelp has no titles," and Burton Strauss, the Vice President reminded Dorothy, "Your late husband would never have approved of an administrative position for you. You're too emotional!" Even though the Board had never considered anyone else for the director's position, many were still ambivalent about Dorothy.

Dorothy explained, *"If my husband had lived I would never have become the administrative director. We moved close to the Selfhelp Center so I could be there all day. But, I had to be home when he came home, he wouldn't have liked it otherwise. He would never have let me work Saturdays and Sundays. He did want me to work at Selfhelp after his death, however. Otherwise, I would have cried all day long and I promised him I wouldn't do that."*

She had been the chairman of Sinai's Planning Committee, and had headed the Southside Neighborhood Group. She had founded both Senior Groups and had spearheaded the idea of building a Home. She had recruited hundreds of volunteers and raised thousands of dollars for the organization; but for her husband, Dorothy had always remained the delightful, intelligent and gregarious girl he had loved and married. Regarding women, he endorsed the views of his time. He disliked independent women because he thought that they were too masculine. He encouraged Dorothy to work as a volunteer but not as a paid employee. The fact was that she couldn't afford to work solely as a volunteer because she needed an income. In Bill's mind, paid work was considered beneath the status of a doctor's wife. However, Dorothy had always valued the work of a volunteer much more than that of a paid employee.

Administrative Director of the Selfhelp Center

At the next meeting, the Board appointed Dorothy to the position of Administrative Director. She continued to work as closely with the residents as before she became the director. But as a paid administrator, she had to relinquish her vote. She never missed a Board meeting and continued to intercede for the residents as well as for the employees who now worked under her supervision. Though not wanting to lose good people to other retirement homes which paid a slightly higher salary, she didn't hesitate to ask the Board for an increase in the employees' pay, but she had difficulty negotiating a salary for herself. Dorothy explained:

"I was never a regular employee because I always remained a volunteer. I got paid for an eight-hour day, and I volunteered another eight hours. First I worked for nothing. I wanted to work for nothing. Then I worked for $300 a month. That was the amount of rent I paid for my apartment. Some of my closest friends on the Board were Hedy Strauss, Gerry Franks, Rolf Weil and Jenny Wolf. They should have told me that I wouldn't be able to live on $300 a month. Then they paid me $50 dollars more. They got a real bargain!"

Dorothy Becker, the director, was the heart and soul of the Selfhelp Center. In addition, she was the business manager, the activities director and the public relations expert. But first and foremost she was a mother, a friend and a confidant to the 70 residents and an equal number of employees. She was the best fund-raiser, and the daily round of socials and parties made the home an extension of the community and the community an extension of the home. She kept her own apartment, but she stayed at the Center most nights.

One evening, while picking up her mail at home, a man standing next to her suddenly touched her arm. From that moment on, she was afraid to go home at night. The residents who went on vacation or to the hospital offered to let her stay in their apartments. For about eight years, she slept in a different apartment every week. It was better than going home to her empty apartment. Staying at the Home also enabled her to go to the hospital with the people who got sick at night. She thought that was important because that was when people needed her.

On Friday evenings, Dorothy invited the people who came back from the hospital to sit with her at the round table for the celebration of the Sabbath. People who came back from vacations as well as guests would join her there. According to Dorothy, "It was a table for 10, but we could always make room for at least another 10."

She picked out the tablecloth for the central table herself. People gave her most of the embroidered cloths that they had brought with them from Germany. She liked fresh flowers which she picked in Selfhelp's garden until late fall. Mitzi and Martin Marx, longtime friends and volunteers, brought a bouquet of flowers whenever they joined Dorothy at the round table on Friday evenings. People listened for the joyful lilt in Martin's voice when he said kiddish, the prayer over the wine. He shared this privilege with Mr. Kahn, Mr. Fruehauf or Mr. Steierman, who felt honored when Dorothy would ask them to say kiddish.

People dressed festively for the Sabbath dinner. All of the men wore suits and ties, plus a yarmulkah, the head covering. The regal Mrs. Hilde

Wiesenfelder, sat at the head of her table like a baroness, her shining white hair sculpted into a French twist. All of the women wore dresses or suits. Even on the coldest, sub-zero day, Mrs. Becker would smile at an unwitting visitor and say, "You would look so much nicer in a dress."

Front Table: (2nd) Dorothy Becker and Jenny Wolf
Back: Table: Martha Steierman, Julie Freudenthal, Hedy and Julius Steierman

Mrs. Greta Harnick was the first resident to enter the Selfhelp Center. She never tired of telling Dorothy how happy she was to live at the Home. The Selfhelp family rose when Mrs. Harnick, the matriarch of the Home, lit the Sabbath candles.

In a matter of minutes, the kitchen staff served the steaming bowls of homemade chicken soup and matzoh balls to each of the residents and guests. People at each table passed the platters of baked fish or chicken, along with heaping bowls of creamed spinach and real mashed potatoes.

215

Earlier that day, several dozen cakes filled with apples, apricots or plums had been baked for dessert that evening.

Over a final cup of coffee, people decided if they wanted to attend the after-dinner record concert sponsored by Dr. Epstein, a Viennese music lover, who played the hits that people had sung and danced to during the 20's and 30's. Dorothy would have preferred to play American folk songs but she knew her people enjoyed the music they grew up with. She wiped away a tear when she recalled those early years in Berlin when she and Bill had gone with the Hartmans to the premiere of "The Merry Widow."

She wore only Bill's favorite colors. In the privacy of her room, she celebrated their birthdays. She felt as much married to him now as when he was still alive and she vowed to remain married to him for eternity. She still missed Bill terribly and would abruptly leave the lounge, run to the elevator and knock on Mrs. Hartman's door. In her friend's presence, Dorothy could cry or just sit and stare, without having to say a word. Later, Mrs. Hartman would open her spare cot, make the bed and sit with Dorothy until she fell asleep.

A Day in the Life of Dorothy Becker

"I was there for the people. I loved it. I was absolutely unorganized. I would go to the hospital with someone in the afternoon and stay until the person was tucked into bed. Sometimes I'd come home at sunrise and I'd go up to the roof garden to see the sunrise. It was the only time in my life when I'd see the sunrise. It was beautiful. I'd go to bed and would tell the housekeep-

216

ing supervisor not to wake me up, unless it was an emergency. Sometimes someone would get sick and I would have to get up again and go to the hospital. Years later, when I broke my hip, so many of the nurses at Weiss Memorial Hospital remembered me. 'You're the one who brought the people - day and night.' They remembered me or they had heard about me.

"Usually I woke up at 8:30 and I'd make tours through the whole house to make sure everyone was all right. By the time I went to my office there were six or seven people waiting for me to show them the Home.

"Some people came to see me because they couldn't afford to pay for their medicines. We had a special fund for that. Leni Weil, a long time volunteer, was the treasurer of Selfhelp Inc. and she handled these cases. Leni's husband, Rolf, was in charge of the scholarship fund for needy students. Selfhelp Inc also gave financial and emotional support to a woman with a serious mental illness. For years, Mitzi and Martin Marx drove to Elgin on the weekends to visit this lady at the mental hospital. With the help she got from Selfhelp Inc. she was eventually able to live on her own - but near the hospital. Selfhelp Inc. continued to help the woman until she died 14 years later. [Appendix R]

"I arranged all the parties and all the decorations. The parties were as important as the medicine people took. When we opened the Selfhelp Center, I had the people from the Senior Group come to the Home every Tuesday and Thursday afternoon. The people from the Senior Group and the residents at the Home got to know one another. All or most all of the members of the Senior Group became residents of the Home.

The Selfhelp Choir under the direction of Julie Freudenthal

"We celebrated birthdays individually and had at least one party everyday. The residents together with the Senior Group arranged the parties and planned the entertainment. People wrote poems and some told anecdotes about the birthday child. Mrs. Bellak, a professional singer, could entertain an audience for an hour. Mrs. Freudenthal and her choir sang whatever songs people wanted to hear. They always requested: 'Freut Euch des Leben Weil Noch das Lampchen Gluht.' The English equivalent is: 'Enjoy Yourself, It's later Than You Think.' My greatest enjoyment was bringing in the cake and seeing the glow of the candles bring a smile to someone who seldom smiled.
[Appendix S]

Some people were afraid to go to the doctor by themselves. They were real happy that I went with them. I never followed a schedule. Things came up which I thought were more important.

"I always ate lunch with our people. I loved it. If someone wasn't eating, I would try and find out why they didn't have an appetite. The funny thing is that people would say, 'You need a break; I'll take you out for lunch so you'll see something else.' I told them, 'No, I'm perfectly happy to eat here. In fact, I'm only happy when I'm at the Home.'

Ella Bachenheimer's 89th Birthday

"I could cry sometimes when I re-read the thank you letters I got. [See Friedel's Letter on page 311] In the evenings I did all of my office work. I worked 'till 11:00 o'clock. I learned something from Fred Aufrecht. He taught me to keep track of the checks I received by writing down the name and number of each check. That was the only thing I learned from him that was good. In fact, it was the only thing I learned from him."

219

Hedy Strauss and Dorothy Becker

Hedy Strauss and her husband Ernst lived in Dorothy's building. Hedy was the top bookkeeper at her firm and her employer knew he could depend on Hedy to account for every transaction to the last penny. Hedy, who didn't share her husband's interest in sports, had lots of time on her hands. One Saturday, over a piece of birthday cake, Dorothy asked Hedy if she could do some of the bookkeeping at the Selfhelp Center. Hedy agreed and for the next 40 years, Hedy was not only the Selfhelp Center's main accountant, but she also served on the Board of Selfhelp. Hedy was the Treasurer of the Selfhelp Center and Leni Weil was the Treasurer of Selfhelp Inc. Both women and their husbands volunteered for Selfhelp for decades and were Dorothy's most loyal friends.

Foreground: Lotte and Fred Aufrecht, Rolf and Leni Weil

Leni Weil and her husband Rolf had already gone to Dorothy's fund raisers as teenagers because their mothers were active in the Neighborhood Group. Dorothy had wanted Leni to sell raffle tickets because she maintained that, "People buy more tickets from pretty girls." Dorothy would contact Leni, the Treasurer, if people needed a tuition loan. Leni kept track of a maze of different funds. She balanced the books for the Medication fund, the Bonem fund, the Anna Marx Fund, the Scholarship Fund and others. The money that went to Selfhelp Inc. could not be used for the Home. According to Dorothy, "We don't have as many hardship cases as we used to have, but Selfhelp Inc. continues to provide financial and emotional support to several people."

The woman who could not function well outside the hospital and only wanted to have contact with Mitzi and Martin Marx needed new teeth. Selfhelp not only paid for them but subsidized her rent for many years. Dorothy said, "I think we should eliminate the Scholarship Fund because most families can afford to pay for their children's tuition. The people who need financial assistance today are Russian and Polish people. I think the Jewish Federation should help them." The money that went to Selfhelp Inc. could not be used for the Home. Every month, Dorothy collected the rent checks Hedy Strauss deposited into the Selfhelp Home Account.

Dorothy never asked for a salary increase for herself, but she didn't hesitate to let people know that in order to keep the monthly assessment low and the quality of the food high, the organization depended on its membership for contributions.

Instead of giving gifts, Dorothy encouraged people to support the Selfhelp Homes with donations to their favorite funds. The Happy Day Fund and the William F. Becker Fund were the two main accounts that supplemented the two Selfhelp Homes. But most of the donations were made in honor of Dorothy Becker. Dorothy was proud that they never had a deficit until they added the nursing care facility.

"As long as we've had the nursing care facility we've had a deficit. It used to be about $100,000 dollars. In 1993, it had increased to about $600,000 dollars. This was figured into the budget. The Happy Day Fund and the

membership dues always covered it."

"Every week we paid our employees. At first I did it, but after a while, Marlise Katzenstein took over because there was too much time involved. The people who worked with the residents had different hours every week. Some worked 39 hours, others 39.5 hours, other 40, and a few 40.5 hours. After 40 hours, they were paid overtime. It got to be too much work for me. I did it until Marlise took over as a volunteer."

Marlise Katzenstein

When the Selfhelp Center opened in 1963, Dorothy asked Marlise Katzenstein, who lived across the street from the Center, to unlock the door for one of the delivery trucks. Marlise, was glad to do that favor for Dorothy, not realizing that she would volunteer for Selfhelp for the next 40 years. After work and on the weekends, Marlise made sure that the weekly payroll was correct. Marlise typed the government reports, while Dorothy wrote the requests for donations - with excellent results!

"*Every week I ordered fruit, canned goods and meat. We ordered the same supplies every week. Lotte Aufrecht was excellent. She helped me a lot. We had cards which listed the quantities of meat, produce and staples we had to order every week. We had a method. She didn't think I knew how to hire good housekeepers. She didn't think they cleaned well enough. I told her they can always learn how to clean the floors, but it's harder to teach them to be nice to our people.*

"*Lotte's mother and aunt were in the Home. The mother was very outspoken and the aunt was as sweet as she could be. She was always nice and said 'yes' and 'amen' to everything. I loved the feisty one so much more. It's very funny, but the nurses all felt the same. With the outspoken one I knew where I stood. The other day, I found a letter she wrote me. I showed it to Lotte Aufrecht who said, 'That's my mother.' She wrote:*

'Dear Mrs. Becker, I appreciate that you knew you made a mistake when you placed me at that certain table in the dining room. But I appreciate even more that you admitted the mistake and assigned me to a different table. It's just like you to do such nice things.' I loved the outspoken mother and Lotte loved her sweet aunt. Lotte was a good daughter. She visited her mother everyday and bought her the things she needed. She made sure she was always dressed nicely, but they both kept their distance.

"*The mother began to scream all the time, 'help me, help me.' When I visited her in the hospital I didn't have to ask what room she was in. I could hear screaming as soon as I stepped out of the elevator. I said to Lotte, 'Why don't you embrace your mother once.' She shook her head and said, 'We are not a kissing family.' But I embraced her mother and kissed her and she loved me for it. She was so happy; she always stretched her arms out and wanted to embrace me whenever I visited her. Magda, Lotte's sister-in-law, felt the same as I."*

Dorothy's Mother

"My mother complained that I spent so much more time with everyone else. I didn't have to prove to her that I liked her, but I had to show the other residents that I loved them. I liked some people better than others, but people said I was fair. I tried to be twice as nice to the people I didn't like so that they wouldn't know how I felt. My mother would always chide me and say, 'You could be nicer to me.'

"My mother entered the home in 1963 and loved it. We had a current events group and she would ask lots of questions. When she thought that the speaker was twisting the facts, she would say, 'This is the answer of a politician. I want to have a real answer.' She died just before her 86th birthday. She always said, 'I don't want to become older than 85 because then you become a nuisance.' She had angina, but she was perfect mentally. She would sit glued to the radio and later television, but mostly the radio, because she couldn't see too well. She was so modern, much more modern than I was."

Dorothy, who made a habit of talking to each resident everyday, noticed the slightest changes in their appearance, appetite or demeanor. For several days she had observed that Mrs. Goldschmidt, her mother's roommate, had become more quiet and withdrawn. One day she saw that Mrs. Goldschmidt was crying and took her aside to talk with her. She assured her, "I'm here for you as much as for my mother," and asked her why she was crying?

Mrs. Goldschmidt remained silent, keeping her eyes fixed on her hands. Not getting anywhere with Mrs. Goldschmidt, Dorothy asked her mother if she knew why her friend was crying. Her mother explained that because Mrs. Goldschmidt had difficulty hearing, she had always told her the story line whenever they watched television together. One night, Dorothy's mother didn't have the energy to raise her voice loud enough so that Mrs. Goldschmidt could hear her. Since that incident, she cries more often and refuses to talk.

The doctor attributed Mrs. Westmann's fatigue to a heart condition. She tired after the least exertion. The doctor prescribed more medicine and advised frequent rest periods. During the autumn of 1967, Mrs. Westmann fell and broke her hip. Dorothy, her brother Kurt, and his wife Hilde, visited her at Weiss Memorial Hospital everyday. The doctor set the hip without surgery, and the fracture appeared to be healing well on X-rays.

After several weeks, he transferred her to Weiss Pavilion, where she received physiotherapy daily. With encouragement from the physiotherapist, Dorothy's mother progressed to the point where she could put weight on the leg. The pain was excruciating, but she seldom complained. She had lost her appetite and began to lose an excessive amount of weight.

Dorothy and Kurt stayed by their mother's bedside 'till late into the evening. Shortly before her 86th birthday, the valiant Mrs. Westmann lapsed into a coma and died.

After her mother's death, Dorothy stayed with Kurt and Hilde for several days. Thereafter, she resumed work, but stayed at night with Mrs. Hartman, to avoid the dreaded emptiness of her own apartment. She then escaped into work and describes the week following the funeral as the most hectic time of her career. A series of crises pulled her in four different directions at the same time.

The day following her mother's death, her best friend, Mrs. Hartman, began to complain of severe abdominal pains. Later that evening, Mrs. Cohen, another resident, became seriously ill. That same day, Dorothy received a call from her friend, Ellen Sandmann, who had been Marian's kindergarten teacher in Germany. Ellen's husband had died that day; she had called to ask if Dorothy would stay with her that night.

Dorothy packed an overnight bag and took a cab to Ellen's apartment. Ellen had just poured Dorothy a cup of tea when the phone rang. The nurse's assistant from Selfhelp told Mrs. Becker that Mrs. Hartman was complaining of severe pain in her abdomen, and that Mrs. Cohen was having trouble breathing. Dorothy explained her dilemma to Ellen and decided to return to the Selfhelp Center immediately in the event she would have to take Mrs. Hartman and/or Mrs. Cohen to the hospital that night.

Dorothy worried especially about Mrs. Hartman. The location and intensity of her pain reminded her of Bill's symptoms before he underwent surgery. By the time she returned to the Center, Mrs. Hartman had made an appointment to see her doctor the following day. She then rushed to Mrs. Cohen's bedside and decided to take her to the hospital immediately.

Dorothy called Mrs. Cohen's daughter who said that she would take her mother to the hospital herself. "You lost your own mother several days ago; you need your rest," insisted Mrs. Cohen's daughter. By noon, the daughter, Mrs. Seckelson, called to tell Dorothy that her mother had died shortly after she had been admitted to the hospital. She thanked Dorothy for the personal attention and care she had given her mother.

"I loved your mother," replied Dorothy who didn't hear from Mrs. Seckelson again until the morning of her birthday when she called to tell her, " I'm sending you the largest bouquet of flowers you have ever received in your life." "I doubt it," replied Dorothy, "because on the morning of my birthday, my late husband greeted me with an arm load of roses to equal my age. Mrs. Seckelson assured her, 'You'll see.'

Later that day, the janitor knocked on her door to tell her that a landscaper had delivered a large tree with blooming red flowers for: "Mrs. Becker from: Mrs. Seckelson." She could hardly encircle the flowering tree with her arms. Not a day passed that Mrs. Becker didn't think of Mrs. Cohen and her daughter because the magnificent tree took root, grew and blossomed right outside her office window.

The last incidence to occur on the busiest day of her career involved a distressing phone call from Alice, the girl Bill and Dorothy had taken into their home after her mother had died and her father had been admitted to Downing psychiatric Hospital in 1957. Dorothy loved Alice like a daugh-

228

ter even though the girl never helped with the dishes, cleaned her room or picked up after herself. Dorothy refrained from correcting the girl because she thought that Alice needed love more than criticism. For the Becker's 25th wedding anniversary, Dorothy asked their friends to give money - instead of gifts - towards Alice's college tuition. After she had been accepted at the university, the Jewish Federation agreed to pay for her education.

During the ten years her father had been hospitalized, Alice had married, and was raising two children. She now called to tell Dorothy that her father had been discharged from the psychiatric hospital. Alice had never told her children about their mentally ill grandfather and feared he might suddenly appear at their home.

Dorothy had more to fear than Alice because over the years he had confused her with his wife. From the hospital he had written Dorothy many love letters. She called the hospital immediately and asked to speak with his social worker. Both the doctor and the social worker were aware of the problem because they had read all the letters their patient had written Dorothy. The social worker assured her that the doctor had made sure Alice's father fully understood that if he as much as called Mrs. Becker, the police would bring him back to the hospital immediately. The doctor advised Dorothy not to send him cards or gifts for his birthday or at Christmas. Alice's father never contacted his daughter or Mrs. Becker. Shortly after his discharge from the hospital, he died.

The Snowstorm of 1967

Since Bill's death, Dorothy had worked day and night tending to people's endless needs and expectations. She fell into bed exhausted every night only to get up a few hours later to take a sick resident to the hospital. She continued this hectic pace until the gargantuan snowstorm of 1967 brought every earthbound mode of transportation to a wheel spinning halt. Dorothy's brother-in-law, Richard, called from Florida and suggested she join him and his wife Thea for a vacation in North Carolina. When Bill was alive, she had always enjoyed their annual vacations with them.

Instead of the warm sunshine they had anticipated, the weather turned uncomfortably cool. It was too cold to go swimming, she had neglected to bring a book - and to her surprise - the gift shop stocked neither magazines nor newspapers. Richard spent the entire day on the golf course, while his wife, Thea, who contracted a cold, stayed in bed most of the time.

This was the first time in her life that Dorothy had ever eaten alone. She felt totally abandoned and couldn't hold back her tears. She sensed Bill's comforting presence and recalled his words, "Don't sit and cry, work for Selfhelp."

When the airplane landed, the Chicago snow, piled high along the curbs, was beginning to melt. As soon as she entered the Selfhelp Center, a flock of residents welcomed her with kisses. Hedy Strauss couldn't understand how she could stand to have every one kiss her. She loved it, and told another colleague who reminded her that it was the flu season, "I just eat a dozen oranges at the first sign of a cold."

The mountain of mail in her office could wait; Dorothy first had to see

Mrs. Hartman, who assured her that the new pain medicine worked better and enabled her to sleep much better. Dorothy admitted she had gotten lots of rest, not having to get up to take residents to the hospital. The days however had been long and lonely. She described the worst vacation of her life in terms of, "No people, no sun, no swimming, and nothing to read." Richard had told her that she had done nothing but cry, and promised he would never ask her to go on a vacation with them again.

A Shocking Accusation

While getting through the heaps of mail covering her desk, Dorothy received a call from Ellen Sandman, Marian's kindergarten teacher. Her elderly father was beginning to have more difficulty taking care of himself, and she had discussed with him the possibility of moving into a retirement home. Ellen's father agreed to give up his apartment on one condition: if he could go to the "Selfhelp Center where Dorothy Becker is the director." She reiterated: He only wants to be with Dorothy.

Ellen had been a friend since Marian's kindergarten days, but neither Dorothy nor any one else could bend the rules either for relatives or friends. Dorothy explained regretfully that Ellen would have to adhere to the admission policies and place her father on the waiting list. Ellen reminded her that they had been friends for 35 years. She had gone with Kurt to Hamburg when the Beckers left Germany to go to America.

Dorothy agreed that Ellen had been one of their most loyal friends, but she would not be able to change the admissions policies. Dorothy explained that people were considered for admission to the Selfhelp Center according to their place on the waiting list. However, her father probably could be admitted in a short time to the Southside Home, which had a shorter waiting list. "He doesn't want to go to the Southside Home, he wants to be with you," snapped Ellen.

Shortly thereafter, Ellen began to accuse Dorothy and Maria Ikenburg, the chairperson of the Admission Committee, of erasing names on the waiting list and inserting the names of applicants who had contributed large sums of money to Selfhelp. The following weekend, Ellen attended a wedding reception with Agnes and Burton Strauss; both were officers on the Board of Selfhelp. Ellen insinuated in a loud voice that certain influential people in charge of admissions were giving preferential treatment to applicants by erasing and inserting names on the waiting list. Upset by her accusations, Agnes and Burton abruptly walked out!

At their next meeting, the stunned Board members listened as Burton Strauss described the abrasive tone Ellen had used to accuse them of tampering with the admission's process. When Burton asked to see the admissions list, the enraged Maria Ikenburg told the Board, "If people don't trust me, I'll resign from the Admissions Committee."

Dorothy was equally outraged and called Ellen from the privacy of her office. "Did you really tell Burton and Agnes Strauss you suspected me of erasing names from the Admissions List?" "Yes! I said it, and I believe it. Don't pretend to be holier than thou. Your husband would turn in his grave if he knew what you're doing."

Dorothy knew it was no use to reason with Ellen. To say anything would be futile. She hung up the phone in disbelief. Ellen's attempt to align herself with Bill in defiling her integrity felt like sacrilege to Dorothy. Just as fanatics justify murder by invoking the name of God, Ellen had invoked Bill's name to justify wrongly accusing Dorothy Becker of cheating and lying.

Realizing she had no other choice Ellen did place her father's name on the waiting list. Within the month, the Board approved his admission to the Southside Home. One year later when his name came up, he was transferred to the Selfhelp Center. Dorothy treated the father as she always had, with respect and kindness, but the hand embroidered pillows Ellen made for Dorothy's birthday, did not restore their friendship.

Shortly after this incident, a wealthy woman applied for admission to Selfhelp, and once again tested the integrity of the Board and its president, Fred Aufrecht. A 90-year old woman, who had never placed her name on the Admissions List before, offered to pay the organization a sum of $100,000 dollars for immediate admission to the Selfhelp Center. Her lawyer called Dorothy to substantiate his client's decision and asked if she would like him to deliver the check.

The lawyer was surprised when Mrs. Becker explained the admission policies to him, but promised she would speak to the Board about his client's offer. "We could use the money," lamented Dorothy, but every Board member, including Dorothy, agreed to adhere to the admissions policy. Fred Aufrecht, whose last name means, "upright," spoke for every member when he declared, "No one receives special privileges or favors at Selfhelp - neither family, friends or millionaires."

The woman's lawyer told Dorothy that this was a once in a lifetime experience for him. He had never known any organization to say "no" to $100.000. Dorothy promised to process the woman's application but she died before her name came up on the Admissions List.

Throughout the 1960s, requests for admission to the Selfhelp Center skyrocketed. People usually waited two years before Dorothy notified them about a prospective opening at the Center. Mrs. Hartman, predicting the Board would have to build an addition to the Center, urged Dorothy to obtain her administrator's license.

For two years, Dorothy enrolled in the required courses on gerontology and administration, for state licensing. Dorothy and Mrs. Edith Stern, the director of the Southside Home, took classes together to become licensed nursing home administrators.

The classes came alive as Dorothy told of her experiences with the elderly. She told them about Dr. Mueller, 94 years young who told attractive young women when they asked how he was feeling, "When I see you, I feel better!" Another "young" octogenarian when coaxed to eat her salad, muttered, "Eating rabbit food won't make you live to be a hundred, it'll just seem that long."

Dorothy waited until the last minute to submit her application for the licensing exam for nursing home administrator, which the state offered once a year. Had it not been for Mrs. Hartman's continued prodding, Dorothy would have missed the deadline for sending her application to the state. She had just begun to fill out the form when she received a call from Marian, who had returned from their vacation with a lingering sore throat. Her doctor had recommended hospitalization because her symptoms resembled those of a "Chinese" disease he had heard about years ago when he was still in medical school.

Worried about Marian's health, Dorothy lost interest in taking the licensing exam. She handed the application to Marlise Katzenstein, who filled it out and mailed it to the Department of Professional Regulation in Springfield, IL. Within a week, Marian recovered and went home. Relieved to hear her daughter didn't have to take anything stronger than aspirin, she decided to take the nursing home administrator's exam.

One of the first to finish the exam, she handed her paper to the proctor and proceeded to walk out. Having checked her application against the title of the exam, the examiner called her back and informed Dorothy she would have to take another exam. The test she had just completed would only enable her to obtain a license for the State of Illinois. Unwittingly, Marlise had checked off "national" instead of "state" on the application form she had filled out for Dorothy.

In vain, Dorothy explained to the examiner that she only needed a license for the State of Illinois, since she would never work for any other organization except Selfhelp. Bureaucracy triumphed. Dorothy had to take a second exam, which would enable her to be a nursing home director in every state of the nation. She took the national exam and passed.

Two months later, she hurried to Mrs. Hartman's apartment, holding the long-awaited envelope from the Department of Professional Regulation.

Preparing herself for the worst, Dorothy opened the envelope, inspected its contents with apprehension, and pulled out the newly printed license with a triumphant flip of her wrist.

Mrs. Hartman inspected the gold engraved piece of paper savoring each word of the name and title: "Dorothy Becker, Nursing Home Administrator." Sharing the joy of Dorothy's accomplishment seemed to have a salutary effect on the sharp pains, which had begun to plague her again in recent weeks.

The Loss of Her Best Friend

Three years earlier, when Mrs. Hartman had first begun to complain of abdominal pains, she had undergone extensive tests which confirmed the presence of cancer cells. At that time, the doctor had promised Dorothy he would refrain from disclosing the diagnosis to his patient. As the disease progressed, Dorothy wondered whether her friend suspected she was dying.

Excessive weight loss had widened the dark, sunken eyes, highlighting the delicate contours of her face. When the pain became unbearable, the doctor admitted her to Weiss Hospital. Dorothy spent most of the Holiday Season at Mrs. Hartman's bedside. She slept until the pain medicine wore off. Clutching Dorothy's hand, she waited impatiently for the nurse to give her another injection. As she drifted into an artificial but painless sleep, Mrs. Hartman's fingers gradually released their hold on Dorothy's hand.

Leaning back in her chair, Dorothy began to relax somewhat herself as she listened to the hypnotic sound of Mrs. Hartman's breathing. Dorothy wiped away a tear as she recalled scenes from their intertwined lives. During the 42 years they had known each other, neither differences, disagreements or adversity had ever been able to loosen the bond between them.

She recalled the joy of celebrating their first New Year in America together. On that New Year's Eve of 1940, 35 people had arrived at the Beckers' apartment in tails and evening gowns. Dorothy and Lissy had served a sit-down dinner, and Bill had made the punch. Dorothy maintained, "It was the most elegant party in town."

In time their New Year's Eve parties had become legendary. At the Home, a team of residents, wearing latex gloves and caps, made platters of open-faced sandwiches while the decorating committee put up the balloons and streamers in the dining and recreation rooms. Dorothy's joyful celebration of the New Year was contagious and concealed her painful longing for Bill. She wore the dress she knew he would have picked out for her. Every New Year, she renewed her resolve to continue to lead her life in accordance with Bill's wishes. When the clock struck midnight, the entire Selfhelp family raised their glasses and wished one another a healthy, Happy New Year. She embraced and kissed everyone, but no one except Mrs. Hartman knew that she spent the rest of the night crying.

As she sat by the bedside of her dying friend, Mrs. Hartman's frantically groping hands roused Dorothy from her reverie. She didn't respond or open her eyes, but as soon as Dorothy enfolded the shriveled hand into her own, the agitated clutching at the bed linen stopped. Inaudibly, Marian and Phil entered the room. Stroking her hand, Marian softly called Mrs. Hartman's name, but she did not respond.

They watched helplessly whenever the rise and fall of her chest stopped momentarily, and respiration would resume again with raspy, short breaths. Her peaceful expression seemed to ignore her body's feeble attempt to continue the fight for life. With a final sigh, the gentle, steadfast hand slackened, and slipped away forever. Dorothy's best friend, confidant and mentor died on New Year's Eve, 1970.

Famous Betty Bellak performs on New Year's Eve - just as the clock strikes Midnight...

Within a period of seven years, Dorothy Becker had lost her husband, her mother and Lissy Hartman. Once again, she found in the work of Selfhelp the source of her comfort and strength. Ron, her grandson, who was studying journalism and music in Colorado, thought a trip to the Rocky Mountains might do her good. But the mountains would remind her too much of Bill, who had belonged to a mountain-climbing club in Germany. It was so thoughtful of Ron to invite her, but she couldn't go. Instead, she immersed herself in the whirlwind of projects with the energy and drive that belied her 60 years.

Concerned members of the Board warned she might be doing herself a disservice by taking people to the hospital at night. Fred Aufrecht advised her to ask family members to accompany a sick resident to the hospital, but she ignored his suggestion. Mrs. Becker was determined not to leave before she had tucked the person into the hospital bed. After a few hours of sleep, she dressed, ate breakfast, and was in her office at 10 for her first appointment.

Whenever Marian and Phil invited their mother for the holidays, midway through dinner, without fail, the phone would ring. She had trained her staff to notify her of any problems occurring while she was out of the Home, especially at the first sign of illness. She usually called a cab and returned to the Selfhelp Center before Marian had a chance to serve the dessert.

Several colleagues encouraged her to take some time off, and many friends suggested she take a vacation with them. She declined their well-meaning invitations, explaining: "I'm only happy when I work." When Hedy Strauss asked, "Why do you kill yourself?" Dorothy replied simply, "I only live *because* I work."

11

FROM SELFHELP CENTER TO SELFHELP COMPLEX

By the early 1970's, over a 1000 names on Selfhelp's waiting list convinced the Board to build an addition to the Northside Home. Since the original home first opened 20 years earlier, the average age at both Selfhelp - South and Selfhelp - North had risen to 84. Most of the older people at Selfhelp - South and some of the residents at Selfhelp - North needed more care and supervision. Rather than transferring these residents to another nursing home, the Board decided to close the Southside Home, expand Selfhelp - North and build a nursing care facility on the 7th and 8th floors of the new addition. Though most of the elderly people regretted having to leave the Southside Home, they were happy that Mrs. Stern, would be moving north with them and continuing to be their director at the new nursing care facility.

The new Selfhelp Center, which included the health care facility, would be large enough to house a total of 180 residents, 140 in the independent living facility and 40 in the Nursing Care Facility. Architects from the firm of A. Epstein and Sons estimated the new nine-story building, including the roof garden, would cost around two million dollars.

Fred Aufrecht and Rolf Weil, the respective Board President and Vice President, were successful in obtaining a low interest mortgage of $1,714,000 from the Federal government. United Help of New York contributed $50,000 to Selfhelp of Chicago.[10] In addition, Dorothy and hundreds of volunteers sprang into action to raise the rest of the money. The Selfhelp community came out in full force that year to attend the annual May Party and the elegant Fall Banquet, and most of the donations to Selfhelp's building fund were made in appreciation of Dorothy Becker.

The new nine-story addition was designed to blend seamlessly with the three floors of the original building. In addition to a nursing care facility, the new wing would add another 70 apartments to the independent living facility. In 1963, Selfhelp had pioneered kitchenette apartments, enabling the residents to remain as independent as possible. In 1973, Selfhelp was one of the first retirement homes in the state to have a nursing care facility on the premises.

Another innovative program for its time was the day program that Dorothy had initiated for people who spent the day at Selfhelp, and went home in the evenings. At meetings with the architect, Dorothy had put her bid in for a library and a recreation room large enough for celebrations with the entire Selfhelp family including the children, grandchildren and staff.

Dorothy hoped the design for the new addition would include a guest apartment for visitors from out of town. For years, she had dreamt of a roof garden with a view overlooking Lake Michigan. It was a dream the organization could hardly afford.

When the new addition was near completion, Fred Aufrecht announced at a Board meeting that they didn't have the $40,000 needed to build the roof garden. The 30 members of the Board groaned and looked morose but no one spoke. Rudi Meyer, a successful business man moved his chair closer to his wife, Margot, and whispered to her. She beamed a smile at her husband, and nodded in agreement before Rudi announced, "We're going to have our roof garden!"

He went on to explain that Margot had enjoyed tending their large garden in Germany, but since they had moved to Chicago, her garden consisted of the flower boxes on their window sills. His wife would welcome the opportunity to set the top of the new Selfhelp Center in bloom. The Board responded with cheers and applause.

Rudi and Margot made the necessary financial arrangements, and handed Fred Aufrecht a check for $40,000. Every summer since, the residents have enjoyed the planters of trees and flowers Margot planted on the Rudi and

Margot Meyer Roof Garden. Two residents, Hilde Wiesenfelder and Mina Jonas, volunteered to water the plants not only on the roof garden but throughout the Home.

Margot and Rudi Meyer

The blueprint for the expanded Selfhelp Center also included an apartment for Dorothy Becker. At one of the Board meetings, Agnes Strauss, one of Dorothy's good friends, remarked that, "Dorothy lives like a gypsy. Sometimes she stays in Mrs. Hartman's former apartment or else people who go on vacation offer her the use of *their* apartments." Without further debate, the Board agreed to build an apartment for Dorothy. It had a living room, bedroom, bath, kitchen and a walk-in closet.

When the time came for Dorothy to move into her new apartment,

Gerald Franks, a long-time officer of the Board, asked if she planned to live like a nun for the rest of her life. Dorothy's loyalty to her late husband could be compared to that of a nun. In her mind she was and always would be married to Bill. She only wore the colors that he had liked. She couldn't understand how any widow, regardless of age, could ever want to marry again. When Bill knew that he was dying, he told her repeatedly to continue to work for Selfhelp but he could never have imagined that Selfhelp would become her *reason* for living.

Two friends dining with Agnes Strauss

Since her husband's death 10 years previously, Dorothy had slept more nights at Selfhelp than at her own apartment. She wanted to be available to residents who got sick at night, while at the same time, the Home provided a refuge from the loneliness of her own apartment.

Moving demanded sorting through years of accumulated cards, outmoded clothes, and wrinkled tablecloths. Dorothy looked at the gifts, souvenirs and the hundreds of cards people had sent her throughout the years and couldn't part with a single one of them. Marian offered to help. She packed her mother's belongings and gently persuaded her to give most of the hard-to-iron tablecloths to the Salvation Army. She re-read all of the cards people had sent her throughout the years and couldn't part with any of them.

She helped Marian wrap each exquisite piece of the porcelain dinner set that had survived the trip from Germany unscathed, 37 years previously. She closed the door to her apartment for the last time and hurried to her office at the Selfhelp Center where a long line of people were already waiting to see Mrs. Becker for the initial interview of the admission process.

Dorothy's friend, Marlise Katzenstein, a Selfhelp volunteer who handled most of Dorothy's secretarial work, kept track of the mail piled high on her desk. Months prior to the opening of the Selfhelp Complex (the expanded Selfhelp Center), Irmgard Heymann, the Chairperson of the Admissions Committee, called Dorothy repeatedly throughout the day to verify the information submitted by people who applied for admission to the Home. Irmgard wanted to double check even though she already knew what Dorothy would say, "Yes, I've known the family since they first came to Chicago. I went to court with them when they became citizens." Dorothy usually knew the applicants, their families and every detail of their life stories. The Admissions Committee and Dorothy worked feverishly to process the 70 applications for the independent apartments plus another 40 applications for the Nursing Care Facility.

The Opening of the Selfhelp Complex

The modern Selfhelp Complex had more than doubled its capacity and attracted the attention of prominent politicians and community leaders. Rabbi Herman Schaalman from Temple Immanuel and Rabbi Ira Sud lauded Fred Aufrecht, the Board President and the members of the Selfhelp Board for their determination to provide for the needs of their aging German Jewish population.

Mrs. Rosalie Maier, the Home's poet laureate, spoke on behalf of her fellow residents when she said that every member of the Selfhelp family shares in making Selfhelp not just a real home but the hub of the German Jewish community. She added," Every one of us is needed and appreciated." In Dorothy's vision, the residents were the family of origin who maintained close ties to their extended family in the community. Mrs. Maier maintained that Dorothy's love of people, combined with the "personal touch" of Mitzi Marx and her corps of volunteers, distinguished the Becker Home from all other retirement homes.

A House Divided

For 11 years, Dorothy Becker had been the sole administrator of the Selfhelp Center, affectionately called, "The Becker Home." When the population at the Home consisted of only 70 residents and an equal number of staff, Dorothy, the Executive Director, had been Business Manager and Nursing Supervisor as well. She was the first to respond when people got sick and was considered a superb diagnostician by the doctors attending the elderly. When the Board decided to hire more directors, Dorothy agreed that the enlarged complex needed additional administrators and welcomed the opportunity to work cooperatively with them; but she had no reason to doubt that she would remain the head as well as the heart of the Home.

Before Edith Stern and the people from the Southside Home moved to the Nursing Care Facility at Selfhelp North, Fred Aufrecht told Dorothy, "Edith Stern doesn't want to work under you and Ruth Turk doesn't have to." When Dorothy asked why Edith felt that way, he said that she had told him, "Whatever I do, and I try to do a good job, it doesn't seem to matter. People come to me and tell me what Mrs. Becker does and what Mrs. Becker likes… and nothing else. When she comes to the Southside Home, everyone stretches his or her arms out to her and smiles. I work myself to death and I can't get a nice word from anybody." Years later, when Mrs. Stern was asked about her experiences as Director of the Southside Home, she reflected for a moment and said, "I gave the residents lots of love and I received lots of love."

In the winter of 1974, Edith Stern and the people from the Southside Home moved to Selfhelp North where Edith Stern would be in charge of the new Nursing Care Facility. Dorothy and Edith had attended classes together to obtain their licenses in nursing home administration. Dorothy gave Edith high marks for treating the people under her care with patience and kindness.

Dorothy hoped that Marlise Katzenstein, who had volunteered in her office for 10 years, would become the new Business Manager. To Dorothy's surprise, Fred Aufrecht and a small executive committee chose Ruth Turk, the wife of the late Dr. Ernest Turk, for the position of Business Manager. Lotte Aufrecht admired the efficient Ruth Turk who had been the Administrative Secretary to Fred Weissman, the Director of Selfhelp of New York. The Beckers had been friends of the late Dr. Turk and his wife for years. Dorothy recalled, "I thought it would be wonderful to have a friend work in the office with me."

Edith Stern

Until 1974, the Board under Fred Aufrecht's watch, had always expected Dorothy to assume full responsibility for the internal operations of the Home but they only grudgingly gave her the title of Executive Director and the authority that went with it. Dorothy, who did not want to disparage anyone, later conceded in a barely audible voice, "It was all about power!" In general, however, the Board had always supported her, with or without the title.

Strangely enough, it was Fred Aufrecht, who had previously told Dorothy that "Except for the President, Selfhelp administrators didn't have titles," who now issued a directive on 3/18/73 which made Edith Stern, Executive Director-A, in charge of the Nursing Care Facility and Dorothy Becker, Executive Director-B, in charge of the Independent Living Facility. Ruth Turk, in her position as Business Manager, was placed at the same administrative level as the two executive directors. The expanded Selfhelp Center, which had more than doubled in size, would now be run by three administrators responsible for their respective departments but without any one of them being in charge of the overall operations of the Home. [Appendix T]

This unusual administrative structure, which lacked a designated head, fragmented the Home socially and could prove hazardous in an emergency. In case of a fire, who would coordinate the evacuation of the Home? Who would assume responsibility for the control of communicable diseases? Who was the person in charge when city, state and government inspectors visited the Home?

During the 10 years she had been Executive Director, the Selfhelp Center was rated as one of the best retirement homes in the state. But more than that, the Board had given Dorothy and her Selfhelp family the credit for the joyful vitality that permeated the Home. She was a strong advocate at Board meetings, but above all, she was a team player who overlooked differences if people worked for the good of Selfhelp. She couldn't understand why Fred Aufrecht and his "ad hoc committee" thought that she would not be able to work cooperatively with the new administrators. For decades, she had gotten along with some of the most rigid members on the Board of Selfhelp. She wondered why now people thought she wouldn't be able to work cooperatively with the new Director and Business Administrator?

The change in Dorothy's authority was difficult to detect because on Selfhelp's letterhead she still held the title of "Executive Director Selfhelp Center," while in reality her authority was restricted to the independent living facility as "Executive Director of B." In the past, the supervisors had reported to Dorothy whereas now the three administrators, including Dorothy, had to report to either Fred Aufrecht, the Board President, or to a "Management Committee." [Appendix T]. Generally, the Board oversees the finances, handles the legal affairs and prepares to meet the challenges of the future and leaves the responsibility for the internal operation of the facility to the Executive Director of the Home.

The job descriptions of the three administrators as stated in the Board President's directive of 3/18/73 insulated and isolated the three administrators in their respective domains and left Dorothy feeling dispossessed and demeaned.

What upset Dorothy even more were the lengthy do's and don'ts of their respective job descriptions. Dorothy received a detailed directive from the

Board which stipulated that she, "should place her emphasis on the social and recreational activities," while Edith Stern, "should place her emphasis on the psychological and physical well-being of the residents." [Appendix U]

Dorothy Becker who believed in the unity of mind, heart and body, was now instructed to restrict her services primarily to people's social and recreational needs. Was she to ignore their physical and psychological well-being? Her holistic philosophy - her warmth and understanding - enveloped the total person. To place peoples' needs into separate compartments, she thought, would not only do a disservice to the people under her care but could be potentially harmful.

Lotte Aufrecht, the Chairperson of the House Committee, was known to complain that Dorothy hired maids and janitorial staff with poor housekeeping skills. When interviewing prospective job applicants, Dorothy did place priority on a person's attitude toward the elderly. She thought new employees could always learn to upgrade their housekeeping skills, "But how do you teach compassion?", she asked.

Subsequently, the Board President's directive of 3/18/73 deprived Dorothy Becker, the Executive Director of Unit B, of the right to hire and supervise her own housekeeping personnel. Instead, Ruth Turk, the Business Administrator, was authorized to hire the housekeeping staff and the Housekeeping Supervisor was authorized to supervise them. Also the nursing personnel would be screened first by Ruth Turk instead of Dorothy Becker. [Appendix T]

Yet, Edith Stern, the Executive Director of A *was* authorized to supervise the housekeeping and kitchen personnel of Unit A. [Appendix T]

This same directive stipulated that all mail would be read and placed in cubicles according to subject matter, unless the word, "personal," was written on the envelope. [Appendix U]. Dorothy thought that in America people had not only the right to open their own mail, but it was against the law to open other peoples' mail. She also questioned why the directive of 1973 gave the supervision of her office to Ruth Turk. These new rules undermined Dorothy's authority and demoralized her. Powerful emotions emboldened her to stand up for herself and the people under her care. She put her requests in writing to the Board President:

"I do not think it practical for the nursing personnel to be screened by the Business Manager. The initial interview should be given by me. Kitchen personnel may be seen first by the Business Manager, and, after screening, referred to me for interview. I should have the right - if I am dissatisfied with the household personnel - to be heard and have a say-so in whether or not an employee should be dismissed. This is important because of complaints from our residents about the way they are being treated sometimes by our maids. I'm referring you to paragraph I which states that I am responsible for the well-being of our residents. Therefore, this request should not be refused by the Business Manager." [Appendix V]

"When residents of Selfhelp Center are being moved to the health care floors -either on a temporary or permanent basis - and are taken to the hospital or are seriously ill, I would appreciate being informed. This has been done until now by Dr. Kaluzny. If any of our residents should need more frequent linen changes because of bed-wetting or losing stool, I would like to

be informed immediately since this may be a medical problem and not only a matter of additional charges." [Appendix V]

Soon after Edith Stern and her 45 people from the Southside Home moved into the Nursing Care Facility, Fred Aufrecht and his small ad hoc committee began to issue additional directives Dorothy could neither understand nor accept. He told Dorothy not to set foot inside the Nursing Care Facility.

Some of the people who would be transferred to the Health Care Facility had been under her supervision for years. Because of their declining health, she had monitored these residents closely and had established regular contact with their families. How could she possibly agree not to visit her people after they were transferred to the Health Care Facility? She told Fred Aufrecht: "My working hours are from nine to five. After that, my time is my own, and I can visit whom I want."

After the Selfhelp Complex opened, the Board President began to call Ruth Turk in the evenings, instead of Dorothy, as had been his habit for years. Many times, Dorothy was not notified of meetings the Board President had scheduled with the other two administrators. She recalled, "Initially, I taught Ruth Turk everything, but later she made a secret out of everything."

Trust between herself and the other two administrators eroded, and communication dwindled to icy politeness. Isolated and excluded from the administrative network, she obtained important information directly from the residents and the employees, who loved and supported her.

Dorothy tried to understand the road blocks that were placed in her way. The Board's loss of confidence in her angered and confused her more than her loss of power. Her power came from the residents and the staff who continued to trust her implicitly. And this may have been a large part of the problem between the Aufrechts and Dorothy who explained that,

"Both Fred and Lotte worked so hard for Selfhelp but very few of the residents knew Fred, even though he had been Board President for 11 years. The residents saw Lotte, the Chairperson of the House Committee, almost everyday, but explained Dorothy , "She was not one to engage in small talk and only said 'Hello' in later years."

The Aufrechts had been close friends of the Beckers while Bill was alive. After his death, their relationship with Dorothy became more strained. In an afterthought, Dorothy said, "Fred Aufrecht taught me how to keep track of the checks people gave me and that was a good thing I learned from him."

Despite the conflict, Dorothy respected Fred Aufrecht and admired his relentless dedication to the organization. After her husband died and he became President, she promised to give him the support she had given Bill when he was Board President. And she kept that promise!

Dorothy described Edith Stern as, "A nice woman, a caring director and a chic dresser." She was respected and well liked for the gentle way in which she coaxed people to take their medication or eat another bite of food. Like Dorothy, she lived at the Home, and was available day and night to the people under her care. Mrs. Stern was also a widow, but unlike Dorothy, she took Saturdays off. Concerning her relationship with Dorothy she said, "I didn't think that I could ever meet Mrs. Becker's expectations."

Striking personality differences existed between Dorothy Becker, the "people's person" and the business-like Ruth Turk. Unlike Dorothy, whose desk rose to the ceiling with mail, the meticulous Ruth Turk personified order and efficiency. Their opposite personalities had not impaired their friendship while their husbands were alive because, as Lotte Aufrecht explained, "Bill had kept Dorothy in check." The refrain that Dorothy could only be held in check by her husband was expressed by other members of the Board as well. Dorothy wondered if people thought that Ruth Turk, as well, could only be "held in check" by her late husband.

Fred Aufrecht did attempt to initiate discussion of the problems by inviting Dorothy and the other two administrators to a restaurant for dinner. Dorothy declined the invitation. In the absence of an impartial mediator, she doubted that they could reconcile their differences.

For the first time since Bill died, she longed for the solace of her own apartment away from the Selfhelp Complex. Except for the death of her husband, these were the most difficult years of her life. But she was determined not to let the power struggle at the top interfere with the well-being of the people under her care.

One can speculate as to the causes of this counterproductive clash. Was the animosity fueled by jealousies or motivated by the competition for turf or power? Did the perception that Dorothy was too emotional or assertive and could only be controlled by her husband arouse anxiety in her colleagues on the Board? Did they fear not being able to stand their ground - especially when a few tears rolled down her cheeks? Some thought Fred Aufrecht was a kind, mild mannered man, who had been too gullible.

Years later, Fred Aufrecht explained to Dorothy that he had asked her not to visit the Health Care Facility in order to give Edith Stern a better chance to establish herself in the new facility. Perhaps differences in personality and lifestyle did contribute to the tensions existing between Dorothy and the other two administrators. We may never know the real and imagined fears, the exaggerations and misperceptions that, according to one longtime member of the Board, caused this conflict to have "nearly brought down the Home."

What we do know is that neither the people involved in the conflict nor an impartial mediator initiated discussion of the issues. No one questioned the assumption that the new administrators would not be able to establish themselves at the "Becker Home" when these real or imagined fears could have been discussed and resolved in advance. Her track record showed that if it was good for Selfhelp, she could resolve differences and work cooperatively with the most rigid people. No one questioned the restrictive job descriptions that undermined her authority, eroded trust and distorted communication. Had an impartial member of the Board assumed the role of a fair and objective negotiator, the conflict could have been resolved. In the absence of a skilled ombudsman, the stressful situation became intolerable, and resulted in changes that could have been prevented.

Changes in Leadership

In November, 1974, eight months after the Nursing Care Unit opened, Edith Stern resigned. Many of the elderly people who had been with her for nearly eight years wept when she left Selfhelp. Dr. Kaluzny, a foreign-born physician awaiting his license from the State of Illinois, became the new Director of the Health Care Facility. Dr. Kaluzny told Mrs. Becker that he respected her judgment, and couldn't understand why the President of the Board told him: "Don't listen to Dorothy Becker. You're the doctor." One year later, the Board asked Dr. Kaluzny to resign.

After Dr. Kaluzny left, Fred Aufrecht begged Dorothy Becker to take charge of the Health Care Unit. She agreed until the Board hired an "associate director" for the Nursing Care Facility. Shortly after this incidence, in January of 1976, Fred Aufrecht resigned and Rolf Weil became President of the Selfhelp Board.

Rolf Weil, the new President of the Selfhelp Board, had been the Chairman of the Finance Committee for over a decade. As President of Roosevelt University, he had survived the student riots of the 1960s with the negotiating skills of a diplomat. To him, there was a distinct difference between the respective role of the Board President and that of the Executive Director of the Home. He valued the many facets of Dorothy's leadership ability, and she admired his intelligence and wit. With Rolf Weil and Dorothy Becker at the helm, Selfhelp entered the decade of the 80's with renewed energy and enthusiasm.

A temporary executive director was hired for the Nursing Care Facility, Ruth Turk remained the Business Manager and both administrators had to report to "Dorothy Becker, Executive Director, Selfhelp Center." From September 27, 1976 and every year thereafter, Rolf Weil wrote Dorothy a letter regarding her annual salary increments which included his personal expression of appreciation, " I want to thank you on behalf of the Selfhelp Home as well as myself personally for your great humanitarian service to our residents." [Appendix W]

Three years later, Ruth Turk, the Business Manager died suddenly. In her will, she stipulated that after her death, Dorothy Becker could chose any memento from the items on display in her apartment. Dorothy asked for the small portrait of the late Dr. Turk and said, "He was a good friend of ours."

Strangely enough, some of Dorothy's closest friends on the Board remained silent throughout these traumatic years. Since she officially had retained the title of "Executive Director," they may not have realized that her authority had been significantly reduced. Perhaps they hadn't seen the "Directive of 3/18/73," and if they had read it, they probably didn't under-stand the convoluted hiring, firing and reporting instructions. Not that Dorothy had expected any of her women friends to back her publicly because they seldom spoke up at Board meetings. Dorothy recalled, "In my 40 years on the Selfhelp Board, I seldom heard another woman say anything and if she did speak, nobody paid attention to her." Yet this silent group of friends and colleagues continued to support Dorothy wholeheartedly.

The Becker Circle

A handful of Dorothy Becker's closest friends not only served on the Board but as Selfhelp volunteers for 35 plus years. Most of these people, she had merely tapped on the shoulder years ago and simply "held onto" for the next 40 years. They did much of the accounting work, submitted the government reports and wrote the social histories; they served on the Board as financial and legal consultants. They were committed to Selfhelp for life. Dorothy could count on them to perform some of the essential functions which freed her to work directly with the people entrusted to her care and supervision.

Hedy Strauss, Dorothy Becker, Mitzi Marx

At a time when the organization struggled to stay within its operating budget, this group of people saved Selfhelp millions of dollars. To replace people like Fred and Lotte Aufrecht, Irmgard Heymann, Marlise Katzenstein, Mitzi and Martin Marx, Hedy Strauss and Rolf and Leni Weil, the organization would have had to hire high-priced social workers, bookkeepers, accountants, financiers, administrative secretaries and supervisors.

Upon completion of the original Selfhelp Home in 1952, Fred Aufrecht told his wife Lotte: "Selfhelp is an organization I could work with. They all pull together in the same direction." That year he joined Selfhelp and served

10 years on the Finance Committee. He became Vice President first, and later, as President of the Board, obtained the government loans that enabled Selfhelp to expand and build a Nursing Care Facility. After Bill died, Dorothy wanted Fred to become President and she backed him 100 per cent. Her personal conflict with him was restricted to a period of three years and didn't diminish her appreciation for his 40 years of service to Selfhelp.

Lotte Aufrecht promised Dorothy she would work for Selfhelp as soon as her youngest son turned 9. She welcomed the opportunity of working alongside her husband, Fred. She served on the Selfhelp Board for decades and worked with Jenny Wolf on the House Committee before she became its chairperson. Under her watchful eye, the furniture was repaired, the appliances were primed to run smoothly, and the drapes were cleaned on schedule. Her sky blue-eyes beamed when she said, "The volunteers don't have time for busy work. At Selfhelp we are needed!"

Irmgard Heymann, the Chairperson of the Admissions Committee, worked full time as a social worker and spent weekends and evenings completing the social interviews for people awaiting admission to the Home. She called Dorothy in the 1950's to request a tutor for one of her clients who was confined to a wheelchair. Within the week, Selfhelp provided her client with an excellent tutor. What impressed Irmgard was Selfhelp's freedom from bureaucratic delays. She told Dorothy, "If you need a social worker, give me a call."

Bill Becker was impressed with Irmgard's ability to write reports which the government never returned for more information. When Bill told

Dorothy, "We need a person like Irmgard." Dorothy asked Irmgard to work on Selfhelp's Admissions Committee. For the next 35 plus years, Irmgard did most of the pre-admission interviews for Selfhelp and served on the Board of Selfhelp as Chairman of the Admissions Committee. After she retired from her salaried job, she remained Chairperson of the Admissions Committee and, in addition, devoted Mondays to counseling residents who were referred to her by Dorothy.

In the late 1980's, Irmgard was the person who first suggested changing Selfhelp's admissions policies. She argued that for the organization to remain competitive, Selfhelp needed to change from a predominantly "German Jewish Home" to a "Jewish Home." The Board agreed with her and after a few years, the residents residing at the Selfhelp Home were predominantly Jewish people born in America. Dorothy was glad that the German Jewish immigrants had become more independent and said, "I'm glad we're now in a position to open our doors to other Jews as well."

In May of 1986, Irmgard and her two cats moved into an apartment at the Selfhelp Center. At 75, she developed a new talent and began to create stained-glass creations with exceptional artistry and mathematical precision. In 2000 she won the, "Honored Senior Artist Program Award." for her three-dimensional glass art - original designs - in kaleidoscopic colors.

Marlise Katzenstein had been volunteering for Selfhelp since 1963, when Dorothy asked her to wait in front of the new Selfhelp Center for the moving truck. In addition to raising a family, Marlise worked in Dorothy's office, typing the employees' work schedule, the weekly payroll and much of

Dorothy's correspondence. For years, she edited the "Selfhelper," and was in charge of the annual May parties. After retirement, she occupied the desk across from Dorothy to make sure that Selfhelp's largest fund, the "Happy Day Fund," was well stocked. In her spare time, Marlise played the violin with the Chicago Lake Shore Orchestra. When asked how she found time to volunteer, she replied, "When I'm busy I don't think about my problems."

Martin and Mitzi Marx

Mitzi Marx felt honored when Dorothy said that Mitzi's tolerance, empathy and humor most resembled that of her closest friend, Lissy Hartman. After the Beckers moved north, Dorothy asked Mitzi to take charge of the Southside Neighborhood Group. For decades, Mitzi organized and oriented the Selfhelp volunteers, who were known for their, "Personal Touch." In the evenings, Mitzi updated her list of volunteers, while Martin balanced the books for Selfhelp's gift shop. On Friday evenings, they arrived at Selfhelp with a bouquet of fresh flowers to join Dorothy at the "round table" for Shabat dinner. People listened for Martin's lilting rendition of the Hebrew melodies.

During idyllic summers at the Indiana Dunes, Martin, a professional photographer, took prize-winning photographs of Mitzi and their three children. Mitzi's favorite was the photo of Martin and herself entwined in each other's arms, watching the sun set beyond the horizon. The love they radiated continued to live in the hearts of their children, grandchildren and all who knew them.

Hedy Strauss, the Treasurer of the Selfhelp Home and Leni Weil, the Treasurer of Selfhelp of Chicago, Inc. worked for the organization in near obscurity within the confines of their homes. Besides her full-time accounting job, Hedy devoted another 40 hours every week balancing the large accounts for the Selfhelp Home. She worked late at night to type the W-2 forms for over one 100 employees. When asked what drove her to do accounting work in her spare time, she threw her hands up and exclaimed: "I love figures!"

She was one of Dorothy's closest friends, even though Dorothy couldn't understand what enjoyment Hedy got from trying to outwit the slot machines in Las Vegas. When Dorothy underwent heart surgery, Hedy stayed by her bedside from ten in the morning 'till after supper. Dorothy considered Hedy family, "I can call her at three in the morning and she'll be here."

Leni Weil, with a glow of satisfaction once said, "Rolf and I did everything together." Already as teenagers, Rolf and Leni sold raffle tickets at Selfhelp fund raisers. On the day Rolf received his master's degree in economics, he and Leni became engaged. Rolf served as the youngest president of Roosevelt University. He and Leni had survived the student riots of the 1960's together. They raised their children together and worked for Selfhelp throughout their busy lives. Without the use of the computer, Leni balanced the account of Selfhelp of Chicago to the penny; and she assumed responsibility for mailing monthly supplements to people who qualified for financial help. On Tuesday afternoons, Selfhelp residents and people from the community flock to Rolf's current events group. He covered all the major events of the week, gave a quick summary and ended with a joke. He always loved teaching and students of every age loved him. The Weils and other members of the "Becker Cabinet" established a tradition designed to start every New Year off right. Every year they reserved Rosh Hashana afternoon for Kaffeeklatsch with Dorothy Becker.

Two New Administrators

In January, 1977, Mrs. Ann Hirschberg became the Associate Director of the Health Care Facility and Mr. Charles Lohfeld accepted the position of Business Manager. Both Mrs. Hirschberg and Mr. Lohfeld were directly accountable to Dorothy Becker, who met with them regularly to discuss mutual problems and concerns.

Dorothy Becker described Ann Hirschberg as an "elegant, intelligent woman, who danced the Czardash each year at the Christmas Party. Ann

Hirschberg's only complaint of Dorothy Becker was that she, "Ruled too much with her heart." She appreciated the fact that Dorothy "always discussed the issues with me before a final decision was made." The new Director of the Nursing Care Care Facility came to work early and left late. She could never do too much for the infirm people, many of whom were concentration camp survivors who had lived productive lives despite their brutal experiences.

Charles Lohfeld, Rolf Weil and Ann Hirschberg

Her loyal staff called her, "The Iron Lady," because she insisted on the best care for the infirm elderly. She didn't hesitate to correct an employee herself, but she fiercely defended her staff against any outside criticism. She won their loyalty because she respected her staff and appreciated how hard they worked. Most of them stayed with her for decades. Selfhelp could boast one of the lowest employee turnover rates, a rare statistic for most nursing care facilities.

Mrs. Becker relied on the competent Mr. Lohfeld to handle the organization's business affairs. He appreciated the fact that Dorothy respected people's right to open their own mail. He processed the monthly rent for the 180 residents and submitted the weekly payroll for the growing number of employees. He never lost patience with those elderly residents who came to his office, sometimes, several times a day, to be reassured that their money wouldn't run out before they died. After he retired, he and his wife stayed in contact with Dorothy and spent an afternoon with her whenever they came to Chicago.

A Beehive of Volunteers

Dorothy's untiring commitment to Selfhelp inspired scores of volunteers to work for the organization. Hundreds of women had joined her south and northside Senior Group. Her goal was to bring people together, especially those who had lost their families in the Holocaust. She was convinced that loneliness begot passivity, depression and physical ailments. Her formula for physical and mental health consisted of bringing people together who were involved in meaningful work and a daily round of celebrations. Selfhelp was run by resident and community volunteers who devoted years to putting the "Selfhelp Spirit" into practice.

In his annual address on September, 1984, Rolf Weil, an economist explained that "It would cost the organization $200,000 per year in wages for comparable work done gratis by Selfhelp's volunteers." "Above all," said Dorothy Becker, "Volunteers give the gift of love, and that is its highest reward." [Appendix X]

Dorothy Becker boasted that she could count on 30,000 hours of voluntary service every month. The volunteers were the staple of Selfhelp and the volunteering spirit was at the center of the Selfhelp spirit. It had to do with assuming responsibility for yourself and those close to you rather than expecting to be taken care of. The residents looked out for one another and helped run the Home. "A few of my snow birds went south for the winter," but Dorothy maintained, "I could rely on the volunteers as much as on my paid employees." Some people complained that messages didn't always get through when the residents worked at the reception desk. When some Board members told Dorothy, "You can't teach an old dog new tricks," she replied, "Our people are not dogs and they *do* learn new skills." Rolf Weil, the Board President, considered Dorothy's ability to attract and hold volunteers her greatest strength, on par with her ability to get so many donations that people made "in gratitude to Dorothy Becker."

Lotte Aufrecht said, " Selfhelp is an organization that is run by volunteers. Without the volunteers we wouldn't be able to take care of the elderly at such affordable prices." Both men and women supported the organization with generous contributions of time, energy, talents and money. Men of varying professions served for decades on the Board and on Selfhelp's many "special committees."

Mostly women provided the wide range of direct services the residents needed. Unlike the women before the Second World War, most of the Selfhelp volunteers held full or part-time jobs, took care of their families and volunteered. To give the reader an idea of the many services they performed, the lists of volunteers compiled by Mitzi Marx in 1998 and 1990, have been included in the back of the book. *Unfortunately, these lists omit the names of a countless number of dedicated people who helped make Selfhelp a success, but whose names are unknown to the author.*

Marianne and Harold Weinberg

Dorothy got everybody involved. Many of the volunteers were residents of the Home; others lived in the community. Trude Bing, Ruth Bluethe, Steffie Lax and Esther Mainzer ran the gift shop for years. Eva Grossman met with her knitting group every Thursday to knit baby clothes sold in the gift shop. Several times per week, Donna Broder and others drove the elderly to the doctor, or they went shopping and stopped at a favorite restaurant. Some volunteers ran errands for the homebound. Computer experts updated the membership list. Some residents depended on Marianne Weinberg and Julius Strauss to sort out their insurance forms.

Miriam Levi

Besides taking people to the doctor, Ruth Heilbron, Irma Kamnitzer and many others who lived in the community came to Selfhelp every Tuesday to help serve coffee, to share a bit of news and gossip, and to play cards. Some of the women who visited people confined to their rooms, specialized in telling stories; Jane Gelder and Ruth Gideon told jokes. (Not just the Irish have the gift for gab!) People with writing skills submitted articles, poems and anecdotes to the "Selfhelper," and the "Selfhelp Newsletter." Marlise Katzenstein and Lucille Hauser edited the quarterly publications. Debbie Arendt and Louise Franks organized the new library.

Debbie Arendt, a librarian, gave book reviews as well. For years, after he retired, Dr. Hans Frey, a semi-professional artist, gave art classes at Selfhelp. The impressario among them, Miriam Levi, brought musicians, singers and dancers to the Home. As early as 1954, she introduced the beloved pianist, William Whitaker, to Mrs. Becker.

Center: William Whitaker and Dorothy Becker

William shared Dorothy's humanitarian ideals and respected her dedication to the Holocaust survivors. For 40 plus years, he played his all American concert at Selfhelp every Fourth of July. Mrs. Becker and the entire Selfhelp family mourned when their beloved William Whitaker died on September 6, 1996, two months after he played his last Independence Day concert at Selfhelp.

Rabbis and Cantors conducted services at Selfhelp on the religious holidays. Rabbi Herman Schaalman often chaired the Leo Beck discussions held at Selfhelp one evening a month. Some of the residents like Mr. Nussbaum, Mr. Zeuss and Cantor Fleischer felt privileged when Mrs. Becker would ask them to conduct the Seder.

Talmudic scholars like Dr. Heinz Graupe served on Selfhelp's Religious Committee. They advised Mrs. Becker on the correct observance of the religious holidays. Rosel Stein, a registered dietician, volunteered at Selfhelp for decades. She set up a kosher kitchen and made sure the food was delicious, nutritious and in compliance with the Jewish dietary laws. Dr. Kurt Schwerin, a law professor at Northwestern, and Rolf Weil served on the Scholarship Committee. Dr. Kurt Schwerin wrote the book, "Selfhelp Of Chicago, Inc. Selfhelp Home For the Aged, Inc. A Short History."

Gertrude and Kurt Schwerin

Dorothy was convinced that productive work was essential to people's physical and emotional well-being. Resident and community volunteers took care of the gift shop and cared for the plants throughout the Home. They joined the Birthday Committee, the Entertainment Committee, the Choir, the

271

Flower Committee, the Welcoming Committee, the Companion Committee and the Religious Committee.

Dorothy considered the shared language, culture, history and religion the fertile ground on which the Selfhelp Family flourished. With the passing of years, religion became more important to Dorothy because she realized that faith gives meaning to life and comfort in death. Members of the Religious Committee such as Gustav Freuhauf, Karl Nussbaum, Heinz Graupe and Julius Steiermann advised Dorothy regarding Hebrew prayers and Judaic customs and ceremonies.

Mr. Steierman was a long-time member of Selfhelp's Religious Committee. His daughter, Marion Mayer, wrote, "He and other residents took turns chanting the Friday evening prayers. Several women took turns kindling the candles. My father did much to encourage resident involvement. The Religious Committee, under my father's guidance, was responsible for Yiskor (Memorial) services held at Selfhelp. Every year Dorothy Becker ended the Yiskor Service on Yom Kipur by recalling each one of Selfhelp's deceased residents by name. I am sure he helped decorate the Succah at Selfhelp, since some of the decorations were similar to the ones we made during my childhood. For the Chanukah party, my father encouraged the residents to bring their own menorahs, while the Home supplied the candles. When everyone had kindled them and they all shed their light, it was an unforgettable sight." On the Sabbath and on the Holidays, Mr. Steierman and the other members of the Religious Committee conducted services in the Nursing Care Facility as well.

Groups of women came to Selfhelp to talk and to walk with the people in the Nursing Care Facility. They drove people to the store or went with them to the doctor. They sewed on buttons for residents who had arthritic fingers and helped people with poor vision to write letters.

Every Tuesday and Thursday afternoons, scores of volunteers flocked to the home for coffee and cake, to celebrate birthdays, and above all, to talk. Afterward, they visited the people who weren't able to join them in the dining room and in the nursing care facility.

The well-traveled path from the Home to the community and from the community to the Home allowed the people who lived in the community to become acquainted with the Home, and at the same time, it gave the residents, including Dorothy, a chance to see if prospective applicants felt comfortable with the people residing at Selfhelp.

Jenny Wolf Retires

An aura of respect surrounded Jenny Wolf, the founder of the original Women's Group, the precursor of the Selfhelp Neighborhood Group. She was the first woman to serve on the Board of Selfhelp and remained active on the Board of Selfhelp for 40 years. Initially, she and Dorothy had their differences, but the two women combined their talents to help immigrant mothers and their families. Together, they also threw the best parties in town!

Jenny Wolf, Lotte Aufrecht and other members of the House Committee deserved the credit they received for the beautiful decor of the new Selfhelp Complex. Lotte, a meticulous housekeeper, spotted wobbly tables from a distance and could predict the hour a light bulb was destined to expire, allowing more time for Jenny to focus on the comfort and well-being of the residents. Jenny, an outstanding cook, together with Rosel Stein, the dietician, planned the nutritious and delicious kosher meals served at Selfhelp.

When Jenny Wolf actually *moved* into the Selfhelp Complex, Board rules demanded that she resign from the Selfhelp Board as well as from the House Committee. She confided to Dorothy that she hoped to remain of service to Selfhelp in some capacity. Since Jenny was the founder of the original Women's Group and knew most of Selfhelp's members, Dorothy asked Jenny to answer the phone in her office while she was on vacation. When Lotte Aufrecht saw Jenny sitting at Dorothy's desk, she told Jenny that she had no business in the office. It was against Board rules!

Jenny felt hurt to the core. As founder of the Southside Neighborhood Group, she had first and foremost impressed on the volunteers the importance of confidentiality. She and her volunteers had won peoples' confidence because they maintained strict confidentiality. She confided to Dorothy how humiliated she felt when people suddenly stopped talking the moment she entered the office. After 40 years of service to Selfhelp, Jenny Wolf did not expect to be treated like an enemy alien. Dorothy empathized with Jenny and wondered if she would receive similar treatment when she retired.

Because Dorothy couldn't spend as much time with Jenny as she would have liked, Jenny began to feel estranged from Dorothy, whose responsibilities had increased considerably. The number of residents, employees and volunteers under her supervision had more than doubled. It took time for Dorothy to make contact with each resident everyday, as was her practice. She probably did shortchange her mentor and friend, Jenny Wolf who, nevertheless, continued to support her.

For Dorothy, life was with people from morning 'till night. She thought it was important to celebrate each person's life on the date of his/her birth. She never missed a birthday party and always had an amusing or complimentary story to tell about the "birthday child." Talented residents sang, played the piano, recited poems and told jokes. Selfhelp's choir, under the direction of Julie Freudenthal, succeeded in getting enthusiastic participation from the audience.

Sharing in the work and the fun built the family atmosphere. Another priority for Dorothy was to be with her people during times of sorrow and sickness. Terminally ill people shared their fears with her and hoped that she would remember them after they were gone. She held a memorial service at the Home for every one of her people.

For the average person, this non-stop round of activity would be exhausting but it energized Dorothy. Rolf Weil noted that Dorothy started or ended every other sentence with, "I just love her!" or "He is such a fine, intelligent man." Dorothy explained that she had seldom met a person she didn't like. "The few times I met someone I didn't like, I treated them twice as nice."

Hedy Strauss wondered how Dorothy could stand having people kiss her all the time. The most reserved person, in the habit of greeting his mother with only a hand-shake, would rush up to Dorothy and kiss her. Dorothy simply told Hedy, "I enjoy it!"

Dorothy was able to spend her time with people because of volunteers like Hedy and Marlise who relieved her of much of her paper work. At 11 at night, Dorothy returned to her office to sign the reports and letters Marlise had typed for her. Dorothy summed it up when she said, *"Hundreds of different types of people volunteered at Selfhelp. No one got rich or gained an advantage. It worked because it was done with love."*

The Selfhelp Spirit in Action

Dr. and Mrs. Mueller had moved into the Selfhelp Home in October of 1985. They talked about the Christmas Party for months. Mrs. Mueller, who suffered from depression, claimed the music and dancing had given her a "lift." Dr. Mueller agreed although he could not remember the event since he suffered from memory loss. His wife became increasingly more depressed until the couple could no longer function on their own.

Ten years earlier, Mrs. Mueller had placed their names on Selfhelp's waiting list. Just when they most needed the security of the Home, Mrs. Becker called to let Mrs. Mueller know that an efficiency apartment would become vacant in a month. Mrs. Mueller welcomed the prospect of moving into the Selfhelp Center and readily convinced her husband to agree with her decision.

When Irmgard Heymann, the Chairperson of the Admissions Committee, interviewed Dr. and Mrs. Mueller at their apartment, she must have seen the large statue of the Madonna and Child which stood on the table next to the sofa. She discovered that Dr. Mueller, a Catholic physician, had been forced to leave Germany in 1933, because he refused to divorce his Jewish wife. He fled with her to Brazil until they could emigrate to America.

Mrs. Irmgard and Dr. Joseph Mueller

Irmgard Heymann listened to hundreds of refugees recount similar life stories, yet each had its own twist. Although Dr. Mueller was Catholic, he was eligible to apply for admission to the Home because his wife was Jewish. Ms. Heymann asked Dr. Mueller if he would have any objections to wearing a yarmulkah or cap for the Friday evening meal. He did not object at all. Dr. Mueller liked to read the Bible in its original language. He had learned Hebrew while studying for the priesthood before he decided to change courses to study medicine.

She told them their rent, including three meals and maid service, would amount to $1000 per month for both of them. In 1984, comparable retirement homes charged about four times that amount. Based on their financial ability, they were expected to make a contribution ranging from $2000 to

$10,000 dollars upon entrance to the Home.

After Ms. Heymann's interview, Mrs. Becker invited Dr. and Mrs. Mueller to join her at the center table for Sabbath dinner. Mrs. Mueller had her hair done that morning and wore the red silk dress and gold earrings she reserved for special occasions. She selected a red and ivory tie to add a dash of color to Dr. Mueller's navy blue suit. She was proud of her handsome husband who had left Germany for her sake at a time when so many others had divorced their Jewish spouses. She had been dependent on him through-out most of their lives together. But now, because of his mental decline, he became increasingly more dependent on her. This reversal of roles fright-ened her and caused her to wake up at night drenched in perspiration.

Dr. and Mrs. Mueller felt honored by the special place Dorothy had reserved for them at the center table. Mrs. Mellekson, the housekeeping supervisor, a statuesque, cultured woman, extended a warm welcome to the guests of honor. She smiled as she offered Dr. Mueller a yarmulkah, which he placed on his head without the least hesitation.

Mrs. Becker looked at Dr. Mueller admiringly as she listened to him read the blessing over the bread and wine in perfect Hebrew. Mrs. Becker looked past the fact that Dr. Mueller suffered from Alzheimer's and made a mental note of his ability to say the prayers over the bread and wine in perfect Hebrew. [This is another point on which Dorothy and Betty Friedan agree. According to Friedan, many people with Alzheimer's can continue to live in the community with some assistance.] Dorothy then noticed Dr. and Mrs. Mueller's impeccable manners as well as the amber nicotine stains on Mrs.

Mueller's fingers. Mrs. Mueller, who smoked three packs per day, yearned for a cigarette, but instead, tried to concentrate on the home-made chicken soup and the fresh plum cake which she enjoyed immensely.

A few days later, Mrs. Becker called to tell them that the Board had approved their application. They would be able to move into the Center as soon as their apartment was painted. Being able to bring their own cocktail table, chairs and a cabinet eased the transition from their apartment to the Home. Behind the glass door of the curio cabinet, Mrs. Mueller displayed some Hummel figurines, a gold-rimmed clock, a Rosenthal vase and a copper ash tray, which was a farewell gift from her sister when she left Germany.

The transition from their apartment to the Home was not easy but Dorothy greeted them with a warm embrace and told them at least once a day how happy she was to have them in the Home with her. As soon as Dorothy found out that Mrs. Mueller played the piano, she introduced her to the "Birthday Committee" and said they desperately needed a pianist. Pretty soon, Mrs. Mueller, who hadn't gone near the piano for years, began to entertain people at the birthday parties with popular hits from the 1920s and 1930s. Her husband beamed with pride and Dorothy waited and watched for the mask of depression to drop from Mrs. Mueller's face.

What nearly devastated Mrs. Mueller was the smoking restriction. She knew smoking was not allowed in the public areas on the Sabbath, but anxiety gripped her when she learned that smoking in the privacy of her apartment was prohibited as well. With tranquilizers and a supply of chocolate, she reduced her smoking from 60 to only six cigarettes a day. To avoid detection she would smoke by an open window holding a cigarette in one hand and a can of air freshener in the other. [Most likely, Dorothy smelled cigarette smoke coming from the Muellers' apartment, but she never mentioned it.]

From the day they moved into the Home, the genuinely kind people on Selfhelp's "Welcoming Committee" went out of their way to befriend the personable Dr. Mueller and his charming but insecure wife. Mrs. Wiesenfelder, who got up early to water the plants, would knock on the Muellers' door to take them to breakfast with her. At mid-morning, another woman would ask Mrs. Mueller, an ardent gymnast, if she wanted to go to the exercise class with her.

In the afternoons, Dr. Mueller sang German folk songs with the Selfhelp Choir while his wife accompanied them on the piano. Even after he lost the ability to put a sentence together, Dr. Mueller remembered the lyrics of the songs he had learned in his childhood.

Mrs. Mueller had a weekly appointment with her psychiatrist, and yes, there were several women who specialized in going to the doctor with people. Mrs. Mueller's mood changed from cloudy to sunny whenever she was in the company of the jovial Irma Kamnitzer, who accompanied her to the psychiatrist's office every Tuesday afternoon. During the hour-long session, Mrs. Kamnitzer sat patiently in the waiting room working her crossword puzzles. She said it was a less expensive way of keeping her sanity. She never asked Mrs. Mueller why she had to see the doctor and discreetly avoided any discussion of these weekly appointments. Before they returned to the Home, they stopped at "Lutz," one of Chicago's finest German bakeries, for a piece of hazelnut cake.

While Mrs. Mueller was at the doctor's office, Mrs. Heddie Baer looked in on Dr. Mueller. Both Dr. Mueller and Mrs. Baer came from the Rhineland.

Resident Heddie Baer

The risque jokes she told in the Cologne dialect were reserved only for the ears of Rhinelanders like Dr. Mueller. In the afternoons, Mrs. Henny Straus knocked on Dr. and Mrs. Mueller's door to inquire if they would like to go for afternoon coffee? Usually, the witty Jane Gelder would join them in the dining room. Dr. Epstein, their neighbor, who planned the record concerts on Friday evenings, stopped by regularly to ask Mrs. Mueller if she would help him pick out the music or if she had any special requests.

Dr. Epstein introduced the Muellers to the music appreciation class conducted by a graduate student from Columbia College. Mrs. Mueller had developed a special friendship with the maternal Clara Holzbauer who tried to allay her anxiety about her husband's increasing memory loss. During meals, he occasionally forgot his table manners. Both Dr. Mueller and his wife would lower their heads in shame when the domineering matriarch at their table reprimanded Dr. Mueller for using his finger to pick up a piece of cheese or sausage. They felt demeaned when members of the staff insisted on calling him Mr. instead of Dr. Mueller. These slights added to *his* confusions and bothered *her*, but she didn't dare say anything.

At times, she could assert herself. She complained about the laundry detergent because she thought it aggravated her husband's itchy skin. Mrs. Mellekson, the supervisor, not only had the laundry washed in Woolite, but it was put through an extra rinse cycle. After that, he slept so much better in his "well-rinsed" pajamas.

Mrs. Mueller was afraid to tell Mrs. Becker about the numerous items that had disappeared from their apartment. During their first six months at the Center, she lost a diamond ring, two gold bracelets, a gold pin and her husband's watch. Someone had taken a Hummel figure, the gold-rimmed clock and a blood pressure apparatus. Other residents had talked to Mrs. Becker about this problem but she insisted that stealing didn't occur at Selfhelp.

Dorothy Becker did suspect one resident of stealing. She said, "I usually liked 90% of the people, but this woman I couldn't stand, and this time I showed it!" She first stole from the A&P Supermarket. Her son had a big job as a scientist. I called him and said that I had trouble with his mother. I asked him if he realized that she stole or begged. She always says that she has no shoes and no underwear. Maybe your wife can go with her and buy her these things," Mrs. Becker suggested.

Mrs. Becker admitted, "I really insulted her which I usually don't do. I said, were your parents so "verschnort?" (stingy) She smiled and said, "My parents were very nice people; they gave us all an education." "Did they steal?", asked Dorothy. "I thought she'd be insulted. I'd slap someone if they would ask me these questions." She just smiled. Then she asked Dr. Epstein if she could use his phone. After she left, his favorite cuticle scissors was gone."

The woman Mrs. Becker suspected of stealing was not the culprit, and Mrs. Mueller had no idea who had walked off with the few valuables she had brought with her. She certainly didn't suspect the cleaning woman who supplied them with extra towels everyday. In appreciation, she bought the maid chocolates and gave her the lovely sweaters and coats she had outgrown. But, when her favorite cleaning lady was transferred to another floor, the pilfering stopped. Shortly thereafter, a resident who pretended to be asleep on the sofa, saw the cleaning lady take his watch. He reported the incident to Mr. Lohfeld, the Business Manager. He called the police and fired her on the spot. Mrs. Becker felt sorry for the woman who was raising three children by herself.

The resolution of that problem did not allay Mrs. Mueller's fear that Mrs. Becker would object to their statue of the Madonna and Child. When they first moved into their apartment, Mrs. Becker suggested that a cross would not be appropriate in a Jewish Home, but they could certainly display the beautifully-carved Madonna.

Mrs. Mueller had no real reason to fear Mrs. Becker, but she awoke nearly every night in a state of panic. She continued to see the psychiatrist and took anti-anxiety medication. But what lifted her spirits most were the people they befriended, the appreciation she got for playing the piano and the festive atmosphere of the Becker Home.

Rolf Weil - Lighting the Chanukah Candles

The Chanukah Party

A group of residents, wearing plastic gloves and caps worked feverishly with the kitchen staff to make hundreds of open-faced sandwiches for the Chanukah Party. Najiba, Selfhelp's top chef, baked an assortment of petit fours that dazzled the eyes and delighted the palate. On the night of the party, the residents, their children and grandchildren entered the recreation room early to get a seat as close to the piano as possible.

The chair closest to Dr. Finkel was reserved for Mrs. Becker. Dr. Sanford Finkel's one man show had become a Chanukah tradition. Dr. Finkel, a practicing psychiatrist, who treated people with more than just the "talking cure," explained simply: "I play at Selfhelp because Dorothy Becker asks me to. Who can say 'no' to Dorothy Becker?"

Dr. Sanford Finkel

He sang Russian songs, Yiddish lullabies, love songs in Hebrew and excerpts from "Fiddler on the Roof." The people swayed as they sang, "Du Du Liegst Mir Im Herzen." They hummed along as he sang familiar Chanukah melodies. He closed with a tribute to Dorothy Becker by singing her late husband's favorite song: "Dein Ist Mein Ganzes Herz," or ("My Heart Is Yours Forever.") The applause continued until Dr. Finkel handed the microphone to Dorothy. She thanked Dr. Finkel for giving them his "music cure" which saved them from having to make appointments with him for his much costlier "talking cure."

285

Chanukah Party delicacies

Mrs. Mueller, a connoisseur of herring salad, rated that delicacy the best she had ever eaten, while Dr. Mueller savored the real whipped cream of Najiba's hazelnut cake. Before they returned to their apartment, they thanked Mrs. Mellekson and Mrs. Levitsky for the delicious sandwiches and desserts. Mrs. Mueller let Dr. Finkel know how much she had enjoyed his fiery rendition of the Russian song, "Kalinka." They thanked Mrs. Becker, who beamed when she noticed that the gloom had vanished from Mrs. Mueller's eyes that evening.

Shortly after Passover, Mrs. Mueller complained of severe stomach pain. Mrs. Becker who realized the condition was serious, called an ambulance and went with her to St. Joseph Hospital. That evening, Mrs. Mueller had to undergo emergency surgery. She recovered from the operation, but had to be transferred to a psychiatric hospital because of depression.

Mrs. Becker bought some carnations for Mrs. Mueller and took Dr. Mueller to visit his wife at the hospital. Mrs. Mueller worried about her husband, but Mrs. Becker promised that she would look in on him everyday. Several days later, Mrs. Mueller lapsed into a coma and died.

When Dorothy discovered that a few relatives had come to express their sympathies to Dr. Mueller, she personally came to his room with a thermos of coffee and a platter of cookies. The relatives also appreciated that she attended the funeral mass at Holy Name Cathedral and later that week, invited both a rabbi and a priest to conduct the memorial service for Mrs. Mueller. The presence of the priest gave comfort to Dr. Mueller and he felt honored by the many people who looked in on him.

His niece visited him daily. When a well-meaning resident suggested that he should move to the Nursing Care Facility, Dorothy defended his right to stay in his own apartment. She maintained that maintaining a person's independence and autonomy is more conducive to physical and mental health. [Many researchers on the aging process agree with her on this point.]

Had Dorothy broached the subject, the niece *would* have considered transferring Dr. Mueller to the Nursing Care Facility. Instead, Dorothy proposed a birthday party to celebrate Dr. Mueller's 92nd birthday. His nephew, Fritz Weeg, flew in from Germany to celebrate his uncle's special day on April 23, 1987. One of his most loyal patients, Maria Rivera came to his party as well. Mrs. Becker had ordered an array of spring flowers and a strawberry whipped cream cake. Mr. Bill Whitaker, Dorothy's musician friend, played Dr. Mueller's favorite song, "Home on the Range." Everybody joined the Selfhelp choir in singing, "Enjoy Yourself... It's Later Than You Think."

On a snowy afternoon in November of 1987, Mrs. Becker called his niece to tell her that Dr. Mueller had fallen in his room. He was not in pain or in distress, and she would keep an eye on him. Stalled in traffic, the niece didn't get to the Home until an hour later. She rushed into his room and found Dorothy sitting in a chair next to Dr. Mueller, who had fallen asleep on the floor.

The niece had expected to find one of the nursing assistants in her Uncle's room, but seeing Dorothy taking the time to stay with Dr. Mueller was deeply spiritual. This simple, but genuinely human gesture enabled Dr. Mueller to just relax and take a nap. Her human touch inspired trust and healing; her human touch filled the Home with warmth and joy. However, some professionals criticized her for "treating the residents like infants." The same criticism was voiced by some Board members when she accompanied people to the hospital at night.

The last thing Dorothy wanted to do was to turn people into dependent infants. She equated the word "Selfhelp" with activity, autonomy and independence. Dorothy was convinced that "the human touch" helped people most when they were sick or emotionally distressed. This underlying belief of hers was at the core of most conflicts Dorothy had with other administrators and Board members. It was a case of the human touch versus "administrative professionalism." Dorothy Becker, the ultimate professional, never strayed from the dictates of her educated heart.

When Dr. Mueller woke up, Dorothy called an ambulance and the niece took him to the hospital for X-rays. The doctor found he had a bruised shoulder but no fractures. She was able to take him home that evening. After she tucked her uncle into bed and was ready to leave the building, she noticed that Mrs. Becker was still at work in her office. Mrs. Becker answered the knock on the door without raising her head from the report she was writing.

She asked the niece to sit down, pushed the paper work aside, and asked, "How is Dr. Mueller?" "Like you suspected, he didn't sustain any injuries, just a bruised shoulder. The doctor recommended Tylenol for pain. I gave him some help undressing, and once he slipped under the covers, he fell asleep immediately." The niece couldn't thank Dorothy enough for staying with her uncle until she arrived. Dorothy, who didn't think she had gone out of her way, said simply, " I stayed with him because he knew me."

She asked the niece if she thought that he needed to transfer to the Nursing Care Facility? She thought he might feel less lonely there; he might like it. She offered to introduce Dr. Mueller and his niece to Mrs. Hirschberg, the Director of the Nursing Care Unit.

The following week, Mrs. Hirschberg welcomed Dr. Mueller and his niece to the Health Care Facility on the eighth floor. She showed them one of the rooms that would be available, and introduced them to other members of her staff. If they decided to transfer Dr. Mueller, she suggested bringing pictures and his stereo since he liked listening to German folk songs.

Mrs. Hirschberg took Dr. Mueller's arm and led him to a firmly upholstered chair she had reserved for him in the sitting room. He observed that the other people were sitting in the same kind of chairs and concluded that it must be a classroom.

Mina Jonas on the left

From his central place in the day room, he enjoyed watching the parade of volunteers, nursing assistants, nurses and visitors who strolled past him. He readily extended his hand to those who stopped to say "hello" to him. He seemed much happier in the Nursing Care Facility and his niece realized that her own biases had kept him too long in the confines of his lonely apartment.

The Rainbow Coalition of Employees

Santa Christian, Valentina De Dragin, Denise Christian

He chatted with the lady sitting in the chair next to him who sometimes held his hand. Mrs. Williams and Mrs. Brown, the nurses on the team, used patience and charm to get him to take his medicine. He smiled when he saw

291

Claudette Blaise, Robert and Carmen Gillaume, the nursing assistants who cared for him with respect and kindness. They made him feel at home in the Health Care Facility, but they didn't realize that most of the day he thought he was in a classroom.

He enjoyed the company of the many volunteers who worked with the infirm elderly. With a lady on each arm, he went on in-house walks every morning. He enjoyed the company of two volunteers, a professional seamstress who repaired a zipper on his jacket, and a former secretary who helped him write cards. On balmy afternoons, his two walking companions took him to the roof garden. He could spend hours admiring the large planters brimming with geranium, petunias and marigolds that Margot Meyer had planted. He called the petite Mina Jonas and the slender Hilde Wiesenthal "champion weight lifters" whenever he saw them lift the heavy sprinkling cans to water the flowers. Above all, he liked to sing the songs Mitzi Marx played on the piano. In the evenings, volunteers like Marianne Weinberg arrived to keep people company. Dorothy depended on her volunteers to dispel the lonely feelings that frequently overtook people after their visitors left.

At least 70 employees, mostly immigrants from every corner of the earth, cared for the 140 people residing in the independent living section of the Selfhelp Center. These included cooks from Croatia and Assyria, kitchen and dining room help from Mexico, personal aids from the U.S., India, the Philippines, and Russia, plus an African American engineer and janitorial staff. Before Dorothy hired a person, she made sure the person had a green card. She was interested in his or her family, their background and country of origin. First and foremost, she tried to evaluate if the job applicant possessed the necessary patience and kindness to work with the elderly.

Penna, Clara Mellekson, Dorothy Becker, Najiba Youmaran, Lyubov Levitsky

Many members of her staff never forgot that she had given them their first job despite their limited English. In contrast to the many forms of discrimination they faced daily because of their race, their immigrant status and their broken English, Dorothy showed a genuine interest in them personally. She inquired about their families and found their different traditions and customs fascinating. She loved every member of her staff and believed, "They had to feel loved before they could give love to the residents."

Her philosophy of love was in the air at Selfhelp and fostered a bond between the residents and the employees who readily identified with each other. Because of their shared immigrant background, the respective groups knew the pain of separation from family and friends. Both understood the hardship of finding work in a new country while struggling to learn the language. They shared each other's sorrows and celebrated life's happy events as well. The residents sent sick employees get well wishes and condolences when an employee's loved one died. For graduations, weddings, and the birth of a baby, they included a check with their congratulations.

When the earthquake of 1985 destroyed large parts of Mexico City, Mrs. Becker and the entire Selfhelp family expressed their support for the Mexican members of their staff. Mrs. Becker collected $400 for the Mexican Relief Fund. She wondered if the check had been lost or stolen since she didn't receive any acknowledgment from MRF until one year later.

In like manner, the Selfhelp residents stood united with the African American community when their churches were set on fire in Mississippi during the 1960's. Mrs. Becker again took up a collection of $500 and sent it with a letter to Reverend Jesse Jackson expressing outrage and sympathy on behalf of the entire Selfhelp family. She explained that Selfhelp was an organization founded by Jewish immigrants who had fled from Nazi persecution. The people of Selfhelp considered the burning of the churches as much an attack on themselves as on African Americans.

Again she waited for a reply. Eight months later she received a form letter from Operation Push informing her that the check had been forwarded to the NAACP. More important were the expressions of appreciation Dorothy received from the African American members of her staff.

"I had a wonderful relationship with every one of the staff. Patel wants to be an RN and is close to graduating. She is in charge of nurses. My janitor, Vernon Gary, wrote me after he retired but I didn't have his address so I

couldn't answer. He called recently to ask how I was feeling. He was so gift-
ed - a tall Black man. When Mrs. Mellekson was fired, I was terribly upset.
She was the supervisor of housekeeping for almost 12 years. She is a perfec-
tionist and a very intelligent person. I liked her so much. Najiba is our won-
derful cook. Because of her, Selfhelp has a reputation for its good food. I love
Najiba, our cook and her sister Mariam, who was her sister. Marline, Agnes
Daniels' sister, is beautiful! She told me, 'I love Selfhelp, and I have the most
wonderful family. I wouldn't want to change with any one.' Agnes is a very
intelligent girl. She went to college and has two adorable children. I could
call any one of them in the middle of the night and they would be here."

Agnes Daniels and Dorothy Becker

Dorothy had hired Agnes Daniels, the supervisor of housekeeping, while she was still in high school. Agnes, whose mother had died, invited Dorothy to her engagement party, an occasion almost as important as the wedding in the Assyrian culture. For Agnes, only Dorothy could substitute for her real mother. Many employees sought the advice of their director especially during times of personal and family trouble.

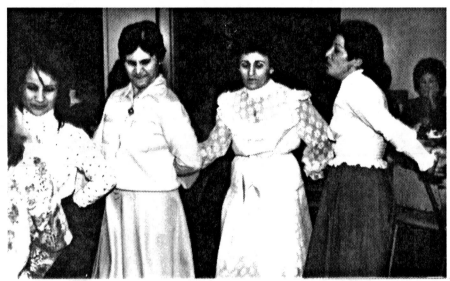

Marline Younan, Penna, Mariam Moshe, Marian Zian

One day Dorothy saw Najiba, Selfhelp's cook, crying, and asked her what was wrong. Najiba told Dorothy that her daughter, who had a three-year old child, had to undergo surgery. Najiba was very worried; she even considered taking time off from work because her daughter and her son-in-law couldn't afford to hire a baby-sitter. Dorothy helped by bending the rules a little. She allowed Najiba to bring her granddaughter, Natasha, to work with her until the child's mother fully recovered. Najiba and her family never forgot Dorothy's kindness during this family crisis. Several months later when

Dorothy hired Najiba's sister, Mariam Moshe, she told the two women she hoped they would stay with Selfhelp for years to come. Every member of her staff, who had the welfare of the residents at heart, was a valued member of her Selfhelp family and she considered a low turnover rate essential to preserving the Home's family atmosphere.

Mariam Moshe would have worked for Selfhelp until retirement had not fate ended her life prematurely at age 50. For 16 years, Mariam cleaned the rooms on the fifth floor, including Dorothy's apartment. Every Mother's Day, she brought Dorothy a bouquet of roses.

Bernie and Linda Fine - Director of Resident Services

Shortly after Mariam was named a supervisor, she became ill and had to undergo surgery. She returned to work with tenacious optimism, but Dorothy worried about her continued weight loss and waning energy. Mrs. Linda Fine, the Director of Selfhelp at that time, granted Mariam an extended sick leave. On several occasions, Mrs. Fine and Mrs. Becker visited Mariam at her home.

Her deep set eyes shone with resignation. Lacking the energy for conversation, she held Dorothy's hand throughout the visit. Before leaving, Dorothy enfolded Mariam in her arms and whispered, "I love you." Shortly thereafter, Mariam died. The people at Selfhelp shared the grief of Mariam with her sister Najiba. The presence of Mrs. Becker and Mrs. Fine at the funeral brought a measure of comfort to the bereaved family.

Before she died, Mariam reminded Najiba not to forget the bouquet of roses for Mrs. Becker on Mother's Day. Najiba kept her promise, and every Mother's Day presented Mrs. Becker with this token of Mariam's love.

The Employees' Christmas Party

Christmas at Selfhelp resembled scenes from, "It's A Wonderful Life." Finding the right gift for every member or her staff took the entire year. *"I gave every employee a present for Christmas. They got a bonus from Selfhelp and then they got a check from the Christmas Fund that the residents collected throughout the year. Depending on how long people had worked for Selfhelp, each got up to $250. Some got only $20 or $50 if they just started working. Rolf Weil was against bonuses. I had to fight for this because the people didn't make much money. He told me that nobody gives bonuses anymore. He said, 'If you have cake and coffee that's enough.' But I stood my ground. To buy individual gifts for so many people was most strenuous. I had to remember what I gave the* *year before. I didn't buy six sweaters; I bought a different present for each one and for the children too. It cost me a fortune. But it was worth-while. They were so grateful."*

Next to each person's name on her employee list, she jotted down their size, color preference, hobbies, mode of transportation, and interests. Whenever she shopped at Marshall Field's or Carson's, she tucked the list into her purse in case she happened to see that special purse, sweater or scarf, for the person she had in mind. For women with a few extra pounds, she usually bought lovely but spacious nightgowns. At the perfume counter she tested a few fragrances her high school and college students might like. She looked at wash-and-wear blouses for working mothers, and bought warm gloves and scarves for people who took public transportation. She paid for the gifts out of her own pocket.

"My brother and sister-in-law came to help me wrap because I'm really not such a good wrapper. I put all of the gifts under the Christmas tree. It was so much work you can't imagine. I was completely exhausted! Every year I swore I wouldn't do it anymore but every year I did it again. After I broke my hip, however, it wasn't so easy to shop anymore. When I retired, Lohfeld took over. He said, 'I'm not crazy like you. We got scarves for everyone.' And "He didn't pay for it out of his own pocket either."

"We put a big Santa Claus in the kitchen and wrote:

HO! HO! HO! YOU'RE INVITED TO THE CHRISTMAS PARTY. PLEASE PUT YOUR ETHNIC DRESS ON AND ENJOY YOURSELF.

My janitor was the Santa Claus. They all came when I invited them to come in their national attire. I wore a sari several employees had brought me from India. We had music. The son of one of our maids played the accordion. He didn't want to come, but he said he would only come for Mrs. Becker. The staff sat in the center and the residents sat at the outside tables. We had red and green napkins for the staff and white and blue ones for our people. The orthodox people loved it. They thought it was the nicest party of the year."

David Youmaran with Natasha at the annual Employees' Christmas Party

People were sipping their last drop of coffee when the lights dimmed and the music stopped. Mrs. Becker stepped up to the microphone. On behalf of the residents and the Selfhelp Board, she wished her employees the best of health and happiness for Christmas and throughout the New Year. She called out the employee names in alphabetical order and asked each one to come to the stage individually. She thanked each person and handed him or her two envelopes - one with a bonus from the Selfhelp Board, the second envelope with a check from the residents. With a warm embrace, she then handed each one of the employees the gifts she had personally selected and purchased for them. Clutching the two envelopes and Mrs. Becker's gift, the last person returned to her seat on a trail of applause and good wishes. The spotlight followed the radiant Dorothy Becker off the stage to the sounds of "Cellito Lindo." Three Mexican caballeros, wearing sombreros, escorted their senoritas to the dance floor with their floral shawls draped across their "off-the-shoulder" blouses, complimenting their full circle skirts. Accenting the beat of this rousing melody, the men tapped their feet while the women resembled swirling butterflies. They exchanged partners, clapping their hands high above their heads and stamping their feet. With the left arm raised and the right encircling each other's waist, they whirled on the wings of their skirts. The audience erupted with applause. It continued while the dancers returned for another bow. The clapping subsided as a line of Assyrian women, wearing party dresses, danced to the center of the stage.

With their arms bent at their elbows below shoulder level, they lightly held each others' finger tips. The first person in line waved to the audience with her handkerchief. Propelled by the hypnotic strains of Middle Eastern music, they executed the intricate steps with grace and dignity. The contrast between the energetic Mexican dance and the Assyrian "Woman's Dance" accentuated the dynamic change of pace. Unexpected reversals from stepping right to turning left captured the interest of the spectators. Like a flower closing its petals, they danced toward the center and opened as they moved back to the edge of the circle. They bowed in unison and danced off the stage with arms bent at the elbow and hands held by the fingertips. Dorothy recalled, "When they returned for another bow, they gave me the handkerchief and we all danced."

Assyrian Women's Dance

"Mrs. Menassus, our nurse, told us how Christmas was celebrated in Holland. Christmas is a church holiday and on December 5th, Santa Claus brings the gifts. Mrs. Menassus then sang a real nice Dutch song. Maria, our cook at that time, sang in Croation, gave a speech in Croation and translated it. The Assyrian girls sang in Assyrian. The Mexicans sang a beautiful Christmas song in Spanish. They all sang "Silent Night" in their own languages. We sang, "O Tannenbaum" in German. Some of them knew it in English. At first, I wasn't quite sure how our orthodox people would feel about it, but they loved it."

302

Santa Claus put on a dance record, and kept the party atmosphere in high gear. People sang and others swayed to the rhythm of a Straus waltz. When he played the Croatian music Maria had brought along, the Croatian people jumped up and danced the "Kolo." For a grand finale, he played,"Hava Nagila."

"We All Danced" - Vicroija, Dorothy Becker and Julia

"At the end, the Jewish people danced with Vernon Gary, our Black Santa Claus, and all the people danced... It was so beautiful.... I wished the whole world could be like this. Where else would you see Jews and Gentiles dancing the Hora with a black Santa Claus? Only at Selfhelp!" That was the "Spirit of Selfhelp"- dancing, singing, working, celebrating - despite sickness, infirmity, the Holocaust and death."

Retirement

After Dorothy broke her hip in 1976, she had to limit her Christmas shopping to one or two large department stores, but the thought of retiring didn't occur to her. Some of her colleagues urged her to reduce her working hours, to do some traveling and reserve more time for herself and her family. She felt that some of the Board members wanted her to retire, but Rolf Weil left that decision entirely to Dorothy and told her to let him know when she was ready for a change of pace. [Appendix Y]

After she broke her hip at age 77, she reluctantly submitted her resignation to the Board. Her friends and colleagues planned an intimate retirement party at the Tower Restaurant in Skokie. They reminisced and joked about their shared experiences. Throughout the 40 years Dorothy had served on the Board, they had engaged in heated debates, they had argued, and even stomped out of meetings. But their commitment to Selfhelp had enabled them to *"pull in the same direction"* and build the best retirement Home in Illinois. After dinner, Fred Aufrecht tapped on his glass to silence the talkative guests.

Fred spoke of the close friendship he and Lotte had shared with Bill and Dorothy since the 1950's. He said, " When I became Board President after Bill Becker died, Dorothy promised to give me the same support she had given Bill. During the 13 years that I was Board president, she never reneged on that promise." A bareley visible tear moistened Dorothy's eyes as she listened to his conciliatory words. When the applause subsided, Gerry Franks took the microphone.

Gary Franks recounted his attempt to dissuade Dorothy from accepting the director's position the Board had offered her in 1963. At that time he was convinced that the youthful, charming Dorothy would remarry in the near future. The Home needed a director for the long term. He knew that she had never forgiven him for this mistaken assumption. He asked the audience, "How was I to know she would marry Selfhelp?" She laughed and conceded that he couldn't have known what was engraved on her heart.

Front: Leni and Rolf Weil, Kate and Klaus Ollendorff, Dorothy Becker
Back: Herbert Roth - Board President and Else Roth, Gerry and Louise Franks, Hedy Strauss

Rolf Weil rose to speak. He credited Dorothy Becker with selling the idea of a Selfhelp Home to the Neighborhood Groups. He considered her a great leader because she had the ability to communicate her vision to others. Not only did she convince hundreds of people to work for Selfhelp, but she never let go of them again. He said that Dorothy was not only a superb administrator, but the residents trusted her like a mother. She was a teacher and confidant to her employees, and she had a social worker's understanding of families. Board of Health inspectors wrote glowing reports when Dorothy gave them a tour of the Home. Last but not least, she was and remained the organization's top fund raiser. Rolf Weil's tribute that evening concluded as follows:

"Mrs. Becker's talents are many, but her most pronounced quality has been that of warmth and human understanding. Her ability to provide a social service based not only on narrowly professional considerations but with a 'heart' distinguished her from most others in the field.

"Her 25 years of service as Executive Director has been unique and will never be duplicated. Her tireless work ranging from hospital visits with the ill and the consolation of the bereaved to the preparation for religious and secular holidays and the arranging for the celebration of happy events has been exemplary.

"There is no recognition that can fully acknowledge the great contributions that Dorothy Becker has made to our community and the example that she has set for all of us which we can only hope to emulate partially. She has truly been what the Bible calls, *'A Woman of valor.'*" With Rolf Weil's words engraved on her heart, Dorothy Becker retired on November 27, 1987.

12

AFTER RETIREMENT

After 26 years, Dorothy Becker cleared her desk, vacated her office and went back to being a full time volunteer. The person sitting at the desk across from Dorothy, busy sorting mail was Dorothy's longtime friend and colleague, Marlise Katzenstein. She handed Dorothy a letter from Dr Walter Friedlander, Selfhelp's first president. Reading his letter, Dorothy smiled and said, "After he retired he was just as busy as before. Students come and ask him for advice. It's good for him too. If you're old and you're busy eight hours a day, that's the nicest situation anybody can have."

Marlise handed Dorothy another letter from one of her favorite people. Evelyn Redel Heidke, who had worked as a high school student in Dorothy's department at Mandel Brothers, never once in 42 years had forgotten to write her for Christmas. Years later, she credited Dorothy with her promotion at Mandel Brothers where she met both of her husbands. In her letter of February 16, 2000, she wrote,

"When I mentioned to Dorothy that I was not pleased with the hours I was required to work, she spoke to her boss and I was hired to work in the Executive Offices. My two marriages and two children were all a result of Dorothy speaking out for me. My memories of Dorothy are lovingly cherished by me."

Dorothy recalled that, "At Rosh Hashonah, I received a letter from a daughter whose mother, Friedel, died 50 years earlier. Shortly before Friedel died, she wrote me a letter in which she asked me to please think of her once in a while after she was gone. I think of her everyday," said Dorothy.

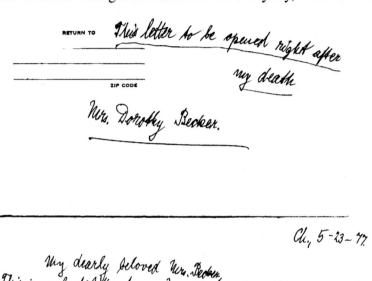

RETURN TO

This letter to be opened right after my death

ZIP CODE

Mrs. Dorothy Becker.

Ch., 5-23-77

My dearly beloved Mrs. Becker,

This is my last letter to you. I just wrote to my children that I want you to sit with the family during funeral and Yiskor services. At the same time I want to thank you once more for your kindness and understanding, for your friendship and love. I cannot write more, because I just cannot concentrate, and my feelings run away with me.

I wish you all the best and all the happiness in the world. And, please, think once in a while of your little friend

Frieda.

"Whenever I'm invited where there are 50 people, at least ten of them had some body ·who lived in the Home. They ask me if I remember when this or that happened. Luckily I have a good memory."

Many of the children of parents who had spent their last years at Selfhelp continued to make donations to Selfhelp in honor of Dorothy Becker. Dorothy was taken by surprise when a woman, named "Gayla," made a substantial bequest to Selfhelp "in honor of Dorothy Becker."

Dorothy had known Gayla for years but Dorothy confessed, "She wasn't my cup of tea. About two years earlier, another couple had willed all of their furniture to Selfhelp. I asked my friend Hedy to go with me to sort out the furniture. I said it's not a nice job, but it may be interesting. We wore old clothes because we knew there was work to do.

Rabbi Steve Westman and Marian Shaffer in 1995

"Here came Gayla, beautifully dressed in a black dress wearing long white gloves. She started to tell us what to do: 'You should clean this out first; you should put that here.' I told her: ' You either work or you don't stay here! Unfortunately we have to empty the apartment, but we don't need advice. I've done this several times before.' Gayla told me that she was allowed to take something. 'Go right ahead, I said.' She took a little picture.

309

When she died, she left us lots of money. Rolf Weil asked, 'Was she a friend of yours?' I told him: 'No, she was not my friend, but she wasn't all bad."

Dorothy never tired of celebrating birthdays including her own. "My 82nd birthday party at the Angus Restaurant was so nice. I couldn't believe that they were talking about me. It seemed like they were talking about a saint. Everybody talked about what I did for them. It was so good what everyone said. I feel bad to hear all of these things because I got as much out of what I did as they did. I felt as if it was a eulogy."

Bob, Mary and Aaron Shaffer in August 2003

"I had a beautiful 85th birthday party at the Ambassador West Hotel. Louise Franks planned it. Marian was there, Steve, my nephew, came in from

Florida. Bob, my grandson, his wife Mary, and their son, Aaron were there. Ron and Vicky were there. About 250 people were there and every one came up to me and asked me if I remembered their mother, grandfather, aunt or uncle. Thousands of people have lived at Selfhelp since we built the original Home, and I remembered every one of them."

"Shortly after my birthday party, I visited Ella Rothschild in the Nursing Care Facility. It was the first time I almost cried. She was the first woman I befriended when I came to this country. She had made the collection boxes that we used to collect money for the Selfhelp Home. She asked me, "Where do you live now?" It was heart breaking for me. She was such an alert intelligent woman. She was 95. She's entitled to be confused, but it doesn't fit her at all. With some, I see it coming; but with her it really hit me. She was perfectly fine before. When I left she asked, 'How are you going to get home now?' It broke my heart."

Dorothy lamented the dwindling number of volunteers. Old age and death had diminished their ranks. Times had changed. More women were working full time. Administrators may find volunteers more difficult to supervise than paid employees. Some employees worked well with volunteers; others, in their well-paying jobs, considered volunteers a threat. Dorothy compared Selfhelp without volunteers to a body without a soul, and declared, "If that ever happens, I hope I'm not alive to see it."

But the Home came alive with the arrival of Jan Schultheiss, a young volunteer straight from Germany. At age 19, Jan was not only the youngest person at the Home but he was born decades *after* the Nazi era. To some of the older refugees, Jan didn't seem quite kosher. But with understanding, tolerance and subtle humor, he soon won over the most guarded residents, including Dorothy Becker. She, Mitzi Marx and a group of residents planned a surprise for Jan on Christmas morning in 1998, when they gathered outside his apartment and woke him up with a harmonious rendition of, "Silent Night Holy Night," in both English and German.

From Left: Dorothy Becker, Mitzi Marx, Alma and Richard Herbst,
Marga Bachenheimer, Ruth Heilbrun, Kora Kaufman, Mildred Sacks.

The highlight of Dorothy's life were the visits from Marian, her grandchildren and great grandchildren.

"My grandson Ron went to Colorado before his graduation. He lived there and studied journalism. He wrote for the newspapers. He wrote articles and took tours with the people. He liked it, but he really wanted to study music. He took me up the mountains. It was terribly hard because my husband loved mountains so much. Marian is like her father; she loves mountains. She was

a great help to me! I hope that I can be a source of strength for Marian. I'm so glad she is so close with her children and grandchildren. She is such a fantastic mother. She is a better mother than I am."

Dorothy Becker's Family   (Photo taken by Jonathan White)
Front: Zach, Marisa and Lori - Back: Marian, Vicky (holding Isabelle) and Ron

Shortly thereafter, Dorothy suffered a stroke and was taken to Weiss Memorial Hospital where she had sat so many nights with sick residents. Many of the nurses recognized Dorothy and said, "You're the woman who always brought the people and waited until they were admitted." The nurses knew her and took care of her as if she were a member of the family.

The stroke had left her speech impaired but she seemed to recognize Marian who sat by her mother's bedside until the end. She did not appear to be suffering, and without struggling, Dorothy Becker died on April 17, 1999.

Researchers Discover The Spirit of Selfelp

Dorothy, the modern woman with uniquely Victorian morals, would be pleased to know that the founder of the "National Organization for Women," Betty Friedan, as well as many other researchers, have substantiated what Dorothy tried to prove decades earlier that, "Old age is not simply a series of losses but that older people can live a satisfactory, dynamic life." [Appendix Z^7]

After extensive interviews and reviews of the literature, Betty Friedan agrees that most seniors do not see themselves as dependent, helpless victims. She wrote, "I was appalled by the overwhelming preoccupation of gerontologists with nursing homes and their sick, passive, childlike and ever more deteriorating, senile patients, when only 5 percent of people over 65 were, in fact, in nursing homes." Friedan questions whether, " we should choose to live our later years in terms of that dreaded 'mystique' of deterioration and decline - which happens to most only in the months before death, if it happens at all. Or should we live the life we want to lead realizing full well that we have the potential for both decline and growth, and that our life will end in death?" [11]

Dorothy referred to the age stereotype in her "Annual Report" of 1973-1974: *"When people think of the aged they usually have the image of a helpless old individual who needs assistance. Most of our residents are mature and able to function. They must not be made useless."* Yet many well-meaning caretakers promote helplessness in the elderly. [Appendix AA^1]

The research by Margaret Bates indicates that "Independent behaviors engaged in by the elderly, twice as often elicited a "dependent - supportive" response from the caretakers. The explicit objective of the institution was to promote and maintain independence as long as possible, but the staff nonetheless, tended mainly to reward dependent behavior."[12]

According to Betty Friedan, the professionals and administrators of a dozen nations at the Salzburg Conference did not want to look at older people in terms of work or productivity. "They ignored Butler Borg and Jim Birren's strong statistical evidence that most older people do not decline in mental or even physical abilities before their eighties, if they remain active in the communities."[13]

Productivity

Dorothy knew from experience that older people could learn new skills. At the Annual Meeting, she asked, " *How many of our residents handled a switchboard or an intercom system and how many took painting lessons or went to gym classes before they moved into the Home?*" She concluded, "*I believe that people stay younger at Selfhelp because we expect them to help with many chores.*" [Appendix BB[1]]

The large study done by Baltes and Kriege included 50-75 percent of all the people 50 - 80 years old living in Berlin and in rural Pennsylvania. Their research showed that growth and deterioration of the brain occur, not just in old age, but throughout life, depending on environmental stimulation.

Baltes concluded, "Certainly there is decline in old age. However, for most normal elderly people there is also great reserve capacity that enhances the potential for new learning and growth... If provided with cognitive enrich-

315

ment and practice, most elderly people up to age 75 and older are capable of remarkable gains in intellectual performance, including memory, where the typical expectation is one of early decline."[14]

"And do *we* have an *enrichment program!*" said Dorothy. Here are just a few excerpts from the "Report of Executive Director, April 1,1984": *"Dr. Hans Frey, our beloved art teacher, retired after 20 years, much to our regret. We were fortunate to find a very able successor in Mr. Charles Freund.*

"We have lots of parties and entertainment. We are grateful to Mrs. Miriam Levi who is always contacting new entertainers. In our midst, we have a professional pianist, Mrs. Paula Staples, our so-talented MC, Anna Hirsch, and Mr. Hausler, our house poet. Many of our residents who never in their lives had given speeches before, come forward now and take the microphone, much to the surprise of their families."

Dorothy understood that every type of productive activity, e.g. chores, new skills, new hobbies and socializing, enhances physical, mental and emotional health. At Selfhelp, people felt needed and appreciated which enhanced their self esteem and enabled them to maintain control of their lives. At the "Annual Meeting in 1973-1974," Dorothy reflected on these ideas: *"Most of our residents are mature and, like younger people, they prefer to make their own decisions. They must not be made useless. Feeling unneeded is often more painful than physical discomfort."* [Appendix AA^2]

Betty Friedan came to similar conclusions. She wrote, "Much research has shown that the most important predictors of vital age are satisfying work, regardless if it is for pay or not.

Those who continue working at jobs that have become mindless and routine forfeit the fountain of age. The possibilities of continued growth can be seen whenever older people continue in work that demands mindfulness."[15]

Control

Ellen Langer of Harvard, and Judith Rodin of Yale, did an experiment on "control" at one of the best nursing homes in Connecticut, where the patients, aged 65 to 90, were randomly assigned to two different floors. The patients on one floor were told by the administrator: "You should be deciding how you want your rooms to be arranged, whether you want to rearrange the furniture, and how you want to spend your time. You can decide which movies to see or not to see." They were asked to choose a plant they wanted to take care of.

The residents on the other floor were told: "We've tried to make your rooms as nice as they can be… We want to do all we can to help you… We're showing some movies next week. We'll let you know which night you're scheduled to go. Each resident was handed a plant to keep, but the nurses will water and take care of them for you."

Three weeks later, the first group showed a significant improvement in alertness, activity and general well-being, as rated by nurses and themselves, while the comparison group showed a negative change. All but one of the active group showed improvement in physical and mental well-being, whereas only 21 percent of the comparison group showed any improvement. This study suggested that, "some of the negative consequences of aging may be retarded, reversed or possibly prevented by returning to the aged the right to feel competent and make their own decisions."[16]

A year and a half later, when Langer and Rodin returned to the nursing home, only 7 of the 47 residents (15 percent) who had watered their own plants and chosen their own movies had died. Twice that number (30 percent) - 13 out of 44 - had died in the group where the nurses did these things for them. There had been no other difference between the two groups, who originally had roughly the same overall health status and had been institutionalized the same amount of time. The survivors who exercised their own choices were now significantly superior to the others on measures of physical and psychological health.[17]

From these studies, John Rowe, then head of Harvard Medical School's Division on Aging, concluded: "To the extent that older people are placed in situations where they lack control over their lives, and to the extent that the forms of support available to them are not control-enhancing, we would predict resultant physiologic changes… with consequent increases in morbidity and passivity."[18]

Integration vs. Depression

Dorothy spent her life building family and community to alleviate isolation and depression. At the "Annual Meeting" on February 20, 1962, she told about, *"An elderly man in another nursing home who suffered from depression. Some of our Selfhelp volunteers and I visited the man, and at first he didn't react to any of our friendly gestures. Life had been too hard for him.*

He said, 'I don't believe in miracles. Why should Selfhelp volunteers be any different from other human beings?'

"Gradually, we got closer to him. He started to come to our Senior Center. Some of the volunteers visited him and they also picked him up and took him to various places. With the change in his mental attitude, his physical ailment didn't seem insurmountable anymore. He began to look forward to moving into our new Home. He appreciated all the kindness that had been extended to him. He not only became active in the group, but was a friend to many. When he passed away he was mourned by many. Through teamwork, we did the impossible!" [Appendix CC[1]]

The study by Margaret Gatz revealed that, "Mental health professionals more frequently recommended drugs than psychotherapy to treat depression in older patients because they believed that psychotherapy is less effective with the elderly. There is no evidence to support this belief. On the contrary, studies show that psychotherapy is quite effective for treating depression; but mental health professionals are more likely to use drugs exclusively to treat depression in the elderly.

Margaret Gatz also found that religious experience that gives meaning to life can help reduce some of the anxiety that accompanies depression.[19] Dorothy understood the importance of religion to the total well-being of the residents and expressed appreciation to, *"Our Mr. Steiermann, the Chairman of the Religious Committee as well as to Mr. Nussbaum and Mr. Hausler. Religion means a lot to the majority of our residents and even the so-called non-believers enjoy the services."*

Above all, the extended hand of friendship, the best antidote to depression, best represents the "Spirit of Selfhelp. At the "Annual Meeting" on April 1, 1984, Dorothy proudly reported, *"Our Home is an example to many. Wherever I go, people rave about our Home. Our residents and their families are the best advertisers. While privacy plays a great role in everyone's life, they all feel secure and know that in case of emergency they can press a button and get help.*

"We have constant inspections. The reports are always excellent and the State of Illinois gives us an extra bonus for being one of the most outstanding homes in Illinois. But our reputation didn't just happen - we worked hard to achieve it."

Independence

Dorothy, whose work depended on the support of the German Jewish community , would probably be as impressed as Betty Friedan was with, "The sense of community that pervades the Live Oaks Home in Oakland, California." Friedan explains, "There's more interaction with family, friends, the people in the independent living section and those in the community. The staff lives at the Home," and writes Friedan " I was struck by the "joie de vivre" of the staff as compared to the oppressive, professional cheeriness of a nursing home staff. I was struck too by the comfort level of the able-bodied residents as they pushed the wheelchairs of the infirm people."

Friedan explained, "Here everyday is different and the elders with disabilities still want to be in charge of their lives. Even people with

Alzheimer's need an opportunity to function and to have choices. The belief is that when people are able to take control of their lives they can get better. The people there probably had the same range of disabilities as in any nursing home, and most were in their eighties. But the ambiance was of a lively, living community. It was a little messy, a little sloppy, but the people, even those using walkers and in wheelchairs, seemed alive and somehow part of each other."[20]

Dorothy maintained that, *"So far almost everyone has felt the warmth and security that permeates our Home and they contribute by being helpful as well. Group living is not for everyone; it is only for those whose lives can be enriched by caring for other people."*

Attachment

Friedan found that, " Since caring, intimacy and love are key to vital aging versus decline, we must be able to evolve beyond the sexual and family ties of youth. The ability to sustain or create bonds beyond the family was an even more important factor than family bonds in successful aging in some studies. Patients' ratings of their recovery from heart attacks, injuries and cancer have been linked to "supportive behavior" from friends, relatives and members of social groups. Women's longevity seems to be related to the bonds of friendship women are able to sustain or recreate."

According to Rowe and Kahn, "The life-and-death importance of friendship was also revealed in studies over many years showing that widowers are 40 percent more likely to die in the first six months after their spouse's death than other men their age. The widower's mortality rate returns to that of other men if he remarries - or after he survives five years alone."[21]

The critical importance of friendship, autonomy and control over one's life to vital aging underscores the close link that exists between physical and mental health. Medical researchers have found that leukemia, cervical cancer and heart disease are linked to a feeling of hopelessness before the onset of the disease. A number of studies have shown that social isolation and feeling helpless contributes to immune deficiencies resulting in lowered resistance to infections.

People agreed when Dorothy said, *"Everyone who enters our Home immediately feels the spirit that prevails, the affection that our residents have for each other. It is with great sincerity that Mrs. Wolf and I thank the members of the two Senior Groups for the socials they plan to make 150-200 elderly friends happy. To see all these elderly people happily united every week would be reward enough, but our people visit and send cards to their elderly friends when they're in the hospital. They even call their families to inquire about them."* [Appendix Z']

Dorothy concluded the *"Annual Meeting" of April 1, 1984 with these words,* *"Again I want to thank every one who works for our Home in whatever capacity, but most of all, our residents whose love gives me the strength to make my sometimes strenuous and difficult job so gratifying. I feel that my love for them is reciprocated by all of them and I hope I will never disappoint them. I hope that I can prove that Old Age is not simply a series of losses only, but that older people can live satisfactory and dynamic lives."* [Appendix Z[7]]

And that is the Spirit of Selfhelp speaking.

SOME OF SELFHELP'S MANY VOLUNTEERS

LIST OF VOLUNTEERS SUBMITTED BY MITZI MARX

1998

Volunteers – Health Care Floors - 7th & 8th:

Edith Strauss – Ruth Markus – Leonore (Lee) Fine - Philip Grundland – Mitzi Marx - Gretel Oppenheimer visited infirm residents for 25 years.

Volunteers Clara Mellekson and Leonore (Lee) Fine

Sewing Name Tags in Clothes:

Kora Kaufmann - Toby Levin – Ruth Heilbrunn – Greta Oppenheimer

Switchboard:

Mina Jonas – Ilse Katzmann - Ilse Lewin, volunteered for 20 years.

Volunteer Eva Grossman

Knitting:

Eva Grossman

Tile Trays:

Rachel Bensinger – Liesel Melber

Volunteers Trude Bing and Ruth Bluethe

Gift Shop:

Trude Bing - Ruth Bluethe - Hedy Strauss – Rosel Stein – Grete Friend – Lilo Wolf – Inge Forst - Esther Mainzer – Lizzy Faff – Ilse Siegler – Liesel Melber

Computer Operators:

Ilse Katzmann – Margot Hertz – Ilse Glaser – Marianne Weinberg –
Ilse Caim

Working with Donations:

Dorothy Becker - Marlise Katzenstein – Gerda Gareny - Elsbeth Salomon

Calling Out Bingo and Other Games:

Annie Gilbert

Volunteer Donna Broder in action

Drivers For Shopping:

Donna Broder – Michael Bayer – Marlene Aufrecht - Martin Lewin

House Committee:

Margot Meyer

Friends of Selfhelp:

Louise Franks

Planting Flowers and Caring For Them:

Margot Meyer – Mina Jonas - Hilde Wiesenfelder

Kaffee Klatsches and Birthday Parties:

Marianne Weinberg

Marian Shaffer with Volunteer Jan Schultheiss in Wyoming

Volunteer From Germany Working With Activity Director:

Jan Schultheiss

LIST OF VOLUNTEERS SUBMITTED BY MITZI MARX

1990

Volunteers Annie Vollmer and Sari Hirsen

Volunteers for:

Switchboard	*Newsletter*
Gift Shop	*Tile Instruction*
Health Care Floors	*Knitting and Crocheting*
Donations to be Processed	*Current Event Class*
Counseling Residents	*Kaffee Klatsch*
Planned Resident Entertainment	*Membership Bills to be Sent Out*
Dietician	*Planting Flowers on Roof Garden*
Newsletter	*Religious Committee*
"The Selfhelper" -	*Computer*
Resident Newspaper	*Drivers: Shopping, Appointments*

May Party Volunteers:

Clare Jericho - Fannie Grunbecker - Sylvia Bartenstein - Lore Frank -

Margot Meyer

Volunteer Lore Frank

Volunteers in Mrs. Loewengart's Clothes Closet:

Dr. Paul and Elsa Hofman

Other Volunteers:

Board of Directors, House Committee, Admissions Committee, Aid and

Scholarship Committees

Switchboard Volunteers:

Ilse Katzmann – Sonya Duke – Edith Sternfeld – Jean Heiman - Paula

Brandis – Ilse Cohn – Ulrich Hork

Ruth and Bruno Fischer – Margot Hertz – Eva Grossman – Gertrude Baran

Volunteers Lillian Bernheimer and Hanna Adler

Resident Volunteers:

Lilian Bernheimer – Mina Jonas – Anny Meyer

Sending Out Donations:

Dorothy Becker – Marlise Katzenstein – Gerda Gareny – Harold Raff

Buying Jewelry for Gift Shop, Getting Chanukkah Presents for

Residents and Running Errands:

Inge Burg – Lilo Wolf

Knitting Baby Clothes for Gift Shop:

Mrs. Walter Friedlieb – Fanny Adler (also aprons and bibs for health care

floors) Bea Spear (crochets) – Gerda Schild (sews scarves for gift shop)

Religious Committee:

Mr. Nussbaum – Dr. Heinz Graupe – Mr. and Mrs. Arnold Levy (made

Kiddush on health care floors every Friday night)

Transportation Volunteers (Doctor appointments, shopping, etc.):

Walter Friedlieb – Eric Heiman – Donna Broder

Volunteer Sonya Duke

Drivers to Funerals:

Lisa and Al Jacobs – Leo Jacobs - Genta and Kurt Hirsch - Lilo Wolf -

Werner Levy – Sonya Duke - Debbie Arendt

Volunteer Debbie Arendt

Gift Shop Volunteers:

Martin Marx (ordering, bookkeeping, etc.) – Beate Alsberg – Inge Forst –
Grete Friend – Selma Marx – Lilo Mullerheim – Lizzie Raff –
Irene Schweitzer – Lisa Jacobs – Sally Loewenthal (showcase decorator)

Resident Volunteers:

Steffie Lax – Trude Bing – Ruth Bluethe – Meta Hirsch – Anny Vollmer –
Hanna Adler – Mina Jonas (pricing merchandise) - Ilse Siegler

Program Chairman:

Miriam Levi (bringing entertainment to Home: concerts, book reviews,
Lincoln Park Zoo, etc.)

Dr. Bernard Baum (engages musical groups for May Party, annual
fundraising party, usually given on 1st Sunday in May)

Editing "Newsletter":

Marlise Katzenstein

Sending Out Annual Membership Bills:

Marlise Katzenstein – Harold Raff

Dietician:

Rosel Stein

Visiting and Counseling Residents:

Irmgard Heymann – Leonore (Lee) Fine

Volunteers of the Now Discontinued Thursday Kaffee Klatsch:

Elly Dukas – Irene Heins – Clare Fleischhacker – Edith Felsenthal –
Gerda Dreier – Edith Gross – Erna Spaeth – Ruth Gideon – Eva Passon–
Margo Schloss (resident)

Kaffeeklatsch Volunteers - Tuesday:

In charge: Nancy Strauss (buys cakes)

Margot Lowenberg – Friedl Newman – Tony White – Sonya Crasso –

Sclea Kantor – Paula Cohn – Rosel Newman – Rosel Sachsel –

Edith Gerngross

Printing, Delivering, Stationary and Garden Party Hosting Volunteers:

Elsa and Hans Levi

Current Event Discussions:

Irene Ernst (once a week – Monday)

Instructions with Knitting and Crocheting:

Eva Grossman – Doris Baer

Instructions with Tile Work:

Rachel Bensinger – Liesel Melber

Mending Clothes on Health Care Foors for Residents Without Family:

Greta Oppenheimer – Elly Dukas – Bertha Zucker

Editing Home Newspaper "The Selfhelper":

Lucille Hauser

Library Volunteers:

Debbie Arendt – Lucille Hauser

Willing to Help Residents with Medicare Papers:

Julius Strauss

Bibliography

1. Craig, Gordon A., GERMANY 1866 - 1945

   (New York: Oxford University Press, 1978). p.406.

2. Ibid., p. 409.

3. Adler, H.G., THE JEWS OF GERMANY

   (Indiana: University of Notre Dame Press, 1969). p. 130.

4. Laquer, Walter, WEIMAR, A CULTURAL HISTORY

   (New York: G. P. Putnam's Sons, 1974). p. 77.

5. Craig, op. cit., p. 573.

6. Schwerin, Kurt, SELFHELP OF CHICAGO, INC.

   SELFHELP HOME FOR THE GED, INC.

   (Chicago: Selfhelp of Chicago, 1989). p. 4.

7. Ibid., p. 4

8. Bowlby, John, ATTACHMENT AND LOSS

   (New Your: Basic Books, 1969 - 1980).

9. Schwerin, op. cit., p. 9.

10. Schwerin, op. cit., p. 14.

11. Friedan, Betty, THE FOUNTAIN OF AGE

    (New York: Simon & Schuster, 1994). pp. 381, 510.

12. Bates, Margret M. and Wahl, Hans-Werner, "The Dependency –
    Support Script in Institutions: Generalization to Community
    Settings," Psychology and Aging, Vol. 7(3) September 1992,
    pp. 409-418.

13. Friedan, op. cit., p. 199.

14. Baltes, P. B. and Kliege, R., "On the Dynamics Between Growth and Decline in the Aging of Intelligence and Memory," in Neurology, K. Poech, et al., eds. (Berlin: Springer Verlag, 1986). p. 8.

15. Friedan, op. cit., p. 222.

16. Langer, Ellen and Rodin, Judith, "The Effects of Choice and Enhanced Personal Responsibility for the Aged: A Field Experiment in an Institutional Setting," Journal of Personality and Social Psychology, vol. 34, no. 2 (1976). pp. 897-902.

17. Langer, Ellen and Rodin, Judith, "Long Term Effects of a Control-Related Deterioration with the Institutional Aged," Journal of Personality and Social Psychology, vol. 35, no 12 (1977) pp. 897-902.

18. Friedan, op. cit., p. 92.

19. Gatz, Margaret, "Ageism Revised and the Provision of Psychological Services," American Psychologist, vol. 43(3) (March 1988) pp. 184-188.

20. Friedan, op. cit., pp. 524-526.

21. Rowe, John and Kahn, Robert, "Human Aging: Usual and Successful," Science (July 1987).

Appendix A[1]

Westmann, Sally in Das Judische Addressbuch in Berlin in 1910

Wertheim, Julius, Rechtsanwalt, Schöneberg, Würzburger Str. 16
Wertheim, Karl, Neu-Tempelhof, Braunschweiger Ring 178
Wertheim, Kurt, W 62, Courbièrestraße 11
Wertheim, Dr. Kurt, Charlottenburg 4, Dahlmannstr. 5
Wertheim, Leon, N 24, Oranienburger Str. 42/43
Wertheim, Leonhard, Dahlem, Auf dem Grat 4
Wertheim, Martha und Paula, N 20, Bastianstr. 20
Wertheim, Max, Charlottenburg 2, Niebuhrstr. 77
Wertheim, Max, Wilmersdorf, Zähringerstr. 14
Wertheim, Oskar, Schmargendorf, Kissinger Str. 14/15
Wertheim, Paula, W 30, Barbarossastr. 23
Wertheim, Recha, N 24, Große Hamburger Str. 30
Wertheim, Rosa, Charlottenburg 4, Dahlmannstr. 4
Wertheim, Rudi, Charlottenburg 2, Goethestr. 1
Wertheim, Siegmund, W 50, Prager Str. 15
Wertheim, Dr. Sigfried, Charlottenburg, Rankestr. 23
Wertheim, Dr. Theodor, San.-Rat, W 15, Meinekestr. 5
Wertheim, Therese, W 35, Magdeburger Str. 26
Wertheim, Wilhelm, Dahlem, Messelstr. 19
Wertheimer, Alfred, SO 36, Beverustr. 6
Wertheimer, Bertha, Dahlem, Gustav-Meyer-Str. 6
Wertheimer, Cilly, Halensee, Markgraf-Albrecht-Str. 6
Wertheimer, Dorothea, Wilmersdorf, Badensche Str. 41
Wertheimer, Ernst, Rechtsanwalt, W 30, Rosenheimer Str. 19
Wertheimer, Gertrud, W 35, Genthiner Str. 29
Wertheimer, Gisela, Wilmersdorf, Mannheimer Str. 38
Wertheimer, H., Halensee, Hektorstraße 8
Wertheimer, Heinrich, W 15, Kaiserallee 206
Wertheimer, Hermann, SO 36, Moosdorfstr. 12
Wertheimer, Hugo, W 15, Pariser Straße 14
Wertheimer, Karolina, Wilmersdorf, Güntzelstr. 48
Wertheimer, Leo, W 62, Kalckreuthstr. 10
Wertheimer, Leo, C 2, Neue Friedrichstr. 59
Wertheimer, Louis, NO 55, Hufelandstr. 6
Wertheimer, Martin, Wilmersdorf, Wilhelmsaue 138
Wertheimer, Otto, Wilmersdorf, Wittelsbacherstr. 5
Wertheimer, Paul, W 30, Rosenheimer Str. 36
Wertheimer, Siegfried, NW 40, Alexanderufer 6
Werthen, Genia, W 30, Rosenheimer Str. 3
Werthen, Michael, W 30, Rosenheimer Str. 3
Werther, Arthur, W 15, Bayerische Straße 31, b. Seligsohn

Werther, Hans, NW 21, Wilsnacker Straße 49
Werther, Dr. Julius, Charlottenburg, Windscheidtstr. 11
Werther, Oskar, Charlottenburg, Weimarer Str. 27
Werther, Dr. Rudolf, Charlottenburg 4, Sybelstr. 7
Wesche, Otto, N 24, Friedrichstraße 107
Wesche, Selma, N 24, Friedrichstraße 107
Weschler, Leib, C 25, Münzstr. 26
von Wesleraku, Ida, Schöneberg, Feurigstr. 52
Wesse, Else, Charlottenburg 4, Pestalozzistr. 10
Wessel, Oskar, W 10, Friedrich-Wilhelm-Str. 6
Wessolowski, Anna, W 50, Passauer Str. 34
von Westerhagen, Julia, W 62, Landgrafenstr. 4
Westermann, Isidor, Wilmersdorf, Kaiserallee 169
Westermann, Markus, W 30, Motzstr. 71
Westermann, Rebeka, N 24, Friedrichstr. 114
Westermann, Tobias, Wilmersdorf, Nikolsburger Platz 11
Westfried, Elisabeth und Jos., W 35, Magdeburger Str. 21
Westheim, Paul, Wilmersdorf, Hindenburgstr. 96
Westheimer, Alex, W 50, Ansbacher Str. 16
Westheimer, Isak, Wilmersdorf, Mecklenburgische Str. 21/22
Westheimer, Max, S 14, Neue Jakobstr. 12
Westheimer, Moritz, N 58, Danziger Str. 96
Westmann, SW 11, Stresemannstraße 84
Westmann, Dora, NW 87, Altonaer Straße 2
Westmann, Else, W 10, Friedrich-Wilhelm-Str. 6 a
Westmann, Julius, Lankwitz, Viktoriastr. 60

Westmann, Sally, O 17, Gr. Frankfurter Str. 4

Westmann, Dr. Stephan, W 15, Kurfürstendamm 22
Westphal, Frau, O 34, Thaerstr. 19
Westphal, Dora, NO 55, Elbinger Straße 60
Westphal, Erna, N 24, Elsasser Straße 76 a
Westphal, Lina, N 58, Schliemannstraße 12
Westphal, Margarete, N 57, Yorckstr. 42
Westphalen, Elise, Friedrichshagen, Waldowstr. 8
Westreich, J., Wilmersdorf, Babelsberger Str. 6, b. Altmann
Westreich, Meyer, N 24, Oranienburger Str. 66
Westreich, Samuel, N 54, Lothringer Str. 99
Westreich, Sara, N 54, Lothringer Straße 99
Wetscher, Paula, N 54, Grenadierstraße 14
Wetscher, Sophie, N 54, Grenadierstraße 14
Wettborn, Frieda, O 17, Rüdersdorfer Str. 36

Wetter, Erna, NO 55, Danziger Straße 37
Wetter, Julius, NO 55, Danziger Straße 37
Wetterhahn, Käte, N 54, Auguststraße 48
Wetterhahn, Riekchen, Halensee, Westfälische Str. 70
Wetterling, Toni, NW 87, Leasingstraße 41
Wetzlar, Eugen, Charlottenburg 4, Leibnizstr. 58
Wetzlar, Gustav, Charlottenburg, Sybelstr. 11
Wetzlar, Rieka, W 15, Bayerische Straße 34
Wetzler, Cäcilie, O 27, Paul-Singer-Straße 93
Wetzler, Johanna, C 2, Klosterstraße 10
Wetzler, Paul, W 50, Neue Ansbacher Str. 11
Wexberg, Else, W 30, Neue Winterfeldtstr. 18
Wexberg, Harald, Charlottenburg, Dahlmannstr. 25
Wexberg, James, Wilmersdorf, Konstanzer Str. 50
Wexberg, Kurt, W 30, Berchtesgadener Str. 59/49
Wexberg, Siegfried, O 112, Rigaer Straße 67
Weyl, Clara, W 30, Luitpoldstr. 30
Weyl, Elly, Charlottenburg 5, Kaiserdamm 4
Weyl, Else, W 30, Bamberger Straße 47
Weyl, Frieda, Friedenau, Südwestkorso 61
Weyl, Louis, C 2, An der Spandauer Brücke 14
Weyl, Ludwig, NW 87, Jagowstraße 44
Weyl, Dr. Max, NO 55, Heinrich-Roller-Str. 26
Weyl, Siegfried, SO 36, Kottbusser Ufer 47
Wezrujtnski, Helene, Charlottenburg 4, Wielandstr. 15
White, Peggy, W 15, Letzenburger Str. [...]

Wiebler, Hermann, NO 55, Woldenberger Str. 28
Wiekert, Marie, Charlottenburg 2, Knesebeckstr. 16
Wiekrun, Mordka, C 25, Bartelstraße 6
Widawer, Georg, Charlottenburg 2, Bismarckstr. 10
Widawski, Samuel, O 17, Koppenstraße 95
Widder, Frieda, N 58, Lychener Straße 133
Widmann, Josef, NO 43, Mendelssohnstr. 12
Widmann, Markus, SW 59, Krankenhaus Am Urban
Widmann, Moritz, W 50, Regensburger Str. 5 a
Wiebe, Karl, NW 6, Karlstr. 10
Wiechmann, Hedwig, Neukölln, Jansostr. 6
Wiedemann, Margarete, Wilmersdorf, Detmolder Str. 21
Wieder, Adolf, Halensee, Kurfürstendamm 108/09
Wieder, Hanny, Halensee, Kurfürstendamm 106/07

Wieger, Camilla, Wilmersdorf, Landhausstr. 37
Wiehe, Klara, O 112, Holteistr. 11
Wieluner, Dr. Fritz, Rechtsanwalt, W 30, Stübbenstr. 8
Wieluner, Moritz, SW 61, Urbanstraße 141
Wien, Rosa, W 15, Emser Str. 39 b
Wiener, Adolf, W 62, Landgrafenstraße 6
Wiener, Adolf, Wilmersdorf, Pommersche Str. 15/16
Wiener, Adolf, SW 19, Seydelstraße 16
Wiener, Adolfine, Südende, Stephanstr. 6
Wiener, Albert, Pankow, Berliner Straße 47
Wiener, Alexander, Charlottenburg 5, Witzlebenplatz 5
Wiener, Dr. Alfred, W 15, Brandenburgische Str. 40
Wiener, Alfred, N 4, Chausseestraße 16
Wiener, Alfred, C 25, Kaiser-Wilhelm-Str. 32
Wiener, Dr. Alfred, N 24, Oranienburger Str. 16
Wiener, Dr. Alfred, Charlottenburg, Zilckistr. 3
Wiener, Amalie, Halensee, Johann-Georg-Str. 16
Wiener, Anna, Charlottenburg 4, Wielandstr. 6
Wiener, Aron, N 54, Fehrbelliner Straße 18
Wiener, Arthur, Charlottenburg 4, Roscherstr. 3
Wiener, Berta, W 30, Aschaffenburger Str. 7
Wiener, Bertha, N 65, Exerzierstraße 13
Wiener, Berthold, Charlottenburg 4, Mommsenstr. 46
Wiener, Dr. Betty, Steglitz, Promenadenstr. 10
Wiener, Camill, N 58, Rheinsberger Str. 43/45
Wiener, Clara, N 58, Choriner Straße 30
Wiener, David, N 54, Schönhauser Allee 173
Wiener, Doris, W 35, Lützowstraße 54
Wiener, Erich, S 14, Alexandrinenstraße 78
Wiener, Ernst, W 57, Potsdamer Straße 73 c
Wiener, Ernst, Wilmersdorf, Zähringer Str. 18
Wiener, Eva, W 30, Bamberger Straße 19
Wiener, Fanny, W 9, Königin-Augusta-Str. 14
Wiener, Franz, W 15, Fasanenstraße 60
Wiener, Franz, Halensee, Joachim-Friedrich-Str. 24
Wiener, Franziska, Lichterfelde, Mühlenstr. 20
Wiener, Frida, NO 55, Straßburger Straße 21
Wiener, Frieda, Charlottenburg 4, Pestalozzistr. 16, b. Henschke
Wiener, Friederike, N 54, Alte Schönhauser Str. 5/5 a
Wiener, Fritz, W 30, Luitpoldstraße 38
Wiener, Fritz, W 30, Münchener Straße 15
Wiener, Georg, W 62, Maaßenstraße 26

Appendix A[2]

Kainer, Herbert in Das Judische Addressbuch in Berlin in 1910

..., Dr. Heinz, W 10, Dörnberg-
straße 7
..., Henry W., W 10, Herkules-
..icke, im Hotel x)
..., Herbert, N 54,
...ontaler Str. 40/41, Aufg. C
..., Herbert, Charlottenburg 4,
...ersdorfer Str. 95
..., Hermann, Schöneberg,
...ner Str. 10
..., Hermann, Schöneberg,
...ner Str. 11/12
..., Hertha, Charlottenburg 4,
...brhstr. 70
..., Hugo, Eichkamp, C 7, Nr.52
..., Hugo, Charlottenburg 4,
...brechtstr. 16
..., Hugo, Steglitz, Mencken-
...traße 10
..., Generalkonsul Dr. Isl,
W 10, Hohenzollernstr. 25
..., Isidor, Charlottenburg 2,
...erliner Str. 153
..., San. Rat Dr. Jakob,
O 17, Strakuer Allee 31
..., Josef, Wilmersdorf,
...hmstedter Str. 12
..., Josef, Charlottenburg 5,
...königsweg 11

..., Julius, S 42, Luisenufer 52
..., Julius, N 58, Schönhauser
Allee 135
..., Käthe, N 113, Schönhauser
Allee 102
..., Karl, Charlottenburg 4,
...bismarckstr. 38
..., Kurt, S 14, Sebastianstr. 72
..., Karoline Lilly, Schöneberg,
...bodensche Str. 10
..., Leo, N 113, Schönhauser
...Allee 108
..., Leon, NO 55, Danziger
Straße 52
..., Leopold, W 50, Prager
Straße 20
..., Lilli, Charlottenburg 2,
Goethestr. 7
..., Lisbeth, S 42, Prinzessinnen-
...traße 1/2
..., Ludwig, Schöneberg,
Wartburgstr. 24
..., Marcel, Grunewald,
Warmbrunner Str. 21
..., Marcus, NW 87, Solinger
Straße 8
..., Martin, Charlottenburg,
Kurfürstendamm 73
b. Werner
..., Max, S 14, Prinzenstr. 39,
b. Werner
..., Michael, S 42,
Prinzessinnenstr. 1/2
..., Moritz, W 15,
Brandenburgische Str. 36
..., Moses, Oranienburg,
Waldstr. 55
..., Nathan Edgar, Charlotten-
burg, Dernburgstr. 2
..., Oliva, Charlottenburg,
Westendallee 63
..., Paul, W 30, Hababurger
Straße 6
..., Dr. med. Paul, Wilmers-
dorf, Hohenzollerndamm 26
..., Paul, W 15, Kurfürsten-
damm 212
..., Paula, W 50, Prager Str. 16
..., Richard, W 10, Königin
Augusta-Str. 49
..., Rudolf, N 113,
Schönhauser Allee 102

Kahn, Sally, W 30, Bamberger
Straße 32
Kahn, Sally, Wilmersdorf,
Pfalzburger Str. 60
Kahn, Saly, Wilmersdorf,
Helmstedter Str. 25
Kahn, Samary, W 50, Regens-
burger Str. 13
Kahn, Siegfried, Tempelhof,
Albrechtstr. 103
Kahn, Siegfried, N 24, Friedrich-
straße 106
Kahn, Siegfried, Halensee,
Karlsruher Str. 23
Kahn, Siegfried, N 113,
Stolpische Str. 18
Kahn, Sophie, Wilmersdorf,
Hohenzollerndamm 34,
Kahn, Dr. Walter, W 30,
Neue Bayreuther Str. 5
Kahn, Zerline, N 65, Exerzier-
straße 11a, Jüd. Krkhs.
Kahnar, Elisabeth, Charlotten-
burg 1, Havelstr. 16
Kahnemann, Clara, W 15, Branden-
burgische Str. 33
Kahnemann, Klara, NW 87,
Flensburger Str. 19a
Kahnheimer Hachest W 10

Kaim, Bertha, W 35,
Potsdamer Str. 106
Kaim, Dr. Hans, Schmargendorf,
Karlsbader Str. 15
Kaim, Jenny, Friedenau,
Hackerstr. 29
Kaim, Leopold, Wittenau,
Neue Str. 6
Kaim, Dr. Martin, W 35,
Potsdamer Str. 106
Kaim, Sigmar, W 35, Steglitzer
Straße 49
Kaim, Wilhelm, W 62, Kleist-
straße 38
Kain, Ella, Schöneberg,
Eisenacher Str. 80
Kain, I., O 112, Frankfurter
Allee 307
Kain, Ludwig, O 112, Gürtel-
straße 36
Kain, Martin, Pankow, Stern-
straße 5

Kainer, Herbert u. Salo, O 17, Große Frankfurter Str. 4

Kainski, Bertha, Halensee,
Hektorstr. 14
Kainz, Horst, Egon, Charlotten-
burg 5, Leonhardstr. 22b
Kainz, Kurt Otto, Charlottenburg 2,
Grolmanstr. 32
Kairies, Marie, N 65, Liebenwalder
Straße 44
Kaiser, Adolf, O 27, Raupach-
straße 15
Kaiser, Alfred, W 15, Sächsische
Straße 3
Kaiser, Alfred, Charlottenburg 4,
Sybelstr. 34
Kaiser, Allee, SO 16, Brücken-
straße 9
Kaiser, Baruch, NW 87,
Lessingstr. 37 b. Levi
Kaiser, Reg.-Rat Conrad,
Schmargendorf, Karlsbader
Straße 15
Kaiser, Dorothea, N 54,
Choriner Str. 73
Kaiser, Edith, N 58, Schönhauser
Allee 162, Waisenhaus

Kaiser, Emil, NO 18, Cothenius-
straße 19
Kaiser, Emil, S 42, Gitschiner
Straße 84
Kaiser, Erich, O 27, Holzmarkt-
straße 64
Kaiser, Ernestine, Charlotten-
burg 4, Giesebrechtstr. 18
Kaiser, Erwin, NO 55, Zelter-
straße 9
Kaiser, Eugen, Halensee,
Hektorstr. 17
Kaiser, Eugen, SO 16, Joseph-
straße 14
Kaiser, Fanny, Steglitz, Kühle-
bornweg 24
Kaiser, Fanny, W 35, Schöne-
berger Ufer 36a
Kaiser, Franz, N 24, Auguststr. 22
Kaiser, Frieda, NO 55, Brauns-
berger Str. 3
Kaiser, Friederike, N 58,
Choriner Str. 44
Kaiser, Georg, Köpenick, Alte
Dahlwitzer Str. 16
Kaiser, Georg, NO 43, Meyerbeer-
straße 5
Kaiser, Gusti, Charlottenburg 2,
Bismarckstr. 115
Kaiser, ...,
Magdeburger Str. 33
Kaiser, Hermann, Reinickendorf-
Ost, Straße 27, Nr. 19
Kaiser, Hugo, Charlottenburg 1,
Berliner Str. 144
Kaiser, Isaak, N 54, Weinmeister-
straße 4
Kaiser, Isidor James, Wilmersdorf,
Ballenstedter Str. 8
Kaiser, Ismar, Steglitz, Flora-
straße 2
Kaiser, Jean, Friedenau,
Taunusstr. 8
Kaiser, Jenny, N 20, Heide-
brinker Str. 7
Kaiser, Käthe, W 15,
Brandenburgische Str. 40
Kaiser, Karoline, Charlottenburg2,
Leibnizstr. 87
Kaiser, Kaufmann, Charlotten-
burg 2, Leibnizstr. 87
Kaiser, Margarete u. Martin,
Charlottenburg 2, Bismarck-
straße 115
Kaiser, Marie, Steglitz, Albrecht-
straße 114
Kaiser, Marie, N 58, Choriner
Straße 20
Kaiser, Martin, NO 55, Greifs-
walder Str. 152
Kaiser, Martin, O 27, Holzmarkt-
straße 64
Kaiser, Max, Steglitz, Albrecht-
straße 114
Kaiser, Dr. Max, Schmargendorf
Karlsbader Str. 15
Kaiser, Max, N 113, Kugler-
straße 25a
Kaiser, Max, NW 87, Wullen-
weberstr. 7
Kaiser, Merton, N 58, Schönhauser
Allee 61
Kaiser, Oskar, Lichterfelde,
Wildenowstr. 30
Kaiser, Otto, NO 55, Lippehner
Straße 3

Kaiser, Richard, O 27, Holzmarkt-
straße 11
Kaiser, Rosa, N 54, Grenadier-
straße 28
Kaiser, Rosa, SO 16, Köpenicker
Straße 36-38
Kaiser, Salli, N 58, Korsörer Str. 9
Kaiser, Sally, O 27, Andreas-
straße 64
Kaiser, Sally, NO 18,
Landsberger Allee 48
Kaiser, Siegfried, W 15, Kaiser-
Allee 44
Kaiser, Therese, Charlottenburg 4,
Kantstr. 38a
Kaiser, Toni, NO 55, Goldaper
Straße 1
Kaiser, Wolf, O 17, Müncheberger
Straße 22
Kaiserblüth, Fritz, W 30,
Bamberger Str. 48
Kaiser-Blüth, Kurt, Wilmersdorf,
Seesener Str. 24
Kaiser-Kyser, Inger, W 15,
Emser Str. 19/20
Kaiser-Lipski, Gerda, Wilmers-
dorf, Kaiserpl. 17
Kaisermann, Feiwusch, N 24,
Kleine Hamburger Str. 17
Kaiser Marie, Charlottenburg 4,
Kajet, Arnold, NW 87, Levetzow-
straße 19a
Kajet, Hugo, NW 87, Jagowstr. 14
Kajet, Leo, Tegel, Veitstr. 41
Kajon, Jacob, W 30, Nollendorf-
platz 7
Kajzer, Fella, N 54, Rosentaler
Straße 39
Kajzer, Tuna, N 54, Rosentaler
Straße 39
Kalabus, Sara, W 15, Düsseldorfer
Straße 13
Kalb, Aron, N 54, Angermünder
Straße 10
Kalb, Erich, Charlottenburg 4,
Leibnizstr. 59
Kalb, Jonas, N 54, Brunnenstr. 196
Kalb, Lina, Charlottenburg 4,
Leibnizstr. 59
Kalb, Michael, NO 55, Prenzlauer
Allee 48/49
..b, Moses, N 54, Dragoner-
straße 11
..lehheim, Jakob, NO 55,
..aarbrücker Str. 6
lehheim, Jonas N 54,
Rosentaler Str. 40/41
Kalehheim, Josef, N 54,
Rosentaler Str. 40/41
Kaleff, Isaak, Schöneberg,
Apostel-Paulus-Str. 19
Kaleko, Dr. Saul, NW 87,
Wullenweberstr. 10
Kalenseher, Eva, N 54, Fehrbelliner
Straße 7
Kalenseher, David, N 65,
Lüttieher Str. 49
Kalenseher, Dorothea, Charlotten-
burg 2, Kantstr. 47
Kalenseher, Helene, C 25,
Katharinenstr. 3
Kalenseher, Dr. Helmut,
Weißensee, Schönstr. 87-90
Kalenseher, Hermann, N 54,
Veteranenstr. 20
Kalenseher, Heymann, Schöneberg
Cranachstr. 41
Kalenseher, Isidor, NO 18,
Friedrichsberger Str. 12
Kalenseher, Minna, O 27,
Dircksenstr. 2

337

Appendix B

Becker, Dr. Wilhelm in Das Judische Addressbuch in Berlin in 1930

Becker, Dr. Wilhelm, NW 87, Lessingstr. 31

Becker, William, SO 16, Michael-kirchstr. 42
Becker, Willy, O 34, Boxhagener Straße 111
Becker, Willy, N 31, Demminer Straße 5
Becker, Willy, Charlottenburg 4, Wielandstr. 29
Beckermann, Abraham, O 17, Breslauer Str. 1
Beckermann, Hans Isak, NO 43, Neue Königstr. 83
Beckermann, Sara, N 54, Gormann-straße 29
Beckhardt, Willy, S 59, Gräfe-straße 15-17
Beckhoff, Dr. Ludwig, Friedenau, Ringstr. 9
Beckmann, Abraham, Adolf, NO 18, Koppenstr. 49
Beckmann, Emil, O 34, Richt-hofenstr. 17
Beckmann, Fritz, SW 29, Blücher-straße 55
Beckmann, Hellmuth, Wilmers-dorf, Sächsische Str. 25
Beckowsky, Hilda, Charlotten-burg 2, Mommsenstr. 69
Becks, Harry, N 65, Adolfstr. 9
Beer, Alfred, Wilmersdorf, Land-hausstr. 44
Beer, Alfred, Direktor, W 10, Friedrich-Wilhelm-Str. 24
de Beer, Alfred Simon, W 15, Sächsische Str. 10
Beer, Alexander, Reg.-Baumeister, W 35, Blumeshof 15
Beer, Anna, W 35, Potsdamer Straße 107
Beer, Anne Liese, Friedenau, Albe-straße 10
Beer, Benjamin, Neukölln, Saale-straße 10
Beer, David, N 54, Grenadier-straße 1 a
Beer, Else, Wilmersdorf, Kaiser-allee 24
Beer, Emanuel, SW 68, Zimmer-straße 50
Beer, Emil, Wilmersdorf, Wetzlarer Straße 5
Beer, Emma, W 57, Potsdamer Straße 80
Beer, Ernestine, Halensee, Katha-rinenstr. 3
Beer, Ernst, Grunewald, Caspar-Theyß-Str. 19
de Beer, Ernst u. Leopold, Wilmers-dorf, Gerolsteiner Str. 12
Beer, Felix, Charlottenburg 9, Lusterburgallee 10
Beer, Franz, W 50, Eisleber Straße 4
Beer, Franziska u. M., W 57, Kurfürstenstr. 9
Beer, Dr. Fritz, W 15, Duisburger Straße 9
Beer, Fritz, Rechtsanwalt, O 27, Schicklerstr. 13
Beer, Fritz, W 30, Schwäbische Straße 6
Beer, Hedwig, Rahnsdorf, Scho-nungsberg 47
Beer, Hermann, N 54, Fehrbelliner Straße 78
Beer, Hilda, NO 55, Christburger Straße 41

Beer, Dr. Kurt, Rechtsanwalt, Wilmersdorf, Rudolstädter Straße 25 a
Beer, Lesline, N 58, Gaudystr. 15
Beer, Lina, N 54, Grenadierstr. 1 a
Beer, Margot, Karlshorst, Heiligen-berger Str. 22
Beer, Margot, Wilmersdorf, Säch-sische Str. 37 a
Beer, Max u. H., Charlottenburg, Dahlmannstr. 16
Beer, Max, N 54, Fehrbelliner Straße 78
Beer, Max, NW 87, Händelstr. 5
Beer, Meier, N 54, Linienstr. 238
Beer, Dr. Oscar, Stud.-Rat, Halen-see, Katharinenstr. 5
Beer, Paul, Wilmersdorf, Kaiser-allee 24
Beer, Paul, NO 55, Prenzlauer Allee 220
Beer, Rosalie, W 30, Nollendorf-straße 29/30
Beer, Sophie, W 57, Potsdamer Straße 78
Beer, Theodor, Friedenau, Varzi-ner Str. 9
Beer, Tobias, SW 19, Köllnischer Fischmarkt 1/2
Beer, Wilhelm, SO 16, Köpenicker Straße 134/35
Beer, Wolf, N 58, Kastanien-allee 72
Beer-Hofmann, Naemah, Char-lottenburg 4, Mommsenstr. 17
Beerensohn, John, Charlotten-burg 4, Wilmersdorfer Str. 92
Beerensson, Adele, W 30, Schwä-bische Str. 21
Beerensson, Rudolf, Steglitz, Kleiststr. 22
Beerensson, Wilhelm, NW 6, Schumannstr. 20-22, Station 29
Beermann, Alfred, W 62, Kalck-reuthstr. 15
Beermann, Alfred, Wilmersdorf, Nassauische Str. 30
Beermann, Arthur, Charlotten-burg, Dernburgstr. 49
Beermann, Bertha, Neukölln, Saalestr. 16
Beermann, Berthold, Wilmersdorf, Kaiserallee 17
Beermann, Cilli, Schöneberg, Grunewaldstr. 16
Beermann, Erna, Wilmersdorf, Trautenaustr. 11
Beermann, Fritz, Charlottenburg 4, Fritschestr. 34
Beermann, Gerschon, Charlotten-burg, Waitzstr. 9
Beermann, Gotthold, NW 87, Waldstr. 25
Beermann, Hans, W 15, Joachims-thaler Str. 21
Beermann, Hans, Rechtsanwalt, Wilmersdorf, Rüdesheimer Pl. 11
Beermann, Julius, Dahlem, Rhein-babenallee 46
Beermann, Julius, Charlotten-burg, Weimarer Str. 19
Beermann, Dr. med. Ludwig, Charlottenburg, Stormstr. 10
Beermann, Magnus, NO 55, Hufe-landstr. 12

Beermann, Martin, W 50, Bam-berger Str. 8
Beermann, Max, Schöneberg, Hauptstr. 34/35
Beermann, Mayer, C 25, Wey-dingerstr. 6
Beermann, Paul, Steglitz, Kaiser-Wilhelm-Str. 8
Beermann, Paul, Wilmersdorf, Motzstr. 49
Beermann, Paul, Charlottenburg 4, Sybelstr. 69
Beermann, Siegfried u. H., Char-lottenburg, Fritschestr. 44
Beerwald, Dr. Joseph, Rechts-anwalt, W 8, Jägerstr. 63
Beerwald, Dr. Josef, Rechtsanwalt, Wilmersdorf, LivländischeStr.10
Beerwald, Lina, Wilmersdorf, Badensche Str. 35
Beerwald, Tobler, NO 55, Metzer Straße 11
Beesen, Helene, N 54, Christinen-straße 7
Behar, Ella, SO 16, Rungestr. 13
Behar, Ella, Wilmersdorf, Land-hausstr. 38
Behar, Emilie. Wilmersdorf Bra-banter Str. 22
Behar, Leon u. Vittoria, Schöne-berg, Innsbrucker Str. 44
Behar, Missis, Charlottenburg 4, Kantstr. 160
Behar, Nessim, Wilmersdorf, Bra-banter Str. 22
Behar, Uriel, Wilmersdorf, Land-hausstr. 38
Behle, Julius, N 58, Schönhauser Allee 30
Behm, Margarete, Niederschön-hausen, Moltkestr. 35
Behmak, Hans, W 15, Xantener Straße 11
Behmak, Wanda, S 42, Branden-burgstr. 44
Behmack, Rudolf, W 15, Lietzen-burger Str. 2
Behnkl, Hans, W 35, Lützow-straße 63
Behnsch, Bruno, Charlottenburg 4, Niebuhrstr. 61
Behnsch, Theodor, Wilmersdorf, Hohenzollerndamm 194/195
Behr, Abraham, Charlottenburg 1, Cauerstr. 9
Behr, Abraham, Wilmersdorf, Prager Platz 4
Behr, Anna, Neukölln, Friedel-straße 9
Behr, Bruno, NO 55, Greifswalder Straße 49
Behr, Emanuel u. Hans, Tempel-hof, Berliner Str. 129
Behr, Frieda, Friedenau, Rubens-straße 14
Behr, Frieda, N 54, Schwedter Straße 263
Behr, Hans, W 15, Branden-burgische Str. 29
Behr, Henriette, N 65, Exerzier-straße 13
Behr, Hermann, SW 61, Teltower Straße 9
Behr, Herta, W 30, Motzstr. 24
Behr, Israel, Neukölln, Friedel-straße 9
Behr, Joseph, W 62, Kleiststr. 5
Behr, Karoline, Charlottenburg, Kantstr. 69
Behr, Kätchen, N 54, Alte Schön-hauser Str. 30

Behr, Lilly, Charlottenburg, Reichsstr. 89
Behr, Louis, Schöneberg, Barba-rossaplatz 2
Behr, Lucie, O 112, Liebigstr. 45
Behr, Ludwig, Charlottenburg 4, Reichsstr. 4
Behr, Margarete, W 15, Joachims-thaler Str. 13
Behr, Dr. Martin, O 34, Frank-furter Allee 14
Behr, Max, N 54, Alte Schön-hauser Str. 30
Behr, Therese, Charlottenburg 2, Grolmanstr. 40
Behr, Wally, Charlottenburg 9, Reichsstr. 9
Behrend, Amalie, NO 18, Elisa-bethstr. 3
Behrend, Blanka, Charlottenburg 5 Garden-du-Corps-Str. 13
Behrend, Cäcilie, NO 55, Greifs-walder Str. 30
Behrend, Charlotte, W 62, Kur-fürstenstr. 97
Behrend, Clara, N 58, Schönhauser Allee 22
Behrend, Dr. Else, San.-Rat, W 62, Lutherstraße 7/8
Behrend, Erich, W 30, Eisenacher Straße 83
Behrend, Erich, N 31, Putthusser Straße 50
Behrend, Friederike, N 31, Lort-zingstraße 37
Behrend, Gertrud, Karlshorst, Hentigstr. 24 a
Behrend, Hanna, Wilmersdorf, Nassauische Str. 21
Behrend, Dr. Hans, W 62, Luther-straße 7/8
Behrend, Hermann, N 31, Put-busser Str. 50
Behrend, Hella, Wilmersdorf, Motzstr. 38
Behrend, Hugo, Rechtsanwalt, Charlottenburg, Kantstr. 67
Behrend, Laura, W 30, Luitpold-straße 24
Behrend, Lilly, Halensee, Pauls-borner Str. 7
Behrend, Margarethe, Lichterfelde, Boothstr. 9
Behrend, Marta, Charlottenburg, Kaiserdamm 36
Behrend, Dr. Mathilde, Charlotten-burg 2, Schlüterstr. 72
Behrend, Max, NO 18, Elisabeth-straße 3
Behrend, Siegfried, W 30, Martin-Luther-Str. 17
Behrend, Walter, Wilmersdorf, Holsteinische Str. 43
Behrends, Erna, W 15, Duisburger Straße 4
Behrendsohn, Adolf, Adlershof, Reckenbergstr. 13
Behrendsohn, Anna, N 54, Chori-ner Str. 69
Behrendsohn, Erich, O 112, Krosse-ner Str. 24
Behrendsohn, Ferdinand, O 34, Rominter Str. 30
Behrendt, Albert, N 65, Amster-damer Str. 5
Behrendt, Alfred, Charlottenburg, Kaiser-Friedrich-Str. 61
Behrendt, Alfred, N 4, Bergstr. 8
Behrendt, Alfred, NW 87, Flens-burger Str. 28
Behrendt, Dr. Alfred, N 4, Tieck-straße 29

338

Appendix C

Selfhelp of Emigres From Central Europe

(Speaker - Professor James Franck)

SELFHELP OF EMIGRES FROM CENTRAL EUROPE, INC.
CHICAGO CHAPTER

presents: THE ANNUAL:

Benefit Recital

All proceeds of the evening go to the Selfhelp Home for the Aged Fund

P r o g r a m :

1. Address   Mr. Richard Emanuel, President
                 Selfhelp Chicago Chapter

2. "A Home for our Aged"   Prof. James Franck

3. Romance............J.S.Svendsen Mr. Hans Basserman and his violin
 Tambourin chinois...F. Kreisler Mrs. Hilde Wetzler at the piano
 Album leaf.........R. Wagner

4. The Broadway hit   Mrs. Ann Birk Kuper, dramatist
 "I Remember Mama"

5. Buffet supper and social gathering

The buffet supper will be served cafeteria style in the North Room adjacent to the theater. There is plenty of food for everyone, and prices are reasonable:

   Cold Plates 50 cents Cake 20 cents Coffee or Cold Beverages 10 cents

Please purchase your food tickets in the lobby, secure your food in the North Room and proceed to the South Room.

If you would like to join Selfhelp, please fill out the form you found on your seat and turn it in to a representative of the membership committee in the North Room or mail it at your convenience.

Due to the fine co-operation and generosity of the firms listed below, we have more than a hundred outstanding prizes for the lucky winners of our raffle. Be sure to look at the display of prizes in the North Room.

Ace Bedding Co., Adams Mfg. Co., Art-Frazen studio, Askows Bakery, Bachenheimer's Foods, Leo Bachrach, Behrman Hardware, Mrs. Bings' Candies, Alfred Blum, Jeweler; Boodlong & Bloom, Buchsbaum & Co., Ernest Carston, Catherine Hat Shop, Chicago Ballantine Distributing Co., Anne Cohen Millinery, Henry Cohen, stamps; Continental Chocolate, Cornell Flower Shop, The Cotton Shop, Carl Eisenthal, Elkan Finer Food Store, Empress Shop, Frank & Newbeck, Ruth L. Friedman, M. Gassman, Gerber's Men's Wear, Glamor Hat Shop, Julius Gumpert, Hagen Stationery Co., Hahn Brothers, Hartman's Food Shop, Kassner's Men's Wear, Erica Kaufman beauty shop; Kenwood Hardware Store, Kronthal's Foods, Loewengard's Diningroom, Lotta Candies, Kurt Low's variety store, Levi Bros., Mabel Dress Shop, Made-Rite Mfg. Co., Meta's Candies, Sol. Moch, R. Mosskowski Studios, Nahm's Stationery Store, Martha Oesterreicher, Rudy Rautenberg, Rico Leather Specialties, Rotenberg's furs, Royal Hosiery, S. Salm, Erna Shafer Hat Shop, Simenauer, interior decorator; Mrs. Stern's Candies, Stessman's jewelry, Stetters Youth Shop, Frieda Stotsky, Swiss American Food Co., University Bakery, University 5 & 10¢ Store, Walters Beauty Shop Supplies, Adolph Wertheim, Weinberg's Delicatessen, Weissman & Sporn, Young California, 47th Ladies Wear, and many others.

Chicago Tribune Article from June 19, 1938

June 19, 1938

NAZIS MENACE POLICE WHO TRY TO CURB MOBS

'Paint Squads' Roam City; Smear Shops.

BY SIGRID SCHULTZ.
[Chicago Tribune Press Service.]

BERLIN, June 18.—Riots developed tonight in the Alexanderplatz district of Berlin. Howling mobs of Nazis surged through the streets, demonstrating against policemen who tried to prevent them from damaging Jewish stores.

The outbreak climaxed a day during which the purge of Jews spread to all parts of Germany.

The disorders started when Nazi "painting squads" invaded the district with buckets of paint and brushes and started smearing the words "racial criminal" and "Jew" on store windows. As long as the "painting squads" confined their activities to this work the police remained in the background.

Mob Besieges Police Station.

But when the accompanying Nazi gangs started pressing against the window panes to break them the police intervened. Two policemen who tried to stop the breaking of windows were nearly mobbed.

When the policemen insisted upon taking two of the ringleaders to a police station the Nazis yelled:

"We'll have you fired for arresting Storm Troop leaders."

The policemen succeeded in reaching the police station with the arrested men. The mob besieged the station and sent for reinforcements, some of which arrived in taxicabs. The besieging forces did not wear the uniforms of Storm Troopers, but they called each other by Storm Troop titles and evidently knew one another well.

Arrested Men Released.

After an hour the two arrested men emerged triumphant from the police station and the daubing of paint on Jewish stores was resumed, with the crowd yelling its enthusiasm.

Many window panes in Jewish owned shops were smashed in the poorer districts of Berlin tonight. The Israel department store was covered with anti-Jewish signs, although the crowd warned the painters to "be careful with Israel's because the owner is English."

In the fashionable west Berlin district a hunchback and two assistants painted "Jew" on ultrasmart Jewish stores and cafés in Kurfuerstendamm. A crowd, including many women, traveled all along the two mile route with them, while in the background stood policemen studiously looking in the other direction.

Aryan Shop Owner Protests.

When the crowd approached a jewelry store famous for its beautiful display on Kurfuerstendamm and the brush wielder began to paint a big "J" on the window, a man leaped out of the shop, crying: "Don't you dare. This is an Aryan shop." The sign painters retreated after a heated exchange of invective.

On Tauenzienstrasse, THE TRIBUNE correspondent saw a mob in front of the Berlin restaurant, a medium price establishment. A pale man was laboriously washing from the window the word "Jew." The mob challenged him.

"How dare you wash off this sign?" they asked.

The man continued to scrub the window in silence. A boy, about 14 years old, who apparently had been left behind to watch the shop, ran off in the direction of the crowd down the street to report to his superior.

Earlier today crowds of Nazis gathered at entrances of Jewish owned shops. They jeered and cried taunts at shoppers who entered these stores. At closing time gangs gathered at the back entrances of Jewish stores and shouted insults at sales girls and other employés, or sang songs such as "Pull Out the Jews," of which there were many verses.

Extend Drive to All Germany.

BERLIN, June 18.—(AP)—A merciless official campaign against Jews, reinforced by mob action, was extended to all Germany today by secret police orders.

Jews were in panic. Foreign consulates were besieged by men and women trying despairingly to get permission to go to other countries.

In Worms, famed as Martin Luther's home, Jews had difficulty get-

[Continued on page 8, column 4.]

Appendix D[2]

Chicago Tribune Article from June 19, 1938

RIOT IN BERLIN; POLICE WHO AID JEWS MENACED

Howling Mobs Daub Paint on Semetic Stores.

[Continued from first page.]

ting food because gentiles were afraid to sell it to them.

Eyewitnesses in Frankfurt said old respectable families were routed from their beds and taken to police headquarters before dawn.

Official estimates of the number arrested were lacking, except a report given the controled press today saying two raids in Berlin resulted in the arrests of 460 Jews, of whom 76 were found to be "heavily incriminated," 26 were "without nationality," and 51 were foreigners "without proper papers."

Some observers believed, however, that raids yesterday and today led to 500 arrests, and that an estimate of 1,000 arrests in Berlin in the last three weeks seemed reasonable. Besides, 1,000 were estimated to be under arrest in the provinces.

Today's official statement said all those arrested were "criminally suspicious persons" and "no political or other motives were behind these actions of the police, which were conducted in the course of regular checkups."

Sent to Concentration Camp.

"A number of Jews had to be taken into protective custody for reasons of personal safety," the statement added.

Official quarters insisted police were looking solely "anti-social and criminal elements."

If a Jew had even as much as the equivalent of an ordinary American parking ticket against him, that fact was seized upon as an excuse for a gruelling questioning, even though the offense was old and minor.

At Buchwald concentration camp, near Weimar, it was reported sixty-five army buses were arriving nightly from Berlin, filled with Jews. Other centers sent smaller contingents to the camp.

Cologne Marks Jewish Shops.

A reliable source said he had seen a decree signed by Reinhard Heydrich, aide of Secret Police Chief Heinrich Himmler, ordering a checkup on Jews throughout greater Germany. Reports from Frankfurt, Cologne, Vienna, Munich and other cities corroborated his assertion.

Anti-Semitism in Cologne meant having Jewish shops designated as such in letters so large nobody could overlook them.

"The characterization of Jewish stores as Jewish must be carried out so plainly that there can be no doubt about their nature," the Nazi press in Cologne declared.

Signs three feet high distinguished Jewish shops in Berlin. Nazid squads smeared Jewish store windows with slogans like: "Jew—whoever buys here is a traitor to his people"; "Jew—our misfortune"; "Avoid this Jew"; "Jew, get out!"; "Don't buy from this Jewish swine"; "Women and girls, avoid this racial defamer."

If there was any doubt as to the nationality of a shop owner, a big question mark was daubed on the front. Three windows of an agency for two American automobile manufacturers were thus decorated.

One group of Nazis was seen to administer a severe beating to a Jew on Frankfurter avenue.

"I witnessed the looting of a shoe store," a middle class tradesman recounted. "A few mob leaders took down shoe boxes from the shelves and handed box after box out through a smashed window. After that, furniture and fixtures were wantonly destroyed."

Demonstrating the swiftness of the mob action was the case of a Jewish merchant in Berlin's exclusive west end who dared box the ears of a member of the Hitler Youth organization.

The boy had smeared "Out with Jews!" on the shop windows. Within a few minutes after the owner had struck the youth a crowd gathered and smashed not only the windows of the Jew's shop but also those of nearby stores.

Appendix E

"Loyalty Drive"

LOYALTY COMMITTEE

OF VICTIMS OF NAZI AND FASCIST OPPRESSION

Chicago Drive

Sponsored by the Council of the Refugee Organizations

of Chicago

Dear Friend:

It is our heart-felt wish to thank you very cordially
for the most active part which you have taken in the
Loyalty Drive.
May we tell you how greatly we appreciated your
cooperation and how grateful we are for your work which
helped to make the drive impressive and successful.

Very cordially yours,

Chairman   District Chairman

Dorothy W. Becker

Of · The · Library

14581 N. Alamo Canyon Dr.
Oro Valley, AZ 85737
February 16, 2000

Dear Mrs. Levy,

Marian, Dorothy Becker's daughter, wrote to me regarding the book you are writing about Dorothy. My husband and I will be at the Arizona address until March 29, and our telephone number is (520) 825-3471 if you wish to call.

You certainly can use my name in your writings. My life was enriched by knowing Dorothy when I started working for her at age 15 when I was in high school. Nine months after graduation during a visit with her I mentioned to Dorothy that I was not pleased with the hours I was required to work at the CPA

Helping Libraries Grow

343

2

form. She then spoke to her boss, and I was hired to work in the Executive Offices. Eventually I was appointed Advertising Controller. However, at age 28 I resigned due to my mother's illness, and Mother came to live with us where I cared for her.

Both my husbands were former Mandel Brothers' employees. My first husband passed away when he was 46. Clarence, my second husband, and I have been married almost 25 years. My two marriages (two children from the first) were all a result of Dorothy's speaking out for me in 1946.

My memories of Dorothy are lovingly cherished by me, and I thank you for writing about her.

If I don't hear from you soon, I'll call when I return.

My best,
Evelyn Redel Heidke

Appendix G[1]

Announcing the Construction of the Selfhelp Home

October 1950

S E L F H E L P,   I N C.

Chicago Chapter

OCTOBER	NEWS LETTER	1950

With the approach of fall comes the good news that construction has finally
started on Selfhelp's Chicago Home for Aged Immigrants at 4941 S. Drexel Blvd.

If plans go according to schedule, the Contractor tells us our Home will be
ready for occupancy in a few months. This is what we have all been working
and waiting for, and we are sure you will share our enthusiasm.

* * * * *

A report by Dr. William F. Becker, President, given at the Annual Meeting on
July 5, 1950 revealed that our neighborhood groups have answered more calls
for assistance in financial help, clothing, living quarters and jobs this
past year than ever before.

He said that much credit must be given to our committee chairmen as well as
to our officers and members who have made great sacrifices during the year
to promote Selfhelp's program of activity. In his own words, "May I express
my personal thanks to all of you who have always so unselfishly helped me to
carry the responsibility of this office. Continue your support and our work
cannot fail."

* * * * * *

Mrs. Bruno Blumklotz, our Program Chairman, announces that a musical treat is
in store for all of us on SUNDAY, NOVEMBER 19th (mark that date on your calendar) when Selfhelp presents a BENEFIT RECITAL. Soloists are Hans Alton,
who will direct and present the Choral Society of Chicago Sinai Congregation;
Bruno Glade, concert pianist; and Lenore Porges, lyric soprano.

The concert will be held at Fullerton Hall in the Art Institute of Chicago at
Michigan Avenue at Adams Street and will start promptly at 8:00 o'clock.
Inasmuch as the Hall has limited seating capacity, we suggest you procure
YOUR TICKETS IN ADVANCE FROM YOUR NEIGHBORHOOD CHAIRMAN. Admission is $2.00.

North Side
Mrs. Elsa D. Franks
3027 W. Fullerton Ave.
SPaulding 2-6315

South Side
Mrs. Alfred Wolf
5454 S. University Ave.
PLaza 2-7392

The evening promises to be well worth your attendance. Hans Alton needs no
introduction, for his association with the choir of Chicago Sinai Congregation has brought him acclaim throughout the city. The choir will be accompanied by Hilde Freund.

Bruno Glade, as many of your know, is on the faculty of the American Conservatory of Music and has given piano recitals in Germany, England and this
country.

Lenore Porges was guest soloist at Orchestra Hall and with the Choral Society
at the Civic Opera House. She has done much radio and club work.

Don't miss out on this fine program. Get your tickets in advance for an even-
you will long remember!

Appendix G²

Marian Becker to Wed Phil Shaffer Announcement

October 1950

- 2 -

HAPPY DAY FUND

Donor	In Honor Of
Mr. & Mrs. Siegmund Lazar	Silver Anniversary of Mr.& Mrs. Leo Levi
Mrs. Leopold Tannenwald	Her son's wedding
Mrs. Ida Loewi	Her granddaughter's wedding
Mr. & Mrs. Henry Gosser	Their daughter's wedding
Mrs. Bierig	Her son's wedding
Mr. & Mrs. Arthur Lowenthal	Their son's wedding.
Mr. & Mrs. L. Wachenheimer	Their son's graduation
Mr. & Mrs. Otto Hanauer	Mrs. Theo Baum's recovery
Mr. & Mrs. Jules Lowengardt	Lotte Frankel's wedding
Dr. & Mrs. William F. Becker	Mrs. A. Gruenebaum's recovery
Mr. & Mrs. Alfred Wolf	" " "
Anonymous	" " "
Mr. & Mrs. Siegmund Steierman	" " "
Mr. & Mrs. Fritz Dreifuss	Mr. & Mrs. Eric Dreifuss' wedding
Anonymous	Bauer-Samson wedding
Dr. & Mrs. William F. Becker	Mr. & Mrs. Arthur Sach's Silver Anniversary
Mr. & Mrs. Alfred Wolf	" " "
Mr. & Mrs. John Monasch	Arrival of Danny Franks
Mr. & Mrs. Gerald E. Franks	Arrival of their son Daniel Lee
Anonymous	Mrs. Olga Scheuer's recovery
Mr. Albert Hanhart	His 70th Birthday
Mr. & Mrs. Alfred Bensdorf	Arrival of grandson James Allen
Dr. & Mrs. Selig	Happy Day Fund
Mr. & Mrs. Ludwig Frankel	" " "
Mrs. G. Aron	Wedding of Mr. & Mrs. Hugo Halle's son
Mr. & Mrs. Alfred Wolf	Mr. Adolf Goldschmidt's birthday
Dr. & Mrs. Charles Wollak of Joliet, Illinois	" " "
Mr. & Mrs. Alfred Wolf	Mrs. Meta Elias' 80th birthday
Mr. Walter Kling	High Holidays
Mr. & Mrs. Henry Levi	" "
Mr. & Mrs. Burton Strauss	" "
Mr. & Mrs. Fred Salomon	Mr. & Mrs. Alfred Wolf
Mr. & Mrs. William Wolfson	Marian Becker's wedding
Mrs. Elsa D. Franks	" "
Mr. & Mrs. Walter Asch	" "
Mr. & Mrs. Richard Emanuel	" "
Dr. & Mrs. William F. Becker	Daughter's marriage to Mr. Phil Shaffer
Anonymous	Mr. & Mrs. Fred Breslau's new apartment
Mr. & Mrs. Walter Kamp	Dr. & Mrs. Julius Schmidt's 20th anniversary
Mr. & Mrs. Fritz Dreifuss	Mrs. Max Schriessheimer's 75th birthday
Mr. Carl Ganz	10th anniversary in this country

Opening of the Southside Selfhelp Home - Nov. 1951 - Page 1(2)

```
                S E L F H E L P ,  I N C .
                     Chicago Chapter

* * * * * * * * * * * * * * * * * * * * * * * * * * * * * * * * * * *
*  November          N E W S   L E T T E R          1951  *
* * * * * * * * * * * * * * * * * * * * * * * * * * * * * * * * * *
```

```
ATTENTION                                           ATTENTION
                        S E L F H E L P
                  presents for the benefit of the
              CHICAGO HOME FOR AGED IMMIGRANTS, INC.

                        C O N C E R T

                 Under the Direction of MAX JANOWSKI
                   At the Piano - MRS. ERNA SAIM

        I.   EXCERPTS from HANDEL'S "MESSIAH"
        II.  EXCERPTS from MENDELSSOHN'S "ELIJAH"

                        INTERMISSION

        III. AIR DE LIA         --     DEBUSSY
        IV.  VON EWIGER LIEBE    --     BRAHMS
        V.   SONGS FOR WOMEN'S VOICES -Arranged by MAX JANOWSKI
                  GRIEG - SCHUMANN - SCHUBERT

                          PAUSE

        VI.  HEBREW SONGS - OVINU MALKENU - SIM SHOLOM -
                     YERUSHALAYIM - CHULU M'CHOL HAHORAH
        VII. HALELUYAH CHORUS


                ON SUNDAY, NOVEMBER 25, 1951 - 7:30 P.M.
                AT COLLEGE OF JEWISH STUDIES AUDITORIUM
                        72 EAST ELEVENTH STREET

    Admission...$1.67            Ticket Sale: Mrs. Richard Emanuel
    Fed. Tax     .33                          Tel. ARdmore 1-1871
       Total    $2.00                         Mrs. William F. Becker
                                              Tel. KEnwood 8-0810
```

The beginning of the 15th year of Selfhelp activity in Chicago will probably go down in the history of this organization as one of its high points. It has been marked by the opening of the Selfhelp House which has given some of our older refugees more than a refuge, more than just a place to live, but a real home, a house where companionship and a friendly homelike atmosphere are the outstanding features.

On July 7th, 1951, approximately 150 people, the representatives of immigrant organizations, the members of the Board of Directors of Selfhelp and of the Chicago Home for Aged Immigrants, Inc. assembled at 4941 Drexel Blvd. to witness the dedication of our home. Rabbi Peritz, Rabbi Schoenberger, Rabbi Wexberg and Rabbi Wolf conducted the religious ceremony. After thanking the rabbis for the arrangement of this beautiful service the president of Selfhelp, Dr. William F. Becker, continued as follows:

"Just 15 years ago Selfhelp was founded by European immigrants from the Nazi dominated countries with the purpose of serving friends who have been uprooted and have been trying to settle down here and abroad. Selfhelp soon recognized that the problems of the aged are much more difficult for the newcomer than for the American. In 1942 a home for aged people was opened up in New York; another such home was established in France in 1945. Today the Chicago home is ready to open its doors for our elderly friends.

"Building such a home has been a new experience for most of us. When we first contacted other Jewish organizations who are familiar with the problems of the aged and homes for aged people we were advised to do some pioneering. We have done it. Only those who go through the aggravations of pioneering know the tensions under which it is necessary to function. The endless problems of finding a suitable building, of fund raising, the planning of facilities within the rigid framework of the Municipal Code, these and a hundred other problems, large and small, complicate this pleasant task of building a home for the aged. But already today the compensations far outbalance the headaches that no one who is privileged to be in the pioneering group really complains. Without the help of the officers and members of the Board of Directors of our 2 organizations, without the work of our ladies from the Neighborhood Groups, without the support of hundreds of friends in our immigrant community, our pioneering job would not have been accomplished. To all those I express my humble thanks."

Death Notice of Elsa Franks - Nov. 1951 - Page 2(2)

- 2 -

3 days later the first permanent residents moved into the home. On September 9, 1951, we opened the doors of our home for the members and friends of Selfhelp. More than 700 people responded to our invitation to an Open House Party. For several hours people swarmed all over the house to see with their own eyes what Selfhelp has accomplished. There were loads of praising comments. Again and again we were told that our Selfhelp Home is not another old age institution but a real home. - And our elderly friends who now live at Selfhelp House are happy and content. They like their home, they like the food, they like their companions, they like the people who take care of them, especially our superintendent, Mrs. Hanna Oschatzke; in other words they like Selfhelp House, their new home in U.S.A.

The home is in operation due to your support. With your help we have done what seemed to many people impossible. We still need your support to keep the home running. Only the combined effort of all the members and friends of Selfhelp and of the "Chicago Home for Aged Immigrants, Inc." can make it possible for Selfhelp House to offer shelter to those who need it.

Do You Want To Help?

Become a member of Chicago Home for Aged Immigrants or Selfhelp.

Contribute regularly to Selfhelp and the Chicago Home for Aged Immigrants.

Send your contributions and membership applications to Mr. Burton Strauss, 4526 N. Beacon St., Chicago 40, Ill.

For information about residency in our home, please contact:
Mrs. Konrad Bloch, 6019 Ingleside, Chicago 37, Ill. (PLaza 2-2792), Or
Mrs. Hanna Oschatzke, BO 8-8860.

On September 17th, 1951, Selfhelp was deprived of one of its most active co-workers. Mrs. Elsa Franks, member of our Board of Directors for many years, chairman of our Neighborhood Group North died suddenly. With great de-
~~hewcomers in need.~~ Selfhelp has lost a great friend.

W.F.B.

Illegible Sentence Read: With great devotion to Selfhelp she rendered helpful services to many newcomers in need.

Our Dedication Book is going to press soon. Have you ordered your AD already??????
If not, HURRY. Contact immediately: Mr. Herbert Wolff, 5219 Kenwood Ave., HY 3-8532 and Mrs. Burton Strauss, 4526 N. Beacon St., LO 1-0483.

Appendix I

Plans to Expand the Southside Home - May 15, 1956

SELFHELP HOME FOR THE AGED, INC.

May 15, 1956

Dear Friends:

The dream of expanding our Home is really coming true. The ground in the rear of the building already has been prepared, and construction of the Annex is about to start. We want you to help us celebrate this momentous occasion in the history of our Home, in the creation of which you have assisted us. Will you, therefore, please join us at the

CORNERSTONE CEREMONY.

The date is SUNDAY, MAY 27, 1956, at 11:30 A.M., at

4941 Drexel Blvd.

We trust you will be impressed with the names of outstanding persons who have volunteered to help make the ceremony an impressive and memorable one. Here is the

P R O G R A M

Star Spangled Banner	Mrs. Manny Adler
Opening Prayer	Rabbi Jacob Weinstein, K.A.M. Temple
Address	Dr. William F. Becker, President, Selfhelp Home for the Aged, Inc.
Psalm 30	Rabbi Court Peritz, Orthodox Jewish Congregation, and Rabbi Joseph Liberles, Temple Ezra
Address	Hon. Barratt O'Hara, Member, House of Representatives, 2nd Illinois District
Address	Leon M. Despres, Alderman, 5th Ward
Prayer of Dedication	Rabbi Bernhard Wechsberg, Congregation Habonim Jewish Center
Address	Julian H. Levi, Executive Director, Southeast Chicago Commission
Closing Prayer	Rabbi Irving Melamed, Hyde Park Liberal Congregation

* * * * * * * * * * * * *

We look forward to seeing you on May 27.

William F. Becker, M.D.
President

349

Appendix J

Dedication of the Annex - April 7, 1957

Dedication

of

T H E   A N N E X

of

SELFHELP HOME FOR THE AGED

Sunday, April 7, 1957

at

1:30 P.M.

_____

P R O G R A M

Opening Prayer . . . . Rabbi Matz

Psalm 30 . . . . Rabbi Melamed

Lernen: "The Home" . . . . Rabbi Peritz

Psalm 15 . . . . Rabbi Katz

Lernen: "The People" and
       Kaddish d'rabbonon . . . . Rabbi Wechsberg

Address by . . . . Dr. Kurt Herz
                United Help, Inc.
                 New York City

Address by . . . . Dr. Fred Weissman
                      Selfhelp
                 New York City

Address by . . . . Dr. William F. Becker
            President, Selfhelp Home
                for the Aged, Inc.

Affixing the Mezuzah and
   Likboa Mezuzah Shehecheyanu . . . . Rabbi Plotke

Sim Sholom - Grant us Peace
          (Composed by Max Janowski)
               Sung by. . . . .Beatrice Horwitz
              Accompanied by . . .Max Janowski

Closing Prayer . . . . Rabbi Liberles

Annual Report of Neighborhood Groups North and South

May 28, 1957

A few weeks ago SELFHELP celebrated at the May Party its 20th Anniversary
in Chicago. We have planned another affair in Fall to commemorate
this event. Mrs. Wolf and I do not want tonight *to talk* about the role
our neighborhood groups played during this period, we shall only
report on the activities of the past year.

Being in our Home tonight, let us start with the accomplishments
right here. The members of our neighborhood groups have been doing an
outstanding job as regional charmen during the fund raising drive for
our Home, collecting in their neighborhoods and from friends, sewing
drapes to make the rooms even more attractive and helping to acquire
needed merchandise as reasonably as possible. We are most grateful
to the Chairmen of the Sewing Committee, Mrs. Tuteur, her co-chairman
Mrs. Baumann and all their fine helpers especially Mrs. Emanuel, Mrs.
Metzger and Mrs. Scheiber. Their work has been greatly admired by all
visitors, you can rightly be proud of it.

Our Happy Day and Memorial Fund is one of the most reliable sources
of income. There are rarely occasions among our group that are
not mentioned by one or the other contributor.. Many a reader is
waiting for the newsletter to find out about the newest event in
our community. While most of the donors give for the good cause, all
of them prefer sending their donations to Selfhelp because of the
assurance that everything will be promptly and correctly taken care
of by our well chosen chairman Mrs. Martha Steiermann. Lots of credit
has to be given to her for the steady riding of *the list of* our contributors.

Our last May Party has financially been one of the most successful
affairs. Our net proceeds amounted to over $1700.00. There is one

III

join us - in thanking all of you who took part in this so important
job. As Selfhelp has not many social gatherings, this is the only con-
ta ot we have with Selfhelp members and friends and it cannot be emphasise
often enough how important our contacts are with those families from
whom we collect. We do need the money more urgent than ever. We have
eases where we have spent several hundreds of dollars and we have constant
calls for help. Our support in some ca ses was supplemented by
some assistance we received from United Help, New York. Several
agencies have called on us and we have established a very good relationship. We have visited again the sick and the old, at home, in hospitals
and State Hopsitals. We were ready for the Hungarion immigration and we
try our best to help everyone who needs our help. ..any of you have
helped Mrs. Wolf and me doing this job but I want to give my special
thanks to Mrs. Metzger, Mrs. Lowenthal xxx Mrs. Lowenstein and Mrs.
Hirschfeld for their wonderful cooperation.
We are also grateful to Mrs. Tuteur and Mrs. Henry Weil for taking
care of the Room Service. We sincerely appreciate the efforts Mrs.
Bensdorf and Mrs. Lowenthal make to sell more and more Good Will
Messages. The end results may not seem too great to either of them
but we all know how important it is to see a Selfhelp Greeting every-
where. It is xxxxxxxx publicity and a constant reminder. A committee
will work out a "new look" to make it even more attractive.
At our last meeting we discussed another new committee which will be
responsible for the activities in our Home. Many new residents have
joined our little family at the Home, we have the responsibility to
keep them entertained and happy. Speakers should be asked to come,
movies should be shown in regular intervals. One of the nicest
affairs last Summer was an invitation by Mrs. Braun. On a
a trip to the country

Appendix L

Informing All Board Members Re a Surprise Party for The Beckers

March 15, 1957

TO ALL MEMBERS OF THE BOARDS OF DIRECTORS OF SELFHELP OF CHICAGO
AND THE SELFHELP HOME FOR THE AGED, INC.

March 15, 1957

Dear Friends:

For once here is a letter going out that has not been prepared by our President and our Secretary, Dr. and Mrs. WILLIAM F. BECKER, and, as a matter of fact, they are not even to know about it. We are sure you will help us keep the secret and make this a perfect surprise for them!

You all know that for many years the concept of Selfhelp and of our Home has been identified with the name of the Beckers. Perhaps you are not fully aware of the fact, however, that it has been ten full years now that the Beckers have been the leading and guiding spirits of the organizations -- and not only that, but actually working hard and sacrificing practically all their spare time to make Selfhelp, and more recently the Home, the much sought and needed support for many people in desperate hours and situations.

We of the Committees -- and we are sure all of you with us -- strongly feel that some recognition should be given to the Beckers for their achievements.

As you probably already know, there will be an open house in connection with the official opening of our Annex, on Sunday, April 7, 1957. In addition to a token of appreciation to be presented to them at this ceremony, a DINNER TO HONOR THE BECKERS has been planned for the same evening,

Sunday, April 7, 1957, at 6:00 P.M.

in the Planet Room of the Country Club Hotel
6930 South Shore Drive.

We would, of course, like very much for as many board members and their spouses as possible to join, but would like to state that, naturally, nobody is obligated to participate. Since we will have to give the hotel an exact count, we would appreciate it very much if you could complete and return the enclosed post card just as soon as possible, in any event no later than March 29. The cost of the dinner will be $6.25 per person, including tax and tip.

PLEASE DON'T FORGET THAT ALL THIS IS TO BE A COMPLETE SURPRISE FOR THE BECKERS, AND DON'T GIVE US AWAY!

Looking forward to seeing you on April 7, we remain,

THE EXECUTIVE COMMITTEES of
SELFHELP OF CHICAGO, INC.
SELFHELP HOME FOR THE AGED, INC.

Enclosure

Appendix M

Letter to Dr. and Mrs. Becker from Fred Weissman - April 9, 1957

Selfhelp of Emigres from Central Europe - New York

TELEPHONE
BRYANT 9-0485

NEW TELEPHONE NO.
BRyant 9-9935

147 WEST 42nd STREET - ROOM 519
NEW YORK 36, N. Y.

Selfhelp

OF EMIGRES FROM CENTRAL EUROPE, Inc.

April 9, 1957

Dr. and Mrs. William F. Becker
5044 N. Marine Drive
Chicago 40, Ill.

Dear Dr. and Mrs. Becker :

Since I made two speeches in Chicago on Sunday,
I do not want to repeat myself too much. I just want
to let you know that I am back at my desk and that I
greatly enjoyed the trip to Chicago and the participation
in the opening of the Becker Wing.

What you achieved is really wonderful. I hope very
much that you will not have too much work in filling up
the Home and taking care of twice as many people as you
had so far.

The climax of all the celebrations, was, of course,
the surprise party on Sunday evening when both of you got
at least a token of the much deserved appreciation you have
earned through hard work with your Chapter. I am just
wondering whether and when I shall be able to make another
speech in honor of the Beckers since there is such a generous
compensation for such a performance.

Hoping to see you soon again in New York, I am,

With kind regards,

Cordially yours,

Fred S. Weissman

CONTRIBUTIONS ARE DEDUCTIBLE FOR INCOME TAX PURPOSES

Programs and financial statements filed under registration No. VFA 021 with the
ADVISORY COMMITTEE ON VOLUNTARY FOREIGN AID of the UNITED STATES GOVERNMENT

Appendix N

Selfhelp of Chicago Newsletter - April, 1957 - Page 1

Opening of the Annex and the May Party

Selfhelp of Chicago, Inc.

NEWS LETTER

APRIL, 1957   NO. 2

Dear Friends:

First of all, although you certainly know about it by now, we want to extend to you, your family and friends, a most cordial invitation to our traditional

MAY PARTY

Sunday, May 5, 1957, at 4:30 P.M.
at
72 East 11th Street

We are sure that you will want to join the fun and bring all your dear ones, the more so, as we know you will be anxious not to miss the especially attractive program which has been planned this year.

ERWIN JOSPE, Director of the Roosevelt University Opera Workshop, has offered us his cooperation and arranged for artists trained in his workshop to present

"SPOTLIGHT ON OPERA"

Included in the presentation will be

"The Telephone" . . . . Menotti
Excerpts from "Tosca" . . . . Puccini
Short Scenes from Other Operas

In addition to this promising performance, another feature has been planned which is particularly appropriate at this time when we just have completed the extension of our Home. You will be most interested to watch a film on the problems of aging entitled

"A PLACE TO LIVE"

Of course, there also will be the much liked, exciting tombola, with fine prizes, and volunteers will provide their well-known culinary delicacies for your enjoyment at the supper.

The price per ticket again is only $2.00, and if you have not yet bought your tickets, please procure them, without further delay, from

Mrs. Alfred Wolf, 6628 N. Talman, SH 3-5681, or
Mrs. Wm. F. Becker, 5044 N. Marine Drive, LO 1-6822.

We are looking forward to seeing every one of you on May 5 and trust that you will help to again make this party a great success. The proceeds of the party, as usual, will be used to support our Home.

OUR HOME

It certainly is not news for you if we tell you that, on

April 7, we celebrated the official opening of the Annex to our Home. Many of you — close to 1,000 persons must have dropped in — were able to put in your personal appearance, at the dedication ceremony or later that same afternoon at the open house, and you saw for yourselves what has been accomplished. Your donations, your purchase of tickets for our May Parties and Theatre Parties, your efforts in soliciting the assistance of others — financially and otherwise — your chipping in to help with the actual work, all have made it possible to afford a comfortable, cheerful, well equipped place to live to an additional 22 persons who have been eagerly waiting for the completion of the structure. The rooms have been tastefully and purposefully furnished; the old building, too, underwent some changes; the dining room has been extended to accommodate the increased number of residents; the kitchen has been modernized and streamlined; a small office has been built in the entrance hall for Mrs. Leo Oschatzke, the Director, so that her former office can serve as an extension of the living room. Additional residents are being admitted gradually, for easier adjustment of old and new residents alike, and shortly every bed will be taken, not eliminating, but at least substantially reducing, our waiting list.

You may have heard that our financial worries, although by no means completely dissipated, could, however, be significantly reduced by a substantial contribution to the construction of our Annex by United Help, Inc., an organization entrusted with the task of assisting worthwhile projects in favor of Nazi victims from Germany, from funds made available by the Jewish Restitution Successor Organization (JRSO) and accumulated from claims on heirless Jewish property in Germany. We were happy that Dr. Kurt Herz, Executive Director of United Help, as well as Dr. Fred S. Weissman, Executive Secretary of Selfhelp, New York, could be with us at the dedication of our new building. They addressed the group during the impressive ceremony conducted by Rabbis Katz, Liberles, Melamed, Peritz, Plotke and Wechsberg. Miss Beatrice Horwitz gave some artistic flavor to the ceremony with her singing of "Sim Sholom", accompanied at the piano by its composer, our friend Max Janowski of KAM Temple. We are most grateful to all of them for making this such a delightful occasion.

A pleasant surprise was sprung on Dr. and Mrs. Wm. F. Becker, our President and Secretary respectively, when during the ceremony Mr. Max Ries, member of the Home's Executive Committee, presented to them a plaque dedicating the new Annex to them as the "BECKER WING."

Nobody has toiled as hard and consistently for the establishment of the Home and its extension as have Dr. and Mrs. Becker, and everybody will rejoice in their having been awarded this token of appreciation. They have been

Appendix O

Selfhelp of Chicago Newsletter, Page 1- November, 1960

Dorothy Becker's 50th Birthday Party

Selfhelp of Chicago, Inc.

NEWS LETTER

November, 1960   No. 3

Dear Friends:

DOROTHY BECKER - FIFTY YEARS OLD

While the 50th birthday of our deeply venerated and respected
Secretary, on October 24, would not be the first item to be reported
on in the sequence of events since publication of our last Newsletter,
we feel that a special spot -- the first page -- be devoted to it.
Knowing her energy, vitality, and how indefatigably she carries on
her manifold charitable activities from morning to night, seven days
a week, it is hard to believe that Dorothy Becker should be embarking
on the sixth decade of her life; but her maternal warmth, unfailing
display of sympathy and understanding, as well as her wisdom and
mature judgment make it more credible that she is not quite as young
in years as her youthful appearance and deportment would make you
believe.

No compensation in kind would be possible, or acceptable, to
Dorothy Becker, for all her acts of kindness, of material and spiritual
aid. But on the occasion of her birthday she received a different,
most gratifying kind of compensation, true demonstrations of affection
and gratitude on the part of many to whom she has extended a friendly
hand. To a large extent it is owing to her ingenuity, enthusiasm and
perseverance that the Selfhelp today can take pride in its Home and
the Northside and Southside Day Centers for our older friends. And
each of these -- along with friends and family -- have feted her with
special parties. The feelings of these groups were expressed in prose
and verse, and we would like to share with you some of the things
that were said at the surprise party at the Home, in which numerous
members of the Neighborhood Groups joined the residents of the Home.

Mrs. John Monasch, as the first Chairman of the Southside
Neighborhood Group, and Mrs. Alfred Wolf, Chairman of the Northside
Neighborhood Group, who shared responsibility for arrangements for
this party with Mrs. Hannah Oschatzke, Director of the Home, were the
first speakers. They expressed their deep appreciation to Dorothy
Becker for her efficient and effective leadership and the hope that,
when the far-off day should come where she may wish to restrict her
activities, she may be fortunate enough to find as capable and devoted
a successor as they did in her.

Lack of space precludes our reprinting in full all that was
said that evening to honor the "birthday child." A few examples,
therefore, must suffice.

356

Appendix P[1]

Letters from Percy and Nell Love - May 23, 1963 - Page 1(2)

Regarding the Death of Dr. Becker

Rabbi Lorge, Members of the Family, Friends:

I consider it an honor to be privileged to pay a tribute to Dr. Becker. It is not easy for me today to speak concerning Dr. Becker, for I am grief stricken at the loss of my friend.

I am not from the Medical Organization but from the factory. There we speak in words and from ideas; when I think of Dr. Becker, I think of ideas, principles, and things of value. I think of these familiar lines: "As a man thinketh in his heart, so is he," and "By their deeds shall ye know them." Everyone is an image in part of everyone whom he has met.

For a number of years I rode home from the plant with Dr. Becker daily. While riding with Dr. Becker, we talked of many things; the concerns of his day, people, industrial proceedings, etc. The greatness of a man does not preclude his need to talk to someone in a quiet, friendly way. I suppose I was Dr. Becker's sounding board. Counselor, friend, we relaxed together as we rode.

All of us know that Dr. Becker was not given to idle conversation. What he said was sincere, and he meant it.

While he was ill, the chief nurse said to me in discussing Dr. Becker's condition, "He was your friend, but he was a father and adviser to many of us." I was very aware of the truth of what she said, for I knew many of his patients. He loved his profession because it gave him the privilege to serve his fellow man, and he truly served them. He was attuned to them both as a specialist in his field and as a human being, genuinely interested in them. He loved his company because it gave him a chance to treat his patients like people who needed not only medical attention, but recognition as persons.

He had a rapport with his patients that served in itself as therapy. He felt that his company was interested in the welfare of the people who came to him for treatment. The company, which provided the facilities and the helps which he needed, thought so highly of Dr. Becker that his methods are used not only at all manufacturing locations, but also at the headquarters of the company in New York. Industrial medicine in this area as well as elsewhere profited from his knowledge and skill. We have only to listen to our lawyers, who appeared before industrial commissions, to realize that Dr. Becker represented the best for both the individual and the company. Many will not believe that industry gave so much recognition to the individual and to Dr. Becker, but he knew it, and loving those who needed him, he loved the company who made it possible for him to aid them. His influence in his sphere can be compared to the ripples created by a stone dropped into a pool. The ripples spread out and out until they touch the very bank.

2.

I agree with the rabbi's remark that Dr. Becker's deep humanness and his approach to religion were far above the average. He was indeed ahead of his time.

I remember once I was asked to say a prayer at one of our annual company dinners. I wanted the prayer to have universal connotations. So I wrote out a prayer and read it to Dr. Becker on our ride home. He liked it because it asked nothing for anyone in particular but for all of us in general. In truth, Dr. Becker was above most of us. His nearness to the important and to fundamentals make me think of him as a forerunner of the brother-hood of man and the universality of all of us.

In conclusion, may I quote: "We shall not see his like again."

Percy Love

May 23, 1963

Dear Mrs. Becker:

I am enclosing a copy of Percy's remarks (which you requested) as nearly as he can recall them.

He regrets that he did not include in his remarks a reference to Dr. Becker's deep attachment to you and your reciprocation of it which he saw evidenced in an incident during Dr. Becker's illness in February. Percy has described the incident to me a number of times, attesting to its influence on him. This is the way he remembers it:

Shortly after Dr. Becker's return home from the hospital in February, Percy was visiting him one day and he needed to be moved. You went to him to help him, and he put up his hand so that you could assist him and looked up at you with a look of absolute affection and adoration which you returned in kind. Percy says that he feels privileged to have witnessed that little scene and that he can't erase it from his mind.

Our best to you, and we hope to see you soon.

Nell Love & also

Love,

from Percy

Appendix Q

Selfhelp of Chicago Newsletter - June, 1963 - Page 1

Dr. William Becker's Death

Selfhelp of Chicago, Inc.

NEWS LETTER

JUNE, 1963   No. 7

Dear Friends:

We know we are not breaking the news to you — you all have heard about the sad fact that our dear, respected and much admired President, Dr. William F. Becker, passed away on May 15. A long, incurable illness caused his untimely death, tearing him away from an active, constructive life. We all deeply mourn this grave loss to the community, to our organizations and those they serve, to his family, and especially to his brave companion in marriage and Selfhelp work, Dorothy Becker. The innumerable testimonials of affection and friendship for both of them during these past months are evidence more eloquent than words of everybody's high esteem and deep concern. The number of communications, by mail and in the form of donations, first, to extend good wishes for the patient's recovery, and now as an expression of sympathy, is so large that, as you will readily understand, Mrs. Becker, to her sincere regret, is unable to thank everyone for them individually and personally. She is deeply touched and grateful in the knowledge that she and our late President have so many friends who share her grief. It will give her the strength to carry on, and we hope that she may soon be able to resume her wonderful, humanitarian work.

Bill and Dorothy Becker's devotion and selfless endeavors to help others have been extraordinary, their strength obviously deriving from their true and utter personal happiness. Without regard for many of the minor joys of life they devoted practically all their spare time, and more, to Selfhelp matters and problems. Due to Dr. Becker's foresight and guidance during the past sixteen years, the small organization of Selfhelp has grown from a small group extending neighborly aid into an important agency. In gaining the respect of the community, it has been able to first create and then expand the home for the aged on the South Side and, more recently, to secure a federal loan for a second, even larger home now under construction on the North Side. With dignity and skill Dr. Becker solved major and minor problems. His forceful example instilled a spirit of emulation and cooperation among those who were exposed to it and were privileged to assist him in realizing his ambitious plans. They are determined to honor his memory by carrying on in the same spirit.

It is hard to believe that Dr. Becker could accomplish all this in addition to his exacting professional work, which he performed with the same concentration of effort and dedication. After leaving Berlin, where he had built up a successful career as an orthopedic surgeon, and settling down in Chicago, he became associated with the famous Hawthorn plant of Western Electric and, for many years, was its Chief Industrial Surgeon. His thorough knowledge and skill and outstanding human qualities won him the deep respect and friendship of all his colleagues as well as national recognition, enhanced by contributions which he made in his specialty to journals and by papers delivered at important meetings. His professional services also were much appreciated by his personal patients who consulted him in the private practice which he was able to maintain on a part-time basis.

Out of the desire to pay tribute to their leader of long standing and following many urgent requests for creating a special means of honoring the memory of Dr. Becker, the Executive Committees of Selfhelp and the Home have resolved to establish a *Dr. William F. Becker Memorial Fund* in the Happy Day and Memorial Fund of Selfhelp. All donations being made now and later in remembrance of our late President will be credited to this fund. Also, in recognition of his great humanitarian achievements, a plaque bearing his name will be affixed in the new home on the North Side. You will be interested to know that a special contribution will be made by a good friend of the Beckers' and of the organizations in the form of a painting of the deceased to be hung in the new home.

The Northside Senior Group most fittingly paid tribute to the memory of Dr. Becker at its first gathering following the sad event. We would like to share with you the thoughts expressed on this occasion by a member of the group Mrs. Frieda Reinsberg:

"Meine lieben Freunde:

Heute kamen wir alle nach hier mit tief bewegten Herzen.

Der Lebenskamerad unserer lieben Praesidntin Frau Becker ist entschlafen.

Der Dahingeschiedene hatte nicht nur als Doktor der Menscheit gedient, sondern hat ausserdem noch so viel fuer die Selfhelp getan. Sein Name wird unvergesslich bleiben. Im Andenken an den Dahingeschiedenen moechte ich Ihnen einige Verse zitieren, die ein Bekannter geschrieben hat. Weil diese allgemeines Interesse haben, koennen sie sich besonders auf Dr. Becker beziehn."

"ZEIT IST GNADE

Sag' mir, was ist doch die Zeit?

Man sieht sie nicht und kann sie nicht fassen.
Und doch ist sie da und immer bereit,
Sich unaufhoerlich nuetzen zu lassen.

Appendix R[1]

Report of the Southside and Northside Neighborhood Groups
by Mitzi Marx - February 4, 1969 - Page 1(2)

Report of the South-Side and North-Side Neighborhood Groups
of Selfhelp of Chicago at the Annual Meeting, February 4th, 69

This is the year of Selfhelp's 30th Anniversary, a special time for
the organization to do some special thinking, and our thoughts are
thoughts of pride, accomplishment and dedication. The name "Selfhelp "
that has become a household word today, signifying therapy for all kinds
of ills, was rather unknown then but picked by our organization 30
years ago. And ever since, we have helped practiced Selfhelp in every
possible way by providing beautiful and comfortable Homes for the Aged
so that they can enjoy the companionship pf people their own age.
Our Neighborhoodxwomen volunteers did the big job of collecting money by
emptying cans every year, these dedicated women made it possible for us
to build our first Home 18 years ago. Now they bring cheer to the residents, arra
arange Kaffeeklatsches" with outside friends, take them to the theater and concerts. They write letters for the ones whose eyesight is failing, or
do some mending for those who need it. They call out a Bingo Game, are
with them on their special birthdays. They drive them to doctors and hospitals and arrange little outings for them.

Besides our work in the Home we have still quite a lot of cases to
take care of. I like to mention just a few. When we heard of a
young man, an Israeli who has lived in this country only a few years, we
learned that his wife was dying of cancer. His 7 year old child was
understably/disturbed about it and refused to go to school. The poor
father did not know what to do first: to see his dying wife, go to work
in order to make money and to pay the hospital bills or to stay with the
child who was using his asthmatic condition to stay home from school.
We were fortunate to place the child within a week on a scholarship
in a Jewish Day School. The public school had due to changes in the
neighborhood some very rough elements attending it and was not a desirable
place for him to be or to make friends. When the sad day came and his
mother died, at least the father did not have to worry where the child
would spend his days.

There was a desperate widow who tried to commit suicide when her hus
band suddenly died of a heart attack, Our Neighborhood Group stood
by hutxasanx to help her to overcome her grief. But soon after it
was discovered that she had a malignant brain tumor. The year

360

Appendix R^2

Report of the Southside and Northside Neighborhood Groups

by Mitzi Marx - February 4, 1969 - Page 2(2)

II

that followed were dreadful. She had no relatives, no close friends.
We Selfhelp women tried everything to make her a little happier
until she died. We only had to pay for the night nurses during the
last days. This was not a financial burden to our organization,
it will not be found in the our ledgers but it is as important as
financial aid.

There was another case where we did need money. It was discovered
at school that an intelligent 8 year old child was not able to read
or write. Tests were made and the findings showed that there was
a brain injury. The child desperately need to be admitted in a
school for exceptional children. There was no father and the mother
had to struggle to take care of her family. She could not possibly
afford to pay the tuition. Selfhelp helped substantially and after
1 semester we received a beautiful letter from this child. the
mother reported that the teachers hope that the child can attend
public schools again in a year or two.

We could mention many more such cases but time does not permit it.

Selfhelp has done much to be proud of, when we think of all the
accomplishments over the last 3o years. We take special pride
in our Neighborhood Group women, they deserve our gratitude and
thanks, each one of them, for putting their self in the background
many times in order to help others who need us.

Mrs. Martin Marx

Appendix S

Schedule of Events at the Selfhelp Center During December of 1970

Schedule of events at Selfhelp Center during the month of December 1970

Date	Time	Event	Place
Sunday, 13th	3 P.M.	Mr. Danziger's 90th Birthday	Recreation Room
Monday, 14th	6:30 P.M.	Mr. Bernard Weisberg will talk about the new Constitution	Recreation Room
Tuesay, 15th	all day	Election Day:go to the Polls	Carmen Street
Wednesday,16th		Mr. Kahn's 91st Birthday	Party will take place later
Thursday, 17th	2 P.M.	Christmas Part for the Staff of Selfhelp Center	Recreation Room
	17th 7:30 P.M.	Glee Club: String Orchestra	Recreation Room
Saturday, 19th	7 P.M.	Mrs. Michel's 90th Birthday *Mrs. Lende - birthday*	Recreation Room *no party*
Sunday, 20th	3 P.M.	Mrs. Heinsfurter's 93rd Birthday	Dining Room
Tuesday, 22nd	6:30 P.M.	Chanukah,lighting the Candles first day	Recreation Room
Wednesday,23rd	evening	Kantor Schwimmer & Mrs. Schwimmer of Ezra Congregation with a children's String-~~QHAYIBIX~~ Orchestra	Recreation Room
Thursday, 24th		Mrs. Sinsheimer's Birthday	no party
Saturday, 26th	7 P.M.	Chanukah Party for Resident with their Children	Recreation Room
		Also: Miss Paula Marcus 90th Birthday-Party	
Tue 29 ~~Thursday, 31st~~	8 P.M.	*Chanukkah Party senior group* ~~New Year's Eve Party~~	Recreation Room

Frieda Berliner - Birthday Party

Thu, Dec. 31   *New Year's Party*

Directive of March 18, 1973 From Selfhelp's Executive Board

to the Executive Directors and the Business Manager - Page 1(3)

(Question marks in margins are made by Dorothy Becker)

3/18/73

SELFHELP HOME FOR THE AGED, INC.

EXECUTIVE DIRECTORS

The Executive Directors of the nursing wing (A) and the remaining portion of the Home (B) are responsible for -

1. The emotional and physical well-being of the residents and for making life as pleasant for them as possible by talking to and spending time with them, individually and in groups, for therapeutic, social and recreational purposes;

2. Visiting hospitalized residents;

3. Liaison with residents' relatives, physicians, psychiatrists, pharmacists, hospitals;

4. Supervision of nursing staff, of administration of medications, of chart-keeping;

5. Hiring (after preliminary screening by Business Manager[a]) and firing of nursing personnel (in A in conjunction with RN Nurse Supervisor) and kitchen personnel (in B in conjunction with Housekeeping Supervisor). Executive Director of A also hires and fires housekeeping staff for that unit (in conjunction with Business Manager);

6. Encouragement of involvement of volunteers and their activities, within and outside the Home, for the good of the residents of the Home and senior citizens in the community[b];

7. Close cooperation with the House Committee, to which they report and with which they meet at regular intervals; the Executive Directors are members of the House Committee;

8. Reporting to and consulting with the appropriate physician and/or a committee ~~for~~ for joint decision regarding necessary action, such as moving residents to and from nursing unit or termination of residence[c];

9. The Executive Director of A will supervise the housekeeping and kitchen personnel for that unit. The Housekeeping Supervisor will be responsible to the Executive Director of A relative to kitchen personnel (and to the Business Manager relative to non-kitchen housekeeping staff of B and janitorial staff).[d]

Appendix T[2]

Directive of March 18, 1973 From Selfhelp's Executive Board

to the Executive Directors and the Business Manager - Page 2(3)

(Question marks in margins are made by Dorothy Becker)

-2-

BUSINESS MANAGER

The Business Manager of Selfhelp Home is responsible for -

1. All record keeping, including accounting records, inventory, payroll, government forms, etc.;

2. Purchasing (in conjunction with House Committee);

3. Supervision of all physical plant matters, including janitorial services, maintenance and repairs, etc.;

4. Personnel functions -

    a) Work schedules of employees (hours, etc.), time keeping (signing in), vacations and sick leaves;

    b) Administrative aspects of staff recruitment - placing ads in papers, preliminary screening[a];

    c) Monitoring of wage and salary levels based on budget prepared by Finance Committee (except for salaries of the three Executives, which will be determined by Finance Committee and paid by Treasurer of Home);

    d) Hiring and firing of non-kitchen housekeeping and janitorial staff (the latter and housekeeping staff for B in conjunction with Housekeeping Supervisor; housekeeping staff for A in conjunction with Executive Director of A);

5. Financial responsibilities - collecting rents and past due accounts from residents;

6. Supervision of office, including secretary and volunteer receptionist[e];

7. Close cooperation with the House Committee, to which (s)he reports and with which (s)he meets at regular intervals; the Business Manager is a member of the House Committee;

8. Assisting President as requested, including staff support for committees.

* * * * * * *

The Executive Directors and the Business Manager are hired by the President in consultation with a small ad hoc committee.

The Executive Directors and the Business Manager execute policies set by the Executive Committee and are responsible to it with regard to policy matters. They are non-voting, ex officio members of the Executive Committee; their names will be listed on the letterhead after the officers and Chairmen of Standing Committees and before the Representatives at Large, in accordance with their own wishes (husband's or own first names).

The Executive Directors and the Business Manager are responsible in administrative matters either to the President or to a small committee (Management Committee), composed of the President

Appendix T[3]

Directive of March 18, 1973 From Selfhelp's Executive Board

to the Executive Directors and the Business Manager - Page 3(3)

(Question marks in margins are made by Dorothy Becker)

-3-

and one or two persons.

The Housekeeping Supervisor is hired by the Executive Director of B jointly with the Business Manager. She supervises the housekeeping and kitchen personnel of B as well as the janitorial staff; she is responsible relative to the kitchen personnel to the Executive Director of B; relative to housekeeping personnel of B and janitorial staff to the Business Manager[d].

The Nurse Supervisor is hired by the President in consultation with the Executive Director of A.

* * * * * * * * *

a) After screening by Business Manager by mail or phone, instead of brief initial interview with Business Manager, Dorothy Becker wishes to conduct that initial interview herself as far as nursing personnel for B is concerned.

b) All donations, especially from residents, to the Happy Day and Memorial Fund, are to be referred to the volunteer resident who handles this assignment - currently Mrs. Jacoby; she may have to have an assistant.

Such matters as newsletter, minutes of meetings, Admissions Committee records, are to be continued as volunteer activities (if necessary, some typing help to be hired). Responsibility for coordination of these and other volunteer activities to be further discussed.

c) A "neutral" physician probably is needed to serve as a consultant; he may be able to make the decision with the Executive Directors in very clearcut cases; he probably should be a member of the committee, which might be called Committee on Residents, and which would make the decision in cases which are not clearcut. There seems to be need to establish some basic policies relative to the question of such moves; the existing ad hoc committee might be the nucleus of such a policy committee, expanded by inclusion of the Executive Directors and a physician.

d) Although the Housekeeping Supervisor is responsible to the Business Manager for non-kitchen housekeeping functions, this does not mean that the Executive Directors cannot communicate directly with the Housekeeping Supervisor on matters of daily routine operations.

e) Office opens mail, except letters addressed "Personal" or addressed to residents (their mail to be put in pigeon holes to be established for each resident and to be called for by each resident from volunteer receptionist); mail addressed to organization or staff is directed to appropriate person, in accordance with subject matter; for some months, Dorothy Becker will sift her mail at the office and remove letters to be attended to by her personally.

Office answers phones during day; volunteer receptionist answers phone after office hours (try to get some younger residents to volunteer as receptionists; possibility that in the long run this assignment cannot be handled by volunteers - also during day time).

Except in emergencies, residents, when not in their rooms, cannot be called to the phone; possibly a message service can be worked out.

Appendix U[1]

Fred Aufrecht's Clarification of Minutes Regarding the Directive of

March 18, 1973 - Page 1(2)

(Question marks in margins are made by Dorothy Becker)

<u>EXECUTIVE DIRECTORS</u>

A -- In charge of 7th and 8th (nursing) floors and nursing unit
kitchen (?) on 9th floor; major responsibility for welfare of
residents - talking to and spending time with residents; liaison
with physicians, psychiatrists and relatives of residents;
supervision of nursing personnel (RN not to be called Director of
Nurses but possibly Nurse Supervisor;) reports to or consults with
appropriate committees of Board regarding necessary action, such as
move of residents to and from nursing unit or termination of
residence (involves unresolved question of who initiates such moves,
who makes decisions on them - possibly in simple cases decision by
physician; otherwise, a special committee; in any event, in cooperation with, but not on sole decision of, both Executive Directors.

The Executive Director is primarily responsible for the well-being
of the residents and for making life as pleasant for them as possible;
for keeping in touch with relatives, physicians, pharmacists and
hospitals for supervision of nurses, administration of medications,
chart-keeping, visits to hospitalized residents; for encouragement
of involvement of volunteers and their activities, within and outside the Home, for the good of the residents of theHome and Senior
Citizens in the community; for close cooperation with the House
Committee, to which she reports and with which she meets at regular
intervals.

B -- The same tasks would apply to the Executive Director for the non-A
portion of Selfhelp Center, for well patients, except that A would
place more emphasis on the psychological and physical well-being
of residents, while B would put more stress on recreational and
social activities. Under B, nurses aides would continue to be
employed, separately from the nursing personnel working under A.

Both Executive Directors and the Business Manager will be responsible
in administrative matters either to the President or to a small
committee, composed of the President plus one or two persons -
a Management Committee (the latter arrangement was favored by the
President and probably a majority of the committee.)

A lengthy discussion developed over the question of participation
of the three Executives in meetings of the Executive Committee,
to which they will be responsible with regard to policy matters -
policy being set by the Executive Committee of the Board, The
compromise result of the discussion was that the three Executives
should be ex officio members of the Executive Committee, without
vote.

P.S. Discussion of the above minutes with Fred Aufrecht indicated
that he felt it was clear from the discussions that the
Housekeeping Supervisor is to be in charge of housekeeping
and kitchens, and that she would be responsible for all
housekeeping functions to the Business Manager and for all
kitchen functions to the respective Executive Directors.

366

Appendix U²

Fred Aufrecht's Clarification of Minutes Regarding the Directive of

March 18, 1973 - Page 1(2)

(Question Marks Noted by Dorothy Becker)

BUSINESS MANAGER

A -- All record-keeping, including accounting records, inventory,
   payroll, government forms, etc.
B -- Supervision of all physical plant matters, including janitorial
   services, maintenance and repairs, etc.
C -- Personnel functions --
   I -- Work schedules of employees (hours, etc.) timekeeping
       (signing in) vacations and sick leaves
   II -- Administrative aspects of staff recruitment - placing ads
       in papers, preliminary screening; ?
   III -- Supervision of non-kitchen housekeeping staff (Housekeeping
       Supervisor would be responsible to business manager)
   IV -- Wage determination based on budget prepared by Finance
       Committee
D -- Financial responsibilities - collecting rents and past due
   accounts from residents
E -- Purchasing
F -- Assisting President as requested, including staff support for
   Committees.
G -- Supervision of office, including secretary, who is to open and
   distribute mail (pieces of mail not to be opened if addressed
   to residents or if addressed "personal to any member of staff;)
   Mail addressed to organization or staff to be directed to
   appropriate person in accordance with subject matter; residents'
   mail to be put in pigeon holes which will be established for
   each resident and to be called for from volunteer receptionist
   as is a hotel (not to be directly accessible to residents so as
   to avoid indiscretion.) Such matters as donations, newsletter,
   minutes of meetings, Admissions Committee records, to be continued
   as volunteer activities (if necessary, some typing help to be
   hired;) may have to get assistant volunteer for Mrs. Jacoby who
   takes in donations.
   Secretary answers phone during day; volunteer receptionist
   answers phone after office hours (have to try and get some
   younger residents to volunteer for receptionist job; possibility
   that in the long run this assignment cannot be handled by
   volunteers, also during day time.) Issue of outside calls for
   residents when not in their own rooms was discussed; except in
   emergencies, it will be impossible to go and look for them; possibly
   a system for a message service could be worked out.

367

Appendix V

Dorothy Becker's Response to the Directive of March 18, 1973

and Fred Aufrecht's Clarification - Page 2

(Page 1 is Missing)

This, I believe, covers your little memo, and now we go to the job description:

Page 1-Section 5

I do not think it practical for the nursing personnel to be screened by the business manager. I did agree with to Dick Sinsheimer that nursing applicants be given the application forms by the business manager. However, the initial interview should be given by me.

Kitchen personnel may be seen first by the business manager and, after screening, referred to me for interview. I should have the right--if I am dissatisfied with the household personnel--to be heard and have a say-so whether an employee should be dismissed. This is important because of complaints from our residents about the way they are being treated sometimes by our maids. I am referringyou to paragraph 1 which states that I am responsible for the wellbeing of our residents. Therefore, this request should not be refused by the business manager.

Page 1-Section 8

When residents of Selfhelp Center are being moved to the health care floors--either on a temporary or permanent basis--and are taken to the hospital or are seriously ill, I would appreciate being informed. This has been done until now by Dr. Kalurny.

Page 1-Section 9

If any of our residents should need more frequent linen changes because of bed-wetting or losing stool, I would like to be informed immediately since this may be a medical problem and not only a matter of additional charges.

Page 2-Section 4 a

I had already suggested in a meeting that vacation schedules for kitchen personnel should be worked out with the girls, Mrs. Schoenbach and me and then be submitted to the business manager.

368

Appendix W

The First Annual Letter to Dorothy Becker from Rolf Weil

September 27, 1976

Selfhelp Home for the Aged

INCORPORATED NOT FOR PROFIT
908 WEST ARGYLE STREET
CHICAGO, ILLINOIS 60640
TELEPHONE 271-0300

September 27, 1976

Mrs. William F. Becker
908 W. Argyle Street
Chicago, Illinois 60640

Dear Dorothy:

This is just a short note to tell you before the end of the month that on the recommendation of the Finance Committee your salary will be increased effective October 1, 1976 to the annual rate of $14,250 plus the apartment and other customary fringe benefits. This is an increase of $750.00 in the annual rate.

Of course, no compensation is adequate to reward you for your dedication beyond the call of duty. I want to thank you on behalf of Selfhelp Home as well as myself personally for your great humanitarian service to our residents.

In friendship,

Rolf A. Weil
President

RAW:lw

Appendix X[1]

Rolf Weil Board President and Dorothy Becker, Executive Director

Address Selfhelp's Volunteers - Sept. 1984 - Page 1(2)

et 5-8 hbn 9-14-84 begin record 4-51- : 2nd quarter news, for listings of April - June, 1984

809400128 newstwo

VOL. XXXVII No. 3   **September, 1984**

Dear Friends of Selfhelp:

The NORTH SHORE GROUP of SELFHELP OF CHICAGO intends to send out a cordial invitation to all Members and Friends of Selfhelp to attend the annual dinner party on SUNDAY, OCTOBER 28, 1984, in the Gold Coast Room of The Drake Hotel, to celebrate twenty-five years of service of this group to the general community of Selfhelp.

Entertainment will be by Charlie Rex and his Orchestra.
Cocktails will be served from 5:00 o'clock P.M., and
Dinner will be at 6:30 o'clock P.M.
Donation per person $50.00.

Those of us who attended the dinner party last year at the Drake Hotel will remember what a good time was had by one and all. Especially, Mr. Charlie Rex and his Orchestra played such catchy tunes with interludes of sophisticated and lively entertainment. He readily supported our own Herbert Teichner when he regaled us by rendering popular songs on his home-made musical instruments, such as a saw or other converted tools! A high light was the drawing of numbers for three exquisite gifts, which made three people in the audience very happy indeed.

Let us hope that we will duplicate the festive spirit this year and help the North Shore Group help Selfhelp of Chicago and Selfhelp Home for the Aged to a good deal of money, which certainly was the case last year as a result of the party at the Drake Hotel.

Individual invitations are being mailed this month to all the Members.

— — — — — — —

August 19, 1984, was selected to be "Honor the Volunteers Day" at Selfhelp Home. Individual invitations were mailed to all the volunteers of Selfhelp and Selfhelp Home with a copy of a pin to be distributed to the Volunteers that came to the party on a warm and sunny afternoon.

Each volunteer wore this pin, and the recreation room at Selfhelp Home was filled with people from outside of the Home, besides, of course, the Residents who are the most important Volunteers. Mrs. Anna Hirsch and Mrs. Else Strauss greeted the assembly and stressed the importance of every individual who comes to the Home and assists both the elderly and the running of the organizations, of which there are so many phases, it is hard to fathom and impossible to enumerate. There were the poets among the Residents, like Mrs. Hermine Allmayer and Mr. Fred Hausler, who in appropriate rhyme greeted the Volunteers and expressed thanks to them for coming in heat and in cold from all corners of the City as well as from the suburbs to serve the Home and its Residents by serving coffee and cake on Tuesdays and Thursdays, by working at the gift shop and by taking over the switchboard and reception desk during most of the daylight hours, including Saturdays and Sundays.

Mrs. Dorothy Becker, Executive Director of Selfhelp Home, than addressed the assembled group and explained the meaning of volunteering. She spoke of her own experience as a volunteer for Selfhelp and the volunteer work of all of her friends whom she met during her 45 or 46 years of working for Selfhelp. She gave praise to the Chairman of the Volunteers, Mrs. Mitzi Marx, whom she let into volunteering for the Home on Drexel Boulevard and who is continuing her remarkable work nowadays on the North Side of Chicago. Mrs. Becker elaborated on the slogan printed on the above mentioned button *"Volunteers give the gift of love"* by pointing out that every person who undertakes to help others is the greatest recipient ·'

Appendix X[2]

Rolf Weil Board President and Dorothy Becker, Executive Director

Address Selfhelp's Volunteers - Sept. 1984 - Page 2(2)

inner awards — it gives you a warm and satisfied feeling inside after you have done your share, either pouring coffee for the golden age center or when you have tried to feed someone in the health care facility who otherwise would not have eaten a thing, and thus having freed some time for the nurses to do more or other essential work.

Mrs. Mitzi Marx, Chairman of the Volunteers, gave the second address and in a similar vein as Mrs. Becker priased the work of the many volunteers who not only come on a regular basis, regardless of weather conditions, but who also bring some very specialized knowledge and training to Selfhelp. There is for instance a recently retired social worker-psychologist who comes at least once a week and has sessions with a number of residents who require this form of therapy very badly. Or there is a teacher of gymnastics who gives group instruction for the elderly — and believe it or not, we all could benefit from such sessions! There are volunteers who come with their cars to take some of our residents shopping or to their doctors' or dentists' appointments; this takes quite some organization, to satisfy everybody in order to make his or her appointment in time and to pick them up again for the return trip home.

Then President Weil took the podium and expressed his gratitude and appreciation to the volunteers collectively. He said, since he is an economist, he would have to express his thanks on a economic basis. He said he had figured out that if you actually added up the figures that it would cost to pay the volunteers, it would probably amount to close to $200,000 per year in wages to be paid. This, of course, would account heavily for the steady volunteers, like the Treasurers both for Selfhelp and for Selfhelp Home, who are actually on the job every day of the entire year. But apart from these perennial jobs, the many occasional volunteer efforts could not possibly be weighed in monetary remuneration. He recited as an example the position of Mrs. Dorothy Becker who spends eight to ten hours every day as the executive director of the Home, and then she puts in another twelve to fourteen hours every day as a volunteer at Selfhelp. At any rate, he stated that Selfhelp could not have developed into the organization that it has become without the steady and constant assistance from the Volunteers who have given the Home just the little "extra" that makes it so outstanding and different from every other home for the elderly.

Turning the meeting back to Mrs. Becker, she then distributed Certificates to all the many Volunteers who were present this afternoon together with especially printed ballpoint pens saying "THANKS TO OUR NICE VOLUNTEER FROM SELFHELP."

The Home's dining room was set up to receive all these many visitors, besides the residents of our Home, and to treat everyone to delicious strawberry punch and home-made cakes and cookies. Some of the volunteers could even sit down and enjoy these treats, contrary to their custom while they are volunteering.

— — — — — — —

Please note that Selfhelp again was the recipient of several sizeable bequests and we are every so grateful to

Arthur and Emma Eichberg,
Martha Hagen, and
Dr. Albert Oppenheimer,

who remembered us in their wills. Mr. and Mrs. Eichberg were a remarkable couple who lived a quiet and rather inconspicuous life. They obviously saved their pennies and having had no children, left a very large part of their estate to Selfhelp. Selfhelp through them gained a very large amount of money.

As we have said before, it is too late for us to express our gratitude to these good members. But we can try to live up to their expectations and conduct a home in the best posible way for as many people as we can possibly house.

SELFHELP CENTER GIFT SHOP — Please take note that the Gift Shop at Selfhelp Center holds numerous gift store items, handmade knitted and crocheted goods, gift cards, and a beautiful collection of chocolates, both imported bars and boxed arrangements, coming from Switzerland and Israel. When you shop for gifts, MRS. BETTY BETTINK or one of her many co-workers will be happy to assist you in your selection.

DRIVERS — We always need drivers who are aboe to give some time and their cars to take Residents to the physician or dentist. If you have a morning or afternoon, please contact Mrs. Martin Marx* or Mrs. Ernest Bensinger*. They will be able to make arrangements for you and give you details.

Appendix Y

Rolf Weil's Letter to Dorothy Becker on Her Retirement

September 6, 1987

Selfhelp Home for the Aged

INCORPORATED NOT FOR PROFIT
905 WEST ARGYLE STREET
CHICAGO, ILLINOIS 60640
TELEPHONE 271-0300

September 6, 1987

Mrs. William F. Becker
~~908 W. Argyle Street~~
Chicago, Illinois 60640

Dear Dorothy:

At this time of the year it is my pleasant duty to thank you for your dedication to Selfhelp, for your guardianship over our residents who are appreciative of your love, and for your efficient administration of our wonderful Home.

As you know, we have searched with your concurrence for a successor to you. We are quite convinced that noone will ever be able to do all the wonderful things that you have accomplished. The search committee will probably make a personnel decision in the very near future, however.

At this time I want to inform you that effective October 1, 1987 and until your replacement takes over your salary will be at the annual rate of $29,400.00. After that you will receive a pension from Selfhelp for life in accordance with my letter of October 4, 1980. An exact calculation of this annuity will be made at ~~the time of your retirement.~~

Again many thanks for your dedication and friendship.

As ever,

Rolf

RAW:lw
CC H. Strauss

Rolf A. Weil
President

Member, Council for Community Services in Metropolitan Chicago, Member, Illinois Association of Homes for the Aging.
Endorsed by the Chicago Association of Commerce and Industry.
Contributions to Selfhelp Home for the Aged, Inc., are deductible from taxable income.

ANNUAL MEETING   APRIL 1, 1984

REPORT OF EXECUTIVE DIRECTOR

We all have heard enough political speeches lately. I have the feeling
that after close to 40 years of reporting at an Annual Meeting that some
things do not change and become repetitious. However, my feelings to
Selfhelp and our residents still are the same and I hope I can convey
to you my pride in Selfhelp and my hopes for the future.

One of the questions I am asked very often is how old-are our residents?
The average age at Selfhelp Center is 85.5 -- 84.4 for women, and 88.9
years for men. There are 19 residents over 90 years old. We are at the
brink of a major change in medical science. It is expected that in
about 50 years there will be 5 million senior citizens. It is predicted
that most people will outlive the fourscore years of life, and that the
period of decline will be minimized. However, in spite of the growing
population of senior citizens, our government makes new laws that
hospitals have to send their patients home as quickly as possible, in
order not to lose money. If, for example, a patient enters the hospital
because of a hip fracture, and gets a heart attack 3 days before his
discharge, the hospital will not be reimbursed for his stay. They set
a limit for each sickness. If the patient can leave earlier, the
hospital will be paid for the length of stay permitted. What will this
do to us? Are we prepared? Selfhelp has always had the foresight to do
the right think long before others planned it. Our Home is an example
to many. Wherever I go, people rave about our Home, and our residents and
their families are the best advertisers. But our reputation didn't just
happen--we try hard to achieve it. Everyone who enters our Home immediatel
feels the spirit that prevails, the affection that our residents have for
each other. While privacy plays a great role in everyone's life, they all
enjoy the special programs that are offered. All feel secure, and know

-2-

that in case of emergency they can press a button and get help. I
usually accompany them to a hospital or doctor. It gives the residents
the assurance that they are loved and cared for. I have often wished
that the days had more hours to do all the things that have to be done,
but we can just try to do our utmost.
Group living is not for everyone---it is only for those whose lives can
be enriched by sharing responsibilities and caring for other people.
So far almost everyone has felt the warmth and security, and they try to
be helpful, too. Last year 20 new residents moved in. The turnover was
quite heavy, because some residents moved to our H.C.F. and others died.
All of our new residents are well adjusted and happy.

We have continued to give as many services as possible. Dr. Frey, our
beloved art teacher, retired after 20 years, much to our regret. We were
fortunate to find a very able successor in Mr. Charles Freund, a gifted
artist and experienced teacher.

Mrs. Funt's Current Events Class always draws a great crowd, and they look
forward to this inspiring weekly discussion group. Mrs. Sichel teaches
crocheting and knitting; Mrs. Bensinger and Mrs. Melber conduct a very
lovely handicraft class. Everything that is made in these classes is
immediately sold and brings money to our gift shop which is ably run by
our volunteers and residents, under the supervision of Betty Bettink and
the chairman of the Gift Shop, Mr. Martin Marx. We also have a gym class;
the teacher is sent by Truman College. This is a well-liked and important
program, as it keeps our residents young and elastic. Not all can
participate, but those who do feel younger every week. We also have a
Music Appreciation Class conducted by Mr. Gordon, who is very well-liked.
He was absent for a while when Truman College ran out of money and could
not pay him any more, at which time our own Dr. Epstein took over, but
Mr. Gordon is now back with us. Dr. Epstein brings great joy to us when

-3-

he arranges a concert every Friday night. Symphonies, Viennese songs, a
operas are on his program. We all sit in our beautiful East Living-Room
and relax in a real Shabbath mood.

As usual we have lots of parties and entertainment. We are grateful to
Mrs. Miriam Levi who is always contacting new sources. We sincerely
appreciate Mrs. Wetzler, Mr. Akos, Mr. Sabransky, Mrs. Salm, Dr. Chas.
Moore, and the Ebstein Family who provide us with beautiful concerts.
We have dance groups, visits from the zoo, magicians, choirs and many
other unique programs. We had a lovely New Year's Eve Party with a live
band provided by the family of our so efficient secretary Marlene Jenson
Last year's Special Event was the 20th Anniv. Party of Selfhelp Center.
Our cook, 3 residents and I were the only ones of the original staff
and residents left but several volunteers had also worked here during
this time. Every one had a marvelous time celebrating. We depend more
on outside entertainment now than before as the only survivors of the
good old times when we had so many stars are Mr. Brownwald and Mrs. Hirs
We have now a professional pianist, Mrs. Staple; and our so talented MC,
Anna Hirsch, is joined by Mrs. Stiefel and Mrs. Allmayer; Mr. Hausler
is still our House Poet. Many who never in their lives had given speech
come forward now and much to the surprise of their own families do it nc
Mrs. Else Strauss, in charge of the culinary art, has lots of helpers to
Without them we would not have had such a great success at our Hanukkah
Party when we had over 300 guests. She also is in charge of resident
volunteers. Our choir with its conductor, Julie Freudenthal, our
Religious Committee with its efficient and diligent chairman, Mr.
Steiermann meet regularly. The choir entertains at all birthday partie:
but they are at their best on holidays. Mr. & Mrs. Joe Leib regularly
conduct the most beautiful Friday Night services--their kindness shines
through in their voices. (We also received a beautiful large menorah

Appendix Z[4]

Dorothy Becker's Annual Report - April 1, 1984 - Page 5(7)

(Please Note that Page 4(7) is missing!)

-5-

he went on a vacation arranged to have Mr. Mills come. This is a great
relief as shopping becomes a chore for many. Our front desk is manned
by many volunteers during the day and in the morning and evening hours
by our residents. Volunteers play a vital role in our daily activities.
We not only save thousands of dollars but they are a great help to our
staff and residents. There is not one department without volunteers.
We plan to give a party in May for them. I personally want to thank
Miss Rooz and Mrs. Bidi Brown for helping me in the office and Irmgard
Heymann whose valuable services I greatly appreciate. She comes every
Monday to counsel several residents and is also helpful in our H.C.F.
Last year I reported that we were looking for younger volunteers for our
Senior Groups and we succeeded in getting some. We got Nancy Strauss
who is as delightful as she is efficient. Ella Rothschild still takes
care of the box collection at the Senior Group meetings. Ruth Gideon, who
became a resident recently, continues in her job and adds spice to it by
telling jokes. To coordinate all this is a big job, well handled by the
chairman of the volunteers, Mitzi Marx who herself does a remarkable
job in our H.C.F., her warmth touching every patient. She was able to
get some wonderful new helpers; Hilde Aron and Ruth Markus are a great
addition to our really fine group. Gretl Oppenheimer is very much
appreciated by Mrs. Hirschberg for doing the office work. The task of
running the H.C.F. is unbelievably tough. The incurable Alzheimer
disease has changed many personalities to such an extent that our staff
has trouble keeping their own sanity. All our patients are well kept
and clean. We have fine instructors and activity persons. It is
remarkable how much they can do with sometimes very difficult patients.
We have constant inspections. The reports are always excellent and the
State of Ill. gives us an extra bonus for being one of the most
outstanding homes in Ill. We are all very proud and thank Mrs. Hirschber
and Mrs. Salins for their very efficient handling of their jobs.

Appendix Z[5]

Dorothy Becker's Annual Report - April 1, 1984 - Page 6(7) and 7(7)

-6-

The staff at Selfhelp Center as well as in the H.C.F. has been steady and good. A happy staff makes a happy atmosphere for our residents. I am always assured by our staff that they, too, belong to "my Selfhelp Family"; our Home is their home, too. They are well trained and supervised by our housekeeping supervisors Mrs. Meleckson and her assistant, Mrs. Vaiman. Both do an outstanding job. We had some trouble in our janitorial department but as the head janitor is very efficient, we were able to manage most of the time. It seems that we now have succeeded in finding the right men in this department.

To finish my report I want to thank our Business Manager, Charles Lohfeld for his cooperation, we both enjoy working together. I want to thank our 2 Harolds (and I do not mean our Mayor) but Harold Weinberg and Harold Raff for helping Mrs. Jacoby in her never ending job getting donations. She does such a tremendous job that we all admire her. You heard the figures that were mentioned by our treasurers. We could never do it without Mrs. Brandis and Mrs. Jacoby. No one realizes what a tremendous job our treasurers Hedy Strauss and Leni Weil do. Hedy Strauss works 30 to 40 hours weekly for us, and I believe Leni Weil does almost the same when you include the work she does for our president. The accountants are always amazed that this work is done by volunteers. Lotte Aufrecht, the chairperson of our House Committee is sometimes exhausted from her tedious job. It doesn't show today as she has just come back from a long badly needed vacation.

I enjoy working with all the committees and with our Board of Directors and I sincerely hope that Selfhelp will always have a president like Dr. Rolf Weil who is deeply committed and does a wonderful job. Again I want to thank every one who works for our Home in whatever capacity but most of all our residents whose love gives me the strength to make my sometimes strenuous and difficult job so gratifying. I feel my love

-7-

to them is reciprocated by all of them and I hope I will never disappoint them. I hope that I can prove that Old Age is not simply a series of losses only but that older people can live a satisfactory dynamic life.

Appendix AA[1]

Dorothy Becker's Annual Report 1973 to 1974 - Page 1(2)

ANNUAL REPORT -- 1973-74
Selfhelp Center

1973/74 was not the easiest year at Selfhelp Center. Cooking on the 9th
floor, bringing the food down hot, climbing over tools and ladders, admitting as many as 16 people on one Sunday with no janitor around--it was
a nightmare. But it also was a glorious year. We admitted about 83 people;
in fact, the majority of our population moved in in 1974. *or 131*

I had given lots of thought how to handle the situation, how to make the
newcomers feel at home as the first impressions are extremely important.
It worked magically; everyone adjusted very fast. The adjustment of the
old residents was harder than I anticipated. We had asked some of them to'
move to S.C. II, but almost no one wanted to change rooms. They were at
home. The newcomers showed preferences to exposure, floors, etc. I was
grateful to our Executive Committee for adopting Dick Sinsheimer's
suggestion to have a lottery concerning rooms. This way no one could accuse
us of favoritism. And after everyone was settled, we became again a happy
family. Each resident found something to do. We continued all our classes.
Some very gifted newcomers joined the painting class of Dr. Frey who certainly is
successful developing hidden talents. Some joined the outstanding Bible class
conducted by Mr. Weinberg. Others whose hands never rest work under the
direction of Mrs. Simons. Our Gym Class folded up *but was resumed now, and*
as we could not find an-
other teacher to volunteer, but we added a choir. To be at the rehearsals for
the High Holidays was a special treat. Where else can you see oldsters--
some of them 95 and 97 years--sing the old beautiful melodies with the en- *member*
thusiasm of teen-agers? We were fortunate having several rabbis with us for *+ some of our Bd.*
Friday Evening Services. Lately, we even had a Sabbath morning Service.
Religion means a lot to the majority of our residents, and even the so-called non-
believers enjoy the Services.

We had lots of entertainment, starting with infants on Thanksgiving Day, Grandmother Clubs at other occasions. We showed movies, enjoyed lectures, had professional entertainment, rented busses to go to Morton's Arboretum, to Highland Par
Park to a luncheon, given by our North Shore Group, to Homewood to a luncheon
given by Female B'nai Yehuda, to Ravinia to a concert and--last but not least--we
had our very own entertainers who are always ready to perform. There is never
a dull moment at Selfhelp Center. When people think of theaged, they usually
have the image of a helpless old individual who needs assistance. Our
residents, though ethnically have the same background, do come from a variety
of backgrounds. Most of them are mature and--like younger people--prefer

378

Appendix AA[2]

Dorothy Becker's Annual Report 1973 to 1974 - Page 2(2)

to make their own decisions, and as long as they are able to function, they must not be made useless. Feeling unneeded is often more painful than physical discomfort. It is important for me to find out what their interests are. Our newly established Gift Shop is a marvelous outlet for several residents. Some find satisfaction in visiting our Health Care Floor; but others again avoid it as they are fearful of their own future. Finding the right occupation for all, establishing a good relationship to have their confidence in times of need is a great task. And when our residents are too sick to stay here, it gives me great consolation to know that they are well cared for by Dr. Kaluzny on our Health Care floors. It is a great feeling to work with people who realize that they have a commitment to our residents. Our President, our Executive Committee, House Committee, Ruth Turk, our Business Manager, our volunteers, our staff, all share with me in the enthusiasm for the wellbeing of our residents.

Selfhelp Home was founded in 1949. At this time there were many doubtful Thomases, but we proved to them then and now, after 25 years, that we had only one goal: "To create a Happy Home for our Aged."

I read the other day the following words from the Talmud: "He who does charity and justice is as if he had filled the world with kindness."

We are not quite as ambitious; we are satisfied when we can do it for our residents to assure them of a happy life.

Appendix BB[1]

Dorothy Becker's Report of Executive Director - April 17, 1983

Page 1(4)

ANNUAL MEETING
APRIL 17, 1983
REPORT OF EXECUTIVE DIRECTOR

Everyone wants to live long, but we all dread being old.
Most people associate old age with senility, sickness, living in
the past, becoming unbending. Even the younger senior citizens are
afraid of an "OLD AGE HOME". They even avoid visiting residents
of Homes. They try to stay young forever and avoid talking about
their age. A few years later they find themselves in a peculiar
position. They cannot keep up with the younger crowd, are more isolated,
become lonely and forgetful, have accidents, and land after a hospital
stay in some nursing home which would not be their choice. They
put their head in the sand; they didn't plan for their future realisti-
cally. Last year, more than ever before, we got frantic phone calls
to admit people who never wanted to be on our waiting list, or postponed their admission when they were called because "they were too
young". Some of the more affluent aged thought they could stay in
their own homes with private nurses but were badly disappointed
when they were left alone on weekends, or when they couldn't find
the right help. They desperately called Selfhelp to save them. I
am always amazed about their attitude. Everyone knows that our Home
is a beautiful place to live and that our residents are treated with
dignity and respect. Those who cook for themselves can lead the same
life as before but with more security. Why do people wait until it
is too late? I believe that people stay younger here because we expect
them to help with many chores. I do not share the misconception that
even some of my colleagues believe, *in other homes* that "One cannot teach an old dog
new tricks".. It may be true for dogs but many of our residents have
been able to learn new things. How many of them handled a switchboard
or an intercom, how many took painting lessons and how many went to
the Gym classes or Curren Event Classes before they came in? We are
grateful to Mrs. Bensinger, Dr. Frey, Mrs. Funt, and Mrs. Melber, who *the*
bring so much joy to our friends. Truman College paid also for some
teachers but due to government cuts, all classes were cut. One of
our residents, 89-year old Dr. Epstein, took over the "Music Appreciation Class" so that our residents are not deprived. He types programs,
plays beautiful records and everyone enjoys his concerts. I will always
be grateful for Mrs. Miriam Levi who is ~~always~~ *constantly* on the go to look for new

-2-

artists for us. We have outstanding entertainment all the time. I
am happy to report that many entertainers like our atmosphere and the
very appreciative audience and call me because they want to come back
with new programs. We often get dress rehearsals before concerts and
we have excellent book reviews and dance groups. Unfortunately, we
do not have as many artists among the residents as we used to have.
I am always sorry that new applicants don't have any background in the
theater or in the musical field. But we still have our Mr. Brownwald,
our master musician, and we have our Anna Hirsch, our so talented MC
who is the life of every party with her clever ideas. Mrs. Stiefel
and Mrs. Allmayer are her able assistants. And if you've seen
Mrs. Else Strauss and her committee prepare goodies for a party, you
couldn't find a better team among people 40 years younger. Every
morning at 6:30 A.M. you can see our "Fruehaufsteher" at the front desk,
letting the staff in, answering the phone, waking up certain residents
who request it. Mrs. Jacoby as usual does a terrific job. She works
40 to 45 hours a week, and I know Mrs. Brandes is very happy to have
such a capable and reliable co-chairman. Both women cannot be thanked
enough for handling this tedious job so efficiently.--Another hard
working lady is Betty Bettink who, under the chairmanship of Martin
Marx, is in charge of the gift shop. She, Mrs. Mendel, Mrs. Lax
and many others from the Home and from the outside do a lot of selling.
The gift shop is open on all days but Saturday and you'll always find
a friendly salesperson behind the counter.

If you go through our Home, you'll see what every visitor
notices first - our gorgeous plants. Mr. Wiesenfelder also has a
40 hour job. He buys new soil, replants and waters the plants and
gives them tender loving care. Mr. Fruehauf takes care of the plants
outside. In summer you can see him lying on the ground, digging and
planting the flowers, which Margo Meyer buys for the garden downstairs
and the roof garden. He continues what Margo Meyer starts when she
brings in all the new plants. Both men bely their age; both are very
active on the Religious Committee of which Mr. Steiermann is the
chairman. The other two members are Mr. Nussbaum and Mr. Hausler.
They do a terrific job for which they are highly respected by all
residents. Friday Night Services, Havdalah on Saturday and high holidays are kept and they play a great role in the lives of most residents.
The high holidays are always the highlight of the year. Rabbi Plotke,
the young cantor Victor Stiebel, and Dr. Kenn Jacoby, our Shofar Blower,
do a magnificent job, At the memorial services on Yom Kippur I

I cannot praise Miriam Levi enough for bringing us ~~such~~ wonderful entertainment. It is getting much harder to find artists who will work without
remuneration. Our residents gave me a V.C.R. for my birthday, and we have
rented several good films. Mrs. Funt's Current Events Class is most
stimulating. Mrs. Grossman's knitting instructions are very much appreciated, and everything is sold in the Gift Shop. Mrs. Bensinger, assisted
by Mrs. Melber, comes every Friday for the Handicraft Class. If you do not
see their products, which are sold in the Gift Shop, it is because they are
so pretty that they are sold immediately. We are all looking forward to a
larger Gift Shop. We now have very good sales ladies, who work under the
guidance of Steffi Lax. I am sure next year's profits will show it.
Martin Marx does the buying; he too is proud of all his helpers.
Twice a week we have Kaffeeklatsches; the two chairladies, Mrs. Gideon
and Nancy Strauss, are very well-liked. Once a week you can see our
residents in the Exercise Class, and you wouldn't believe that you are in
Housing for the Elderly. The teacher is paid by Selfhelp; so is the
Activity Director in our H.C.F., who does an excellent job keeping our
patients busy and happy. Downstairs we rely heavily on our residents.
Mrs. Anna Hirsch, the by now famous M.C., ~~is~~ assisted by Mrs. Allmayer AND
~~Mrs. Stiefel,~~ is very successful in getting even the most bashful residents
involved. Dr. Epstein continues his weekly concerts; new cassettes and
records are always added. The Home is filled with good music thanks to
him. Mrs. Staple, an accomplished pianist, often entertains us with
live music. She is also in charge of the resident volunteers, and is
responsible for seeing that we are covered at all times. Our residents
volunteers start at 6:30 A.M. and work at the desk and switchboard until
9 or 10 A.M. until the outside volunteers come in. They start again at
5 or 6 P.M. and work until 9 P.M. Sometimes, especially during the
winter when so many volunteers prefer a sunnier climate, they work all day.

4

Mrs. Jonas takes care of the roofgarden flowers after they are planted
in the most beautiful way by Margo Meyer. We also appreciate Mrs.
Wiesenfelder's hard work in taking care of the many plants on the first
floor. We all regretted the passing of her dear husband, who put so
much love and effort into keeping our plants so beautiful. Now his son
comes often to help his mother as a memorial to his father, who also was
our Torah reader. Mr. Fruehauf, the new chairman of the Religious
Committee, and its able members keep up the tradition of having once a
month Friday night services and once a month Saturday morning services.
Mr. and Mrs. Leib give all of us great pleasure during Friday night
services; their voices and personalities add so much to the occasion.
During their absence in winter, Mr. Nussbaum was able to get Mr. Mark
Jesselson, which was very gratifying. Several rabbis came to us for
special services. For this we are most appreciative, since otherwise many
of our residents, due to physical disabilities, would be deprived of
these services which are so meaningful to them. Rabbi Robert Goodman
read the Megillah on Purim again, followed by a lovely party. Rabbi
Plotke with the assistance of Dr. Stiebel, as well as our Religious
Committee and Choir led by Julie Freudenthal, made our High Holidays
again so very special. Cantor Fleischer like every year conducted the
Seder; in the next days he'll be here again. Any one of our Board
Members is most welcome to attend our large family Seder. Mr. Bernie
Hahn will again send us lovely plants for the banquet table, as he does
for all holidays. Hannukkah was beautifully and happily celebrated.
I was deeply touched when several guests gave speeches praising Selfhelp
Center.

There are not words enough to thank Mrs. Jacoby, who works 50 hours a week
to take care of our Happy Day and Memorial Funds. After the untimely

Appendix CC[1]

Dorothy Becker's Report on Neighborhood Groups - Feb. 20, 1962

Page 1(6)

REPORT ON THE NEIGHBORHOOD GROUPS NORTH AND SOUTH AT THE ANNUAL
MEETING OF SELFHELP OF CHICAGO, INC., FEBRUARY 20, 1962

Speaking for the Neighborhood Groups North and South, I must say
there is much good will among the 80 active members in both groups.
There is the will to help people in need, there is the will to make
people happy and there is the will to bring people in distress back
to a normal life again.

It is interesting to see that in our land of plenty there are so
few resources to fall back on in case of an emergency How often
during the year we ask: "what would they have done without Selfhelp?" The Jewish Family Service does not give financial help.
The Chicago Welfare Department is not able to take care of emergency
cases. They need their investigators and their money for the permanent cases and it is at such times that we feel the importance of
our work. Records seldom show and can certainly never measure the
innumerable personal ways to so many who cross our paths.

One instance: We heard of an elderly man in a nursing home who had
a depression. At first, he didnt react to any of our friendly
gestures. Life had been too hard for him. He didn't believe in
miracles, as he said. Why should Selfhelp women be different from
other human beings? Gradually, we could get closer to him. He
started to come to our Senior Center. He was visited, he was picked
up and taken to various places. With the change of his mental
attitude, his physical ailment didn't seem unsurmountable any more.
He was looking forward to move into our new Home. He was looking
forward to all the kindnesses extended to him. He not only became
a member of the group, but a friend of many. When he passed away
he also was mourned by many. Through teamwork we did the impossible.

384

- 2 -

Report on Neighborhood Groups - Cont'd.

We gave him hope and self-respect. This is only one example, but
there are many others where we have to add financial support to the
moral support until people are again self-supporting.

There are a number of elderly people whose Social Security checks
plus small pensions are so small that we have to subsidize each month
an amount of $5.00 to $90.00 to be sure that they have enough to eat.

But not only this specific group of elderly people needs us. We
have helped a mother with four children, two families with five
and six children respectively, a family with three children.
Usually, they get into financial trouble when either father or
mother got sick. A large family usually doesn't have the resources
to fall back on when sickness strikes. Selfhelp alone would not be
abel to help sufficiently either, without the grants from United
Help. An application with the case history is sent to New York and
studied carefully by a committee there. Each of our applications
has been considered urgent and we received 2/3 of the amount requested - 1/3 had to be added by Selfhelp.

There was a Hungarian couple; he had a heart attack, she had several
operations, both couldn't work. There was another Hungarian lady
who came over one year before she became seriously sick. There was
a widow with a son; she had to be hospitalized and we helped her to
maintain the household.

These and may more could be helped. Sometimes smaller amounts of
money could be very helpful. An elderly couple lived on such a

Appendix CC[3]

Dorothy Becker's Report on Neighborhood Groups - Feb. 20, 1962

Page 3(6)

- 3 -

Report on Neighborhood Groups - cont'd.

tight budget that they couldn't afford to visit their only child in
a State Institution. Selfhelp furnished the carfare for a weekly
visit until the daughter was released.

A great source of pride are our two Senior Groups, for which about
35 ladies of our Neighborhood Groups, under the chairmanship of
Mrs. Alice Adler and Mrs. Ludwig Batzner give their time, their
efforts and their friendship to make 150 - 200 elderly friends
happy. It is with great sincerity that Mrs. Wolf and I thank them
for making the Senior Centers possible. To see all these elderly
people happily united every week would be reward enough, but this
was surpassed by the remarks I heard during my recent visits to
hospitals where many of them are at present. I heard from each one:
"Guess how many cards I got from the Senior Group- more than 100, I
bet and they all call my family to inquire how I am. Before I
joined this group, I didn't know many people and now I have so many
friends!"

Our handicraft teacher, Mrs. Ritter, is most efficient and her encouragement has given some of the bashful students so much confidence that they are most eager to participate. Selfhelp has been
one of the first to recognize the need for Golden Age groups; in
fact, we started them 23 years ago when we had monthly meetings for
the elderly. Today, the need for these clubs has been recognized
by all over the world and we are proud of our record of being one
of the first groups in Chicago.

Our Kleiderkammer has been most efficiently taken care of by Mrs.
Lewis Proman and Mrs. Fred Salomon. Through the cooperation of the

- 4 -

Report on the Neighborhood Groups - cont'd.

Skokie Neighborhood Group, we were in the position to help children who were in need of clothing and through the help of all members and friends, we are always ready to help. It is not always the most pleasant work to assort used clothes, but Mrs. Salomon and Mrs. Froman work diligently to have everything in good shape.

There are about 70 women whom we have helped with jobs as companions and practical nurses. We had to disappoint some people who called us to get good maids - most of these women are no longer able to do housework or hold 24-hour jobs. In fact, it is a rather limited service they have to offer, but mostly they are very much appreciated. We were able to place a few men and women in other positions and the reports we received from their employers were very favorable.

We have considered to give up our room service which used to be a very important part of our work. But as there are neither many newcomers nor a scarcity of apartments or hotel rooms, there is no great need for it any more. Yet, Mrs. Steiermann on the South Side and Mrs. Tuteur on the North Side were able to help a few. They have the rather difficult task to make people who want to rent their rooms understand that we can only help them if people request these services.

The box collections, our best source of income, have suffered a set-back in 1961 as it was decided not to collect while the Drive for the new Home was on. The $2,200.00 were still the result of the Fall 1960 collection and from individuals who called their collector that their boxes were filled to the brim. Mrs. Rothschild

Appendix CC[5]

Dorothy Becker's Report on Neighborhood Groups - Feb. 20, 1962

Page 5 and 6(6)

- 5 -

Report on the Neighborhood Groups - cont'd.

and Mrs. Aufreeht have a great job ahead of them, whose dimensions only those people can appreciate who ever worked with files. People are constantly moving and the lists have to be changed accordingly, but both ladies are veterans in this work and their competence is unsurpassed.

Teh greeting cards and telegrams were sold by the ladies of our Neighborhood Groups. The respective chairmen, Mrs. Arthur Lowenthal and Mrs. Eric Raegen, ahve done an excellent job to promote sales.

Supporting the fund-raising project of our North Shore Group, Mrs. Karl Rosenfeld and Mrs. Raegen take orders for napkins, matches, etc.

Our newest project, to collect S & H Green Stamps and other trading stamps should help us substantially when we think of our now Home. Mrs. Tutour is the overall chairman and will be supported by those ladies who will be appointed by our Neighborhood Groups. The co-operation of all our Board Members will be greatly appreciated.

Several of our women have attended meetings of the Jewish Women's Organization. We have attended workshops of the Welfare Council of Metropolitan Chicago and other civic organizations. I, myself, have been re-elected to the Reviewing Committee on the Aged of the Community Fund.

It makes us proud and happy that we have such a fine reputation whereever we go, but we certainly feel the proudest when we can

- 6 -

Report on the Neighborhood Groups - cont'd.

in the Senior Groups or when we hear the recipient say: "We have never met a nicer group." And if I express Mrs. Wolf's and my own feelings, I like to finish this report with sincerest thanks to our co-workers and especially to Mrs. Froman and Mrs. Hirschfeld, Mrs. Arnsdorf and Mrs. Lowenstein, our Secretaries and Assistant Secretaries, and add with great emphasis: There is no nicer group or more devoted group than our Selfhelp Neighborhood Groups.

Appendix DD

Tribute to Dorothy Becker by Mitzi Marx - November 28, 1988

(No Reference in Text)

I am writing as a Selfhelp volunteer and as a successor to Dorothy Becker as chairman of our South Side Neighborhood Group whom I got to know and respect working with her for the organization for many years. The years of my friendship with Dorothy Becker have enriched my life in many ways, besides the respect and affection we had for each other, they were years of learning for me and still are. When my day consists of 12 to 16 hours, hers can be 24 hours long, if necessary. She taught me a long time ago that if you are being needed no hour is too late and no job is too big and if you had other plans before, forget them - just be there when your help is needed.

I learned this when Mrs. Becker told me of a family that had recently come from Greece, had been in Chicago, they had no friends yet and had a child in the hospital dying of cancer. The mother needed companionship and moral support. I was willing to be of help, but since I had a doctor's appointment the next day I wanted to postpone my help to the mother. Dorothy convinced me that it was more important to be with the family right then and there and, of course, she was right. I did spend a week with them when unfortunately the child died. This was the first lesson I learned from Dorothy Becker - if someone is in need of your help don't postpone it.

She also taught me about giving. There were times when I would send food packages to families that needed help. Dorothy Becker's idea of giving was to send little luxuries like a flower and some sweets along things that were not a necessity. Her ways of giving comes in so many different ways, holidays will always be made special by decorations, cakes, speeches, having friends and families participate to make the occasion more special.

There is no limit to her giving of herself, to her understanding, her commitment and good judgment and her superb ability of performance. In addition she is blessed with a good sense of humor.

Dorothy's work for Selfhelp was on a strictly volunteer basis until approximately 15 years ago. It has only been since that time that she has been renumerated for her tireless commitment as Executive Director of Selfhelp Home for the Aged. Her work has truly been a labor of love.

It's a privilege to have her for a friend!

Mitzi (Mrs. Martin) Marx
Chairman of the Volunteers

11-28-198

January 14, 1991

Ms. Dorothy Becker
908 W. Argyle St
Chicago, Il 60640

Dear Ms. Becker:

   I am a sergeant in the U.S. Air force on assignment at
Travis Air Force Base in northern California. I'm glad to
be here because it's just an hour drive to my childhood home
near Sacramento, California.
   While I was on duty during Desert Storm at a small,
remote airfield, each of us in our squadron received
packages of good things to eat: nuts, corn nuts, raisens,
sunflower seeds, delicious oatmeal and ginger cookies, and
soothing aloe vera gel to rub on our skin.
   Even though most of us were sick, we carried on our
duties the best we could.
   I'm sorry to have taken so long, but the truth of the
matter is that I thought I had mailed an earlier letter to
thank you for your kind gesture. I just think you should
know that the packages came when we were very lonely,
scared, sick, or confused. Your package pumped some life
into me. It was then that we knew that we weren't alone.
   God bless you!

                              Sincerely,

                              mike

                              T/Sgt Michael Tuccelli
                              7127 Checkerbloom Way
                              Citrus Heights, CA 95610

Order Form

The Spirit Builder

The Life and Times of
Dorothy Becker:
A Breakthrough View of Aging
By Ursula Levy

$14.95 plus shipping & handling of $5

All books will be priority mailed to the address you provide below. Please allow 2-4 weeks for delivery after mailing this form along with check, money order or credit card information to: **Spirit Builder, P.O. Box 473, Skokie, IL 60076.** Make check or money order payable to **"Spirit Builder."** We accept MasterCard, Visa or Discover. All information will be kept confidential.

You can also order the book on our the web site at: www.spiritbuilder.net or call: 847 677 1654. You can communicate with Ursula Levy, the author, at:ursulalevy@spiritbuilder.net.

Please Print

Name:_____

Address:_____

City/St/Zip:_____

Phone:_____ Email:_____

☐ check   ☐ money order   ☐ Master Card   ☐ VISA   ☐ Discover

CC#:_____ Exp Date:_____

Signature:_____

Printed in the United States
17774LVS00002B/37-188